NO DOGS ON THE BEACH

Recollections of a Littlehampton Foreshore Inspector

NO DOGS ON THE BEACH

Recollections of a Littlehampton Foreshore Inspector

By
JOHN MADELL

No Dogs On The Beach

First Published in 2017
This edition published 2017 by John Desmond Madell
Manor Lodge, 162 Elmer Road, Middleton-on-Sea,
Bognor Regis, West Sussex, PO22 6JA, England.

ISBN: 978-0-9955803-0-5

Scriptures and additional materials quoted are from the Good News Bible © 1994
published by the Bible Societies/HarperCollins Publishers Ltd UK, Good News
Bible© American Bible Society 1966, 1971, 1976, 1992. Used with permission.

A catalogue copy of this book is available from
the British Library.

Printed and bound by DPS Partnership Ltd, Burgess Hill, West Sussex.
Visit www.dpsltd.net for further information.

Cover illustration: Barney, the author's dog.

My reason for writing this work was primarily for self-indulgent posterity, yet perhaps specially to communicate with my yet-to-be-born descendants. I therefore request that this book is passed on by my children and grandchildren, to their children on coming of age, *ad infinitum*.

BIRTHDAY GREETINGS   20 March 2017

My Dear Descendant,

I sincerely wish you a very happy eighteenth birthday. We have probably never met and are very unlikely to do so in this life as, no doubt, by the time you read this letter, I shall be pushing up the daisies. I have written this book in the hope that it will not only vaguely amuse you, but also give you a glimpse into the life and times of your old ancestor.

For a few years I have been intermittently scribbling away in the Foreshore Office situated at the west end of Littlehampton promenade, to while away the rainy days and Sundays. It is by no means a comprehensive autobiography, merely a few recollections, which from time to time have been triggered by my capers on the beach. I have enjoyed this period in my life immensely, thanks mainly to my opposite number in uniform, Dave Strong, who has turned many a damp afternoon into bright sunlight by his quick wit and dry sense of fun.

Should you ever write an autobiography you will be amazed how difficult it is to include all the people you have either liked or loved, and perhaps, on the odd occasion, both!

You will notice that I have quoted a Bible verse at the start of each chapter, and a popular tune of my day at the end; both of which, hopefully, reflect the contents bookended between them.

I have added a little musical composition entitled *Last Chance* that I wrote for my band to record; unfortunately, we were unable to couple my lyrics with a suitable tune. Should you happen to have a talent in this discipline, please see if you can write the musical score to fit the lyrics. I don't think it will worry me if you alter them a little to suit your style.

I have just one gem of wisdom to impart: at least once, preferably sooner than later, read the Bible from cover to cover. The knowledge absorbed will undoubtedly have an impact on the way you live.

Wishing you a long and fulfilling life.

Love, and best wishes,

John Madell

This book is dedicated to the memory of Albert and Nora Madell without whose timely intervention my life would have told a totally different story. Love you both.

Your son, John

Mum and Dad outside Brighton Palace Pier on 17/08/1947.
Photographed on the day that I was born.

ACKNOWLEDGEMENTS

A big thank you to the following:

There is no doubt in my mind that I could never have finished writing this, my autobiography, and persevered on to the publishing stage, without the help and encouragement of my lovely wife Jan.

Having no previous experience of writing, until now only penning business letters with some legal undertones, I sought the opinions of my former neighbours, Bernard and Gwenda Hoad, as to whether the book was worthy of publication. They were complimentary enough for me to press on.

Daniel Madell, my youngest son, has looked over every chapter, one by one, throughout the whole laborious process and given me a great deal of helpful critical feedback.

Bob Stokes, a very talented professional artist, has sketched the cartoons in such a way that they have brought every chapter to life, far beyond my original expectations.

Curiously, my home village of Pulborough provided me with two friends named Colin Bailey. One was a founder member of my first band. The other is my oldest friend – his mum showed my mum how to change my nappies. It was he who undertook the onerous tasks of copy-editing and proofreading the book. I was amazed at how poor my grammar, punctuation and phrasing were when he returned each chapter to me with extensive suggestions for improvement. Together, we may have achieved a standard of work worthy of a decent GCSE pass.

Barney, our dog featured on the front cover, whose seaside behaviour has convinced me beyond any reasonable doubt that there should be 'No Dogs on the Beach'.

Furthermore:
Some names have been changed to avoid a smack in the mouth!

Preface

Dedication

Acknowledgements

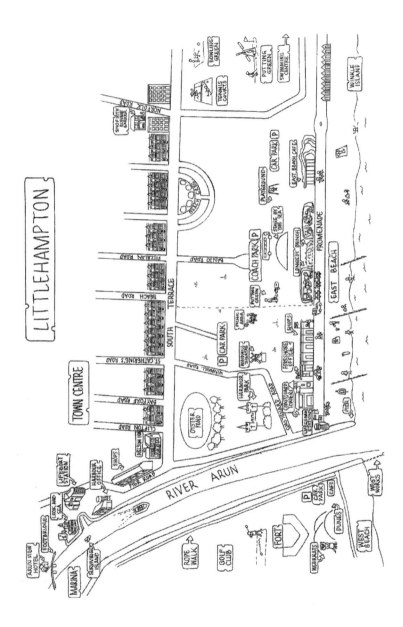

Chapter 1 – Jenny

Psalm 27:10
My father and mother may abandon me, but the Lord will take care of me.

'Jump, you silly bastard.' 'He's not got the bottle.' 'Go on, just do it!' shouted a crowd of hecklers having just stepped out of The Arun View Inn's public bar to witness what they perceived to be an entertaining spectacle. The time was 10pm, the place: Littlehampton harbour slide-bridge over the River Arun, where a nervous young man, sitting centre stage on the edge of the narrow metal bridge, was gripping tightly to the rail with a trembling hand.

On that summer's evening in May the dark, fast-flowing water was cold and uninviting, and perhaps the crowd thought it very unlikely that he would throw himself off the bridge. The police had been alerted and were on their way; surely, someone would talk him down. Though jump he did and immediately disappeared beneath the water, to be dragged down by a treacherous undercurrent. Without hesitation, three brave men leapt into the murky brine and after what seemed an age found the man, and somehow pulled him out. When the services arrived they were confronted by a man not breathing and applied compressions to the technically dead body until the paramedics, following the use of a defibrillator, were able to detect a heartbeat. He was rushed to hospital by helicopter with suspected brain damage. All the rescuers, suffering from hypothermia, were wrapped in foil blankets and whisked off by ambulance to St Richard's Hospital, Chichester.

I was sitting on the seafront with Richard from the Littlehampton Coastguard Station who was relating the details of the previous night's incident less than a mile upriver. I knew Richard quite well as he had the dubious pleasure of teaching my grandson Luke physical education at Worthing High School, when he was not pursuing his first love: the sea along the foreshore. Richard, a very fit and confident man in his early thirties continued, "The would-be suicide is very unlikely to fully recover and could end up a vegetable. How do you think those pissed sods feel now, after goading the poor bewildered lad to jump; I just hope they really hate themselves."

With the sun dancing on the sea in rhythm with a soft background of children's laughter, the distant whirr of a single-engine Cessna light aircraft and the gentle chug of the boat train transporting the enthusiastic holidaymakers along the East Beach promenade; this is the magic of Littlehampton on a warm and unusually breathless day in late May.

As one of three Foreshore Inspectors I find myself in charge of the public's safety and wellbeing between the months of April and September. Now in my fourth season employed by Arun District Council, I treat the job with a mindset that swings from cool relaxation to utter, yet hidden, panic. What will happen next? Lost kids, obnoxious drunks, first aid, illegal immigrants, nuisance skateboarders, itinerant traders, interspersed with a parade of weird and wonderful characters; lost souls seemingly endlessly wandering along the beach, promenade, the river walk and greensward.

The seaside resort of Littlehampton is a hidden gem. With a population of 30,000 and set on the mouth of the Arun, Littlehampton's history goes back many centuries; once a thriving Channel port, now a haven for nautical activities, including sailing, kite surfing, fishing and diving. The town began as the Anglo-Saxon village of Hampton, in the Kingdom of Sussex. The name Little Hampton was bestowed upon it by sailors in the fourteenth century in order to differentiate it from the larger port of Southampton some thirty miles to the west. The forces of Matilda landed here in 1136 when she instigated the civil war with King Stephen. The port was a royal dockyard during the reign of Henry VIII and a quay was built in the mid-1670s. Earlier that century the manor came under the Arundel Castle Estate and successive Dukes of Norfolk continued to own much of Littlehampton until the 1930s.

I recall from visits as a child in the Fifties that both the town and riverside were somewhat tatty, the seafront being the only real attraction. To be fair to the council, the seafront, with a wide promenade, tidy greensward and the newly installed 'longest bench', is still a great place to visit for a daytrip. In addition, the more recently upgraded river walk with neat shops, cafes, and attractive town houses leading from the small wooden pier to the Look & Sea Centre makes a very pleasant place to stroll and take in the seaside air. The town centre, however, like many small coastal towns, is in dire need of a facelift.

Enough of the history lesson – what on earth am I doing here? Now in my seventh decade and with a lifetime in the building industry behind me, I should, by rights, either be in pursuit of my next commercial venture, or retire to a life of charity work and world travel. Or maybe not, perhaps somewhere way back and beyond the sea the answer might be found?

In fact it was beyond the Irish Sea that in December 1946, I was conceived in Dublin's fair city. My father Desmond Tanman, a sergeant in the military police, had for some considerable time been conducting an illicit relationship with my mother Jenny O'Brien. Jenny's husband, Pat O'Brien, had yet to be demobbed from the British Army after his wartime service. When it became clear that Jenny was pregnant and carrying me she was unable to conceal her adulterous affair. Simply, the dates did not line up in her favour. By mid-1947, Jenny and Pat and their two-year-old daughter, Terry, were living in Acton, a run-down area in West London. Pat advised Jenny that he would give the marriage a second chance provided that the child were adopted.

A chat between Albert Madell and a waitress in Lyons Corner House, Piccadilly mapped my future. Albert and Nora Madell were childless, unable to conceive, and looking to adopt. Albert went for his lunch at this restaurant at least twice a week and often chatted with the same checkout lady who became aware of his childless predicament. That waitress, who was in fact Jenny's aunt May, confirmed to Albert that she knew of a soon-to-be-born child who would be made available for immediate adoption. Shortly after my birth in St Mary's Hospital Paddington I was transported, in a sideboard drawer, to Pulborough in West Sussex by Pat and Jenny, and handed to Albert and Nora.

From the very start of my life my guardian angel sprang into action by transferring a six-week-old baby boy from a council flat in Acton to a detached house in a rural country setting. It is interesting to note that there was no overseeing authority or social workers back in the Forties to broker such a deal; just as well, as I suspect that my father, then aged forty-five, would by today's standards, have been judged too old to adopt. Albert, a stickler for good order, ensured that the transfer was ratified by a Court. Desmond O'Brien would from that day on be known as John Madell. From my first memory I was made aware by my 'new' parents that I had been adopted, together with a brief understanding of my roots. Albert and Nora have always been mum and dad and will remain so. As I grew up I became aware that I bore no resemblance to them either physically or in character. This did not really bother me, as by and large, I enjoyed a happy childhood and rarely gave any thought to my natural parentage.

The Adoption c Children (Summary Jurisdiction) ules, 1936.

NOTICE OF AN APPLICATION FOR AN ADOPTION ORDER

in respect of an Infant named (¹)   John Desmond
formerly (²)   Desmond O'Brien

In the [COUNTY] [BOROUGH] OF   SUSSEX

Petty Sessional Division of   Petworth

To   James Patrick O'Brien,
of   35 Emanuel Avenue, Acton. London. W. 3.
~~in the [said] [County] [Borough] of~~
and   Evelyn Jean O'Brien,
of   35 Emanuel Avenue, Acton. London. W. 3
~~in the [said] [County] [Borough] of~~
and   John Desmond Madell,
of   Down View, Sopers Hill, Pulborough,
in the [said] [County] ~~[Borough]~~ of   Sussex
and
The Education Committee of the West Sussex County Council,
in the [said] [County] ~~[Borough]~~ of   of County Hall, Chichester,
Sussex .
~~and~~
~~of~~
~~in the [said] [County] [Borough] of~~

Take Notice:

(1) THAT an application has been made by   Albert Henry Madell
and   Nora Florence Madell,   his wife both
of   Down View, Sopers Hill, Pulborough,
in the [said] [County] ~~[Borough]~~ of   Sussex
for an order under the Adoption of Children Act, 1926, authorising them to adopt the said Infant, being an infant of the ——— male sex, aged   9 months ~~years~~
resident at   Down View, Sopers Hill, Pulborough,
in the [said] [County] ~~[Borough]~~ of   Sussex.

(2) THAT The Education Committee of the West Sussex County Counc
of   County Hall, Chichester,
in the [said] [County] ~~[Borough]~~ of   Sussex.
has been appointed guardian *ad litem* of the said infant.

(3) THAT the said application will be heard before the Juvenile Court sitting at   the Court House, Grove Street, Petworth,
in the said [County] ~~[Borough]~~
on the   7th   day of   July   19 48.
at the hour of   11   in the   fore   noon and that you are severally required to attend before the court ~~[and in case of~~

~~to produce the said infant before the court]~~

Dated the   8th   day of   June   1948.

Justice of the Peace for the [County

At the age of twenty-seven I received a redirected letter addressed to my first home in Pulborough where we had lived until I was twelve years old. It was from Jenny, now residing in the Manchester suburb of Wally Range. The short note stated that she had been most unwell having recently been diagnosed with multiple sclerosis and would very much like to make contact.

It is difficult to describe my emotions when I finally plucked up the courage to telephone Jenny. Disloyalty and betrayal towards mum and dad springs to mind together with an overwhelming feeling of curiosity. Jenny answered the telephone but I have no recall of the conversation; suffice it to say that I agreed to travel up to Manchester at the next available opportunity. When Jean my wife, and I arrived in Wally Range we found Jenny living in a block of flats consisting of eighteen bedsits. The flats were full of students from the nearby university and Jenny was the caretaker. My grandmother Marcella also lived in the building, a floor above Jenny.

It was 1974; Jenny was fifty-four and her mother seventy-six. Jenny greeted me with a huge release of emotion and floods of tears and appeared to be much younger than I had anticipated, a strikingly beautiful slim woman. The only apparent sign of the debilitating MS was a walking stick. Marcella was registered blind, and clearly an educated woman, articulate and very level-headed. On the other hand Jenny appeared shallow, childlike and somewhat bird-brained. Jean found the whole episode surreal with this beautiful stranger sitting on my knee, crying and continuously kissing me, her husband of one year. Well, I quickly learned a great deal about my background, including the fact that I had both a brother and sister living in London. Jenny then gave me a somewhat airbrushed, and as I was later to discover, conflicting, account of my conception, birth and subsequent adoption. Nevertheless, we agreed to meet up again in the near future and I returned home armed with my sister's last known address.

Early the following year Jean and I received a wedding invitation from Jenny. She was marrying Paddy McCartney, a long-time friend, at the registry office in Manchester Town Hall. We arrived in Wally Range on Saturday morning and drove Jenny, Paddy and Marcella to the venue. Jenny announced that the marriage would mean excommunication by the Catholic Church, which I took with a pinch of salt until Marcella confirmed it to be true. Being an outcast would be a very big deal to Jenny who spent half her free time between the Little Alex public house and the church next door, together with 90% of the local Irish community. When we entered the registry office accompanied by quite a crowd of people, Jenny invited me to sit next to her and announced that I would be giving her away. I said, "That's rich Jenny, it was you who gave me away, remember." On reflection, the comment was rather terse and inappropriate. Though in my defence, I was somewhat nonplussed at the prospect of giving away a woman who I had only ever met twice before; three times if you count my birth! Yet the day had just begun and was to prove more intriguing by the minute.

Outside Manchester Town Hall with Jenny and Marcella

For those who know Manchester well, no one in their right mind would enter Moss Side, and certainly not where the reception was to be held at The Moss Side Labour Club. There are more muggings and murders per square mile in Moss Side than anywhere else in Europe; however, to be fair, the reception proved to border on the lavish. A three-course meal provided for over one hundred guests with a top table for the bride and groom, best man, matron of honour, bridesmaids, Jean and me. There was no sign of my brother, sister or any relatives on Jenny's side other than my grandmother Marcella. The drink freely flowed and by the time we reached the sweet course I was feeling relaxed and perhaps a little merry; until Jenny turned to me and requested that I say a few words after the coffee had been served. What on earth does one say under such circumstances? I had been introduced to the assembled throng as Jenny's son, yet I hardly knew the woman. I would like to relate my very clever address word for word; in truth I have no recollection whatsoever of the words I uttered that afternoon. All I now know is that every lecture, presentation or speech that I have subsequently undertaken has been a breeze compared with that day in Moss Side. In typical Irish fashion the celebrations not only carried on well into the night but also seamlessly through to Sunday. Jean and I thankfully managed to escape late on the Saturday night, not that anyone seemed to notice.

The address I had for my sister Terry was in South West London and when, a few years later, I found myself in the locality on business, I knocked on what I thought to be her front door. A dapper Italian man in his late thirties opened the door. He took one long look at me, shook my hand and introduced himself as Mac, and to my utter astonishment stated, "You must be Terry's brother, please come in." I asked Mac, "How on earth do you know who I am, has Jenny been in touch?" Mac replied, "No, I've not seen hide nor hair of Jenny for at least a dozen years; it's simple, you bear such a striking resemblance to Terry you have to be her brother. In any case, I was aware of the 'family secret' that Jenny had another son who was adopted at birth."

Terry was supposedly at work and would not be back until late from her job as a nursing sister at a hospital in London Colney. I spent a couple of very pleasant hours with Mac drinking tea and looking at the family photo album. It was good to see what Terry looked like and to see pictures of their two children: my niece Gillian, and nephew Robert. Mac said that provided Terry was happy to meet me he would arrange an urgent rendezvous.

Precisely seven days later I knocked on the same door, this time to be greeted by Terry and once again I spent a couple of hours in the house chatting with Mac and Terry. My sister and I are very similar and I guess it has been my only real regret about being adopted that we did not grow up together. Terry walked me to the car and said mysteriously that there was something I needed to know which she was not prepared to discuss at that moment. She promised to telephone me at home that evening. When I received her call I was shocked to learn that Terry and Mac had been divorced for a number of years and she was now living in North London with the two children and her second husband Pete. Apparently, Mac, who was ever so kind and caring towards me, had never come to terms with the marriage breakdown and continued to live in total denial of the true situation.

I was never inclined to look up my brother Danny. Terry had told me that he was still living in the family home in Larch Avenue, Acton with his dad Pat O'Brien. I assumed that my reception would prove frosty. As Jenny had informed me that Pat, an ex-professional boxer, was inclined to be heavy-handed with all and sundry, I was not about to add my name to his list; however, in the autumn of 1994 I found myself driving through Acton with my colleague Charles Boughton-Leigh. We stopped at a garage to fill up and I purchased a *London A-Z* to replace my tatty old copy. Purely out of curiosity I looked up Larch Avenue and to my amazement found it to be the next turning on the left.

Within five minutes I was knocking on the door of number twenty-seven. A man in his late thirties answered the door. I said, "Are you Danny O'Brien?" He replied, "Who wants to know?" I continued, "If you are Danny O'Brien, then your brother wants to know." Before he could respond, an invisible voice with a broad Irish accent from within the darkened hall invited me in. The voice belonged to a wizened old man, who could be none other than Pat O'Brien. "Well tell us who you are then" said my mother's ex-husband and I gingerly replied, "I am John Madell, formally Desmond O'Brien, son of your wife Jenny and brother of your daughter Terry; does that sound about right old man?" Pat thought for a moment or two and then turned to Danny and said, "Shake hands with your brother, son."

We moved into the lounge and sat down. Pat stared long and hard at me. He finally broke the silence and said to me in a soft Limerick tone, "I last saw you in 1947 when I drove to Pulborough in Sussex and handed you to Mr and Mrs Madell. Well, tell me, how are you getting on then son?" I said, "Yes Pat, you delivered me in a drawer I believe?" Pat stood up and slowly walked to the sideboard, and removed the bottom drawer. "This was the drawer," he whispered, and smiled. I need not have feared the old man's reaction as Pat bore me no animosity and appeared to be a genuinely caring individual. I saw him one more time before he died in 1999. I see Terry once or twice a year and Danny very occasionally. In 2005 they both attended my son Paul's wedding which was the very first time that the three of us spent a few hours in the same room together.

I first met the Irish side of the family when they crossed the Irish Sea for granny Marcella's funeral in 1986. Jenny casually introduced me to Philip Bosonnet her nephew, my cousin. I came as quite a surprise to Phil as both Jenny and Marcella had spent a great deal of time at his home in the seaside town of Malahide, situated close to Dublin airport, without a mention of me. Jenny's sister, Rose, had four children by her French husband and sadly died in 1967 from cancer. Phil and Tina Bosonnet had been very kind to Jenny since she had been diagnosed with MS and made sure she had many good holidays in their lovely home in Swords Road. Since meeting Phil, together with various members of my family, I have spent time in his home getting to know my Irish roots. It was there late one night after everyone had gone to bed Phil opened a bottle of Paddy Old Irish Whiskey and told me that his father had suspected that Jenny had had another child. Apparently during the war Jenny had developed a long-term relationship with my father Desmond Tanman, and it was thought that both Terry and I were his children. Danny was, most probably, the only child of three that Pat had actually fathered.

Talking of Irish relatives: Marcella's brother, Paddy Darcy, my great uncle, had an amazing experience that he enjoyed dining out on for the best part of his life. It was noon on 24 April 1916, when Paddy popped into Dublin's main Post Office situated in O'Connell Street to buy a stamp. At that very moment the Irish Nationalists rose up against British rule, and 2000 men led by Padraig Pearse seized control of that very General Post Office building and declared Ireland independent, taking both staff and customers hostage, including Paddy, then in his mid-twenties.

After five or six days of prolonged street fighting, the Nationalists surrendered. Paddy was set free. The rebels were less fortunate: taken prisoner, and fifteen of the ringleaders were summarily executed. The uprising became the most significant event in Irish history, and finally, after further insurrection, the Irish Free State was declared in 1921. Paddy lived a long and fruitful life ending up in an old folks' home in Dublin. Even in his early nineties he was able to read without glasses and walk up and down the stairs to his room. Eventually, a lift was installed to facilitate the elderly residents. Sadly, Paddy fell over when the lift suddenly jolted one day, broke his hip and died a few weeks later at the ripe old age of ninety-eight. An Irish story you may say, yet true nonetheless.

It saddens me to write so much about Jenny and so little about Nora. Suffice it to say that Nora was as beautiful on the inside as Jenny was on the outside. I could not have wished for a better mum than Nora.

In 1997, now living back in Ireland, Jenny's MS worsened and she also fell and broke a hip. I last saw her when I visited her with my son Dan in Newry Hospital. Jenny never fully recovered and died at the age of seventy-seven on 12 December. My son Paul, Terry and I flew to Dublin and along with my cousins Paul, Phil, Maud and Ray attended Jenny's funeral the next day. My three male cousins and I carried the coffin to the cemetery and lowered Jenny to her last resting place.

When my father Albert died in 1984 Nora moved in with Jean and me. After two hip replacements and a heart attack she suffered a massive stroke. In need of twenty-four-hour care she moved to a nursing home about two hundred yards from our house in High Salvington. She gradually faded away and died at the age of eighty-five on 13 December. Coincidentally, she died while I was attending Jenny's funeral. The moment I returned from Ireland I found myself making arrangements for Nora. I read the same words from Isaiah at both services. At Nora's funeral I noticed, poignantly, that Paul still had the mud on his shoes from Jenny's graveside.

By the afternoon the Littlehampton weather had deteriorated and a misty rain dripped off my cap as I patrolled the promenade. Only the hard-core of dog walkers and joggers remained. Mike and Lisa had tied up the hire boats in the centre of Oyster Pond and retreated to the Nelson pub for happy hour, to be joined by the two brothers who run the fish and chip stall next door to my office.

Must be time for me to wash down the Kawasaki Mule and lock it away in the boathouse.

The weather I guess can be a little like life, one minute bright and the next dull. Equally, circumstance can instantly change our mood from happy to sad. My old friend Colin has a saying: 'Average is good, average is good'. I think maybe the guy who attempted suicide the previous night might very well agree, if he were able.

La Mer (The Sea)
Performer: Bobby Darin
Composers: Trent and Lawrence
Number 8:   January 1960

Chapter 2 – Madellio

Psalm 150:4
Praise him with drums and dancing. Praise him with harps and flutes.

The year 2009 saw a sudden increase in the number of people raking for shellfish found in abundance at low tide on Winkle Island situated opposite the beach huts on East Beach. Winkles, whelks and clams are out of season between 15 May and 15 September and deemed to be potentially poisonous so collection is outlawed by the Department of Agriculture and Fisheries. As the Arun District Council is responsible for the beach up to fifty yards beyond low tide it falls to the Foreshore Inspectors to control the activity as best we can. To confuse the issue, or dare I say 'muddy the waters', there is a queue of organisations which have a vague interest, indeed oversight as far as our beach is concerned, including the Health and Safety Executive, the Coastguard, the UK Border Agency and not forgetting Sussex Police. Normally I receive a phone call from one of the ninety-odd beach hut owners advising of the presence of rogue pickers.

In all honesty I am not concerned when one or two locals are collecting shellfish out of season, I merely advise them that they are considered poisonous by the Council Health Officer and leave them to continue or not. If they want to take the risk of talking to 'Ruth down the loo', that has to be their decision. The real culprits are gangs of both male and female pickers sometimes over twenty-strong, made up of mostly illegal Chinese immigrants. The pickers are under the control of a gangmaster, often an unscrupulous individual exploiting their own kind and placing the consumer's health at serious risk. A well-organised and highly lucrative business with a warehouse in North London, the food is harvested and sold to West End restaurants via its website.

Armed with an official council notice printed in Cantonese I regularly confiscate the shellfish they have collected together with their bags and tools, and then expel the culprits from the beach. This is not quite as easy as it sounds as the swag is often hidden in the beach foliage or in the boot of the gangmaster's car. Sometimes, I end up chasing the Chinese all over the beach and along the local side roads. With no power of arrest my activity can prove a little frustrating.

From time to time our department will receive back up from the Coastguard and the Police. In fact on one hot and very busy Sunday afternoon the local police sergeant joined me on my beach buggy and we successfully apprehended a number of pickers, it has to be said, not without a Keystone-Cop-style beach chase. Roared on by thousands of intrigued holidaymakers we rounded up and made a number of arrests.

One particular young Chinese man eluded us for approximately ten minutes; weaving in and out of the rock pools he maintained a fantastic pace. The Mule, with a top speed of twenty-five miles per hour, struggled to keep up until the sergeant finally hung out on the vehicle's protective frame and swiped at the poor unfortunate with his stun baton. Charlie Chan fell over and my police friend pinned him to the ground in shallow water. The fickle crowd by now had sided with Charlie and were jeering and booing our success. The soaking wet policeman failed to see the funny side. "Bollocks to this for a game of soldiers, take me back to the wagon; and what are you laughing at John?" he tersely exclaimed, glaring at me, which without doubt made the situation even more amusing. Seven pickers were arrested that day of whom three were subsequently deported as illegal immigrants. I returned over a hundredweight of shellfish to Winkle Island.

My colleague Dave and I have spent many hours driving along the beach and in addition to chasing illegals, we cut fishing nets from the groynes and collect miscellaneous rubbish. Items such as a freezer tossed from a passing ship and the odd dead cat, which can picked up by the tail, stiff as a board. Throughout a season we can easily remove five tons of odds and sods to dump in the skip located behind our office. I consider the mobile patrol a privilege; imagine cruising the beach maybe a hundred yards from the promenade, bright sunshine and a gentle breeze all viewed through cool shades. I can only liken the experience to the very best Disney ride. What's more, I get paid. Sheer bliss! Sheer ballet!

I have no idea why I joined the after-school ballet classes and not a clue why my dad agreed to fund this ex-curricular activity. I was sent to a private preparatory school in Pulborough called Arundale School, run by the formidable Mrs Kelly. The reason I was not sent to the local primary school, according to dad, was the unimpressive sanitary facilities, namely, outside loos. I suspect the real reason was to demonstrate to the outside world his ability to provide private education for his son.

From the age of nine to eleven my ballet lessons taught me deportment, rhythm, timing and coordination. I was the only boy amongst a dozen girls and often called upon to lift, which I found even at such an early age reasonably enjoyable, certainly with the slim pretty ones! We eventually presented shows to our parents including *Swan Lake, Carousel* and a musical version of *Alice in Wonderland*. Strangely, I took to the hard work and discipline that is essential in this art form and considered ballet as another sports activity. Today, I really enjoy the ballet when I visit the Theatre Royal Brighton and see a strong parallel between off-the-ball running in soccer and the intricate and graceful moves performed by the world's top ballet dancers.

Arundale School was a very strange place indeed. Established in 1953, I became one of the first pupils to attend the lessons, which were conducted in the function room behind the Arun Hotel. Within a year Eileen Kelly had acquired the old Springfield Tea Rooms on the east side of the village next door to the Red Lion pub. There I remained for five unhappy years until I managed to fail the Eleven-Plus examination. I did gain an interview, granted to borderline cases, at Steyning Grammar School, which I also failed. At least I was consistent. The property had three storeys, a cellar and a large garden at the rear. I strongly suspected that the school was actually run by Mrs Kelly's mother, always addressed as Nana; it was she who prepared the meals and was head-cook-and-bottle-washer. At lunchtime I consistently found myself sat next to Nana who saw as her mission in life to ensure that I ate every last mouthful of the revolting fare, consisting of such delicacies as macaroni cheese followed by spotted dick and custard.

Mrs Kelly was a contradiction: a left-wing socialist running a fee-paying establishment for the offspring of the local middle-class and gentry. One such pupil bore the improbable name of Prosper Riley-Smith. My best mate at Arundale was Keith Harling, like me one of the few who could never be termed as posh. Keith was a talented musician and eventually became lead cello with the Welsh National Orchestra.

Mrs Kelly was a very good teacher; however, as the number of pupils grew she delegated most of her teaching duties to less able ladies with varying degrees of ability. Being taught by the likes of Mrs Johnson: rather too fond of the gin, and Miss Coles: fast approaching her nineteenth nervous breakdown, it is little wonder that both Keith and I found ourselves at the local secondary modern. The remainder of our classmates also moved on: the boys to further their education at public schools and the girls to Roedean in Brighton or Benenden in Kent. As for Eileen Kelly, she continued to run the school for another quarter-century and thereafter dedicated herself to local community projects and, to her credit, used the profits generated by the school. Three years before she died, in 2006, Mrs Kelly received a much-deserved Order of the British Empire for her good works.

After one academic year at The Weald School, my father, in his wisdom, arranged for me to be transferred to yet another fee-paying school, this time as a boarder at Quays College in Shoreham-by-Sea. The fact that I was doing really well in my first year at The Weald: top stream, good marks and firm new friends, had no bearing whatsoever on my father's decision. To say that Quays College was a carbon copy of 'Dotheboys Hall' and to describe the Headmaster as Wackford Squeers, without the charm, would do a disservice to Charles Dickens' favourite academy so eloquently depicted in *Nicholas Nickleby*. The place was beyond the pale, with bullying rife, appalling facilities and dire educational standards. Worse still, they wouldn't even let me out to watch Brighton and Hove Albion play on a Saturday afternoon.

When I found myself in the bottom stream with boys two years my junior, I had no choice other than to escape, and escape I did. I simply left school with the dayboys at the end of the afternoon session, walked to the train station and ticket-less, caught the first available train home. When I arrived home, I announced my intention to return to The Weald on the following Monday. To my utter amazement my parents agreed, and I did just that. Thankfully, Quays College was never again mentioned.

Quays had been a nasty shock to my system. I realised the need to prepare myself for any future unpleasantness that may come my way. With that thought in mind I joined the local boxing club. The club was held in a Nissen hut situated behind the Village Hall, appropriately next door to the St John Ambulance headquarters. Affiliated to the National Association of Boys' Clubs, it was most efficiently run by Pat Coleman a good-hearted man in his early forties. We met once, or if there was a contest approaching, twice a week for coaching sessions. Initially, Pat taught me the Queensbury Rules, my stance, footwork and how to protect myself, followed by a workout on both the punch bag and punch ball. After a couple of weeks I found myself as a sparring partner for the older boys. In short, I had become their punch bag and ball!

There were a couple of very good boxers at the club in Pat Jones and Len Hookey (what a great name for a fighter). These guys were my height, yet two years older and much stockier than me. In junior contests boys were generally paired off in height and experience rather than in weight or age. Pat pointed out this could work against me when finally, after a few months, my first contest was arranged. Pulborough Boys' Club was away to Bognor Boys' Club. There were to be six three-round contests and I was on second. Each round in my age bracket was of one and a half minutes duration.

I never let on to Pat or my new found colleagues that my ballet training was of great advantage in both timing and footwork. Moreover, being left-handed was also an advantage when taking the southpaw stance; strangely, I was equally comfortable fighting right-handed. I believe boxing to be both mentally and physically the toughest sport of all. To have any chance of success the boxer has to be one hundred per cent fit, confident and fearless. I marginally lost my first fight to an older opponent. Pulborough overall won the contest that night, mainly thanks to Pat and Len.

Over the next couple of years I worked hard, toughened up, and won more times than I lost. I learnt how to take a punch, usually from Pat or Len, how to take a breather, buy time and accelerate my game in short bursts. Pat Coleman was a strict disciplinarian and taught us that our fists were in fact dangerous weapons and to avoid whenever possible using them outside the ring.

On one cold December night in 1961 Pat had arranged a home match in Pulborough Village Hall. The opposition were from a highly-rated club from South London. Dear old Pat was desperate for us to do well in front of a full house. Unfortunately, I had a heavy cold and temperature come on the night before. Dad was totally against me fighting and rang Pat and told him so. When I turned up at the hall that night Pat took me to one side and said, "Your father does not want you to fight tonight; however, I don't think it should be his decision, nor mine; it's your call John." I did feel really under the weather, yet there was no way I could consider dropping out. "Count me in Pat," I heard myself say. Changing in the low-ceilinged room under the Village Hall stage I calmed myself and took encouragement from my teammates. Pat pinned up the order of proceedings on the door. I was on number three of six bouts that night. I didn't care to watch the fights; I just sat in the dressing room in a cold sweat.

We lost the first two bouts and Len who was scheduled number five, opened the door and called me out: "These guys are shit-hot, watch out for yourself John." His words provided little encouragement and my mouth instantly dried up. I thought at least the crowd was on our side, as I climbed into the ring. Names announced and protocol complied with I returned to my corner and waited for the bell. A boxing ring is without question the loneliest place in the world and over the next few minutes time stood still. As the bell rang to start round one, I could see the worried face of my dad out of the corner of my eye and I could hear my mates shouting, 'Madellio, Madellio, Madellio'.

My opponent looked fit and well hard. I was not wrong. As blow after blow rained down on my face and body I could do little to sidestep, hold on or back off. Yet, I stayed on my feet and retaliated with some good body shots. The bell finally rang and I slumped on the stool in my corner. Pat, acting as my Second, sponged down my face and mumbled something about keeping my 'fists up higher'. Ding, ding, and off we went again, for two more minutes of torment. Shit! the headshots really hurt and the next body shot had me down on one knee. I dared not drop to the canvas, as the referee would be likely to stop the fight. Luckily, he gave me the mandatory count, looked long and hard into my eyes and said, "Box on." Shortly after that the bell rang for the end of round two. By now my eyes were streaming; I had no idea where my corner was until I heard Pat yell at me, "John, I'm going to stop the fight." "No Pat, give me the last round. I'll switch my stance. But, for fuck's sake wipe the tears from my eyes; I don't want half of Pulborough to think I'm crying," I begged, just as the bell rang.

My opponent raced over, determined to finish me off. I stood my ground, placing my left foot forward, thereby changing my stance. He seemed quite surprised and froze for a second. This gave me the opportunity to plant a left and a right to his head. The crowd roared and now encouraged, I immediately followed up with two more shots to the head. Like an enraged bull my opponent gave me everything. I protected myself as best I could. My legs had gone and all I was able to do was lean back on the corner ropes to prevent myself from going down. Crack, my nose was broken. A second crack and a rib had gone. As I slumped to the floor, the towel came into the ring just as the referee stopped the fight.

Doctor Ford was in attendance and wiped the blood from my face as he checked me over in the dressing room. I could vaguely hear him tell my dad that the broken nose would 'give the boy character, the rib will heal of its own accord' and 'by the way, have the dentist look at a wonky front tooth.'

Needless to say my career in the fight game came to an abrupt end that night. In my semi-conscious state I did not know whether I was punched, bored or countersunk or perhaps more appropriately, knocked out, stopped or surrendered. The official decision: the fight was stopped. Now there's a surprise!

Dance On
Performers: The Shadows
Composers: E. Murtagh, Adams, and V. Murtagh
Number 1:   December 1962

Chapter 3 – Albert

Proverbs 4:1
Listen to what your father teaches you, my sons.
Pay attention, and you will have understanding.

Immediately behind the Foreshore office is Harbour Park Amusements, covering an area of approximately two acres and consisting of a variety of external rides, such as dodgems, water splash, roller coaster and a Waltzer. Inside the main building complex slot machines, football tables, video games, two cafes and an ice cream parlour will be found. The park is adjacent to the river on the west side and the greensward and car park on the east. It is run with military discipline and efficiency by the owner Gary Smart and his two sons, complemented by a small team of helpful, friendly full-time supervisors. During the high season Gary employs another twenty-plus casual staff between the hours of 11am to 6pm, all members of which are smartly uniformed and well-trained. I have inside knowledge as my youngest son Dan was employed to man the roller coaster and other rides during the summer of 2009 while on holiday from university.

Gary, the nephew of the world-famous circus impresario, the late Billy Smart, was born into the circus and worked in the family business before and after serving with 10th Parachute Regiment, eventually settling in Littlehampton where he acquired the amusement conglomeration from Billy Butlin in 1978. At that time the majority of the rides were under cover and a tad dated. In truth, the site was a little seedy attracting low life and yobs, and on Sunday afternoons, fuelled by drink, they invariably picked fights with all and sundry, requiring Gary and his staff to step in and eject the troublemakers.

In 1985 Gary decided to totally refurbish the site by demolishing the indoor arena and introduced an array of modern activities. At the time it was a very bold move, causing Gary a sleepless night or two pondering the wisdom of his decision; although he need not have worried as this soon paid dividends, making the site far more family orientated, and it quickly built a reputation as a safe and fun environment. The only remaining

Butlin ride is the Waltzer proving to be perennially popular. Billy Smart was a founder member of The Variety Club of Great Britain, a showbiz organisation set up in the late Forties as a charity to help under-privileged children. Gary has continued the family tradition and on the first or second Saturday in June the Park hosts 2,500 children from the Inner London Boroughs to a day at the seaside. They descend on Littlehampton just after 10am, having been collected from home and transported by volunteers in Variety Club coaches to enjoy complimentary rides in the Amusement Park, free ice cream and a goody bag to take home when they leave at 5pm.

Gary told me of a spooky happening in the House of Horrors which replaced the unfashionable Ghost Train. The event was a walk through grizzly waxworks depicting a rather distasteful tableau, including Frankenstein's monster and Dracula. The ride operator reported seeing a bloodstained man in Victorian dress inside the building on the walkway; however, no such character existed. Initially, Gary dismissed the alleged sighting to an over-imaginative member of staff and removed her to oversee other rides. After her replacement reported similar observations he decided to seek independent advice in the guise of a paranormal expert. Although the expert did not personally witness the Victorian man he did uncover that a rather unpleasant homicide had been committed in the vicinity of the attraction one hundred years ago. Gary has since replaced the House of Horrors with a far more mellow attraction called The House of Mystery. Since the alterations the sinister figure has disappeared. Well, for the time being at least!

I just love fairgrounds. Once a year the fair would visit Pulborough and set up on waste ground opposite the station cattle-market. There was little better than riding the bumper cars with the latest Elvis, Everly Brothers and Orbison hits blaring from the distorted speaker system. Hidden in the shadows, the allure of danger was always present: the rickety old rides (no health and safety culture in 1960), menacing yobs, or the hard men in biking leathers; their greased-back hair complete with the obligatory duck's arse, and the inevitable body odour. Dubious glamour came from the long stares of my older peers as I noticed the overt sexuality of their girlfriends.

To be at the fair was a risk indeed, but the considerable chance of being beaten up was outweighed by the sights and sounds:

bright neon lights, noisy unease, pretty girls with lacquered beehives, skin-tight jeans and baggy mohair jumpers. Itinerant gypsy roustabouts collected fares as they swung casually between moving bumper cars; I always handed over the right ride fee knowing full well that any change was most unlikely. Candyfloss: best consumed whilst riding the Ferris wheel. The opportunity to fire an old air rifle to knock down the ducks, and secretly enjoying the tough guys failing to ring the bell when wielding the strongman hammer. Last, but not least, the inevitable penniless walk home.

More recently, three visits to Florida with the boys to take in every theme park and every ride that Disney or Universal had to offer has not cured my thirst for buttock-clenching rides. For me the pinnacle of fairground achievement was winning a kewpie doll on midway at the Texas State Fair in Dallas. Just magical!

In the late Fifties, as a summertime treat, my dad sometimes drove us to Littlehampton for a picnic, to swim in the sea normally off West Beach and end the day in the fun park; I vividly remember the original site especially the Wild Mouse, a roller coaster, part-set on the roof of the indoor arena. The winding track terrified me as a youngster, knowing that when, eventually, we reached the high point, the carriage would lurch sideways and all but tip the fearful occupants into the sea.

Regardless of the fact that my father could be a terrible pain to both mum and me, as a child I worshipped him, indeed he was my idol. As a teenager I clashed with him. When Albert was a youth there were no such irritants as teenagers; a very young man was conscripted into one of the three armed forces and two years later demobbed a man, job done. As an adult I found him distant and difficult and very much resented his attitude towards me. Since his death I have grown to love and admire him. Through my own experiences of life, I am now able to understand the man and find it easy to write off his many faults and idiosyncrasies to eccentricity.

Albert Henry Madell, or as my first wife Jean, aptly in her opinion, nicknamed him, 'AH', was born on 16 October 1902. 'Too young for the First and too old for the Second World Wars.' he often pointed out. He was born in Plumstead, a village in Kent, yet to become a suburb of South East London. As it was for many of his peers in Edwardian times, life was hard for Albert's working-class family, especially with six small children. Along with his mother, brothers and sisters, Albert was regularly beaten by his ex-professional-soldier father, a situation that was commonplace for the time. He claimed he had a miserable childhood, yet was able to enjoy watching the Arsenal play First Division football at the nearby stadium. In fact his best friend was the trainer's son, and both lads had the regular privilege of viewing their favourites from the home bench.

Dad left school at fourteen and found employment in the local munitions factory, the Woolwich Arsenal, out of which grew the football club. Six months after the termination of the First World War, at the age of sixteen, Albert joined the army. After basic training he was posted to Belgium and spent the next two years listing the dead and generally cleaning up the battlefields.

Upon his demob he joined Holland and Holland the well-known gun makers situated in New Bond Street, in the West End of London and there he stayed until 1959. During his forty years' service he undertook most clerical and sales duties, ending his career as Director and Company Secretary. In 1940 he had the onerous task of undertaking regular fire watch duties during the London Blitz on the office roof, which included a strategic ammunition dump in the cellar! He was also a member of The Home Guard in Essex until he moved to Nutbourne in West Sussex in 1943. In 1959, now effectively retired, Albert and Nora purchased The Chocolate Box, a sweet and tobacconist shop, which also sold toys, magazines and newspapers and was situated in the heart of the village of Pulborough, West Sussex. They enjoyed running the shop together until 1973 when they both finally retired.

Dad's army 1941/42. Albert Madell front row wearing German spiked helmet

I have many abiding memories of my father; the one that probably best sums up his eccentricity was his dress sense. For instance, whilst running the Junior Sports Club on Pulborough Recreation ground in the early Sixties, by this time in his late fifties and overweight, Albert ('I'm not portly, just well covered') would sit in the middle of the pitch on a shooting stick. He directed operations from this position whilst dressed in a Panama hat, string vest, long ex-army khaki shorts, even longer brown socks held up by garters, and brown boots. Albert used his ever-present cigar to point at some poor lad who was not correctly performing the given sporting exercise.

I am not certain that he was the greatest tactician as we lost our first game of football 22-0. Thereafter, dad moved into a more executive roll and appointed John Finch, an ex-army PE instructor, to take over training. His next masterly move was to find a president for the club.

Arthur Gilligan was probably one of the most famous cricketers of all time, behind only W. G. Grace and Jack Hobbs. What is more, he lived in Pulborough! Not only did he take a keen interest in our progress in both cricket and football, but also funded and donated a great deal of kit to the club including his own cricket bats. What would they be worth now as sporting memorabilia? More importantly, his name was priceless to the credibility of the club, which was now beginning to attract talented junior sportsmen as well as quality opposition. I found Arthur Gilligan to be a very kind man and the ultimate gentleman. Over the next two years we were unbeatable.

By the time I was about seven or eight dad had unwittingly taught me every swear word in the book. That was from a man who claimed not to swear in company; however, I don't think he viewed me as company. The only times I heard him swear was when he was attempting to start the old Citroen car. The Citroen was the type the Gestapo could be seen driving in old war films.

Dad's Citroen 1954

Invariably, in winter the car refused to start by the normal turn of the key; life in those days was not that simple. The regular format was that I sat in the car and eased the choke, waiting on dad to crank the starter handle. With the least sign of life from the old girl, with my foot on the accelerator pedal, I started revving the engine. If any part of the operation were not exactly right then Albert had to crank the handle again. Cranking the handle from my vantage point in the front seat meant, in reality, dad's head disappearing below the line of the bonnet, and then suddenly with a strenuous jerk, his round bespectacled face instantly appearing again, a split second between success and failure; joy or despair.

Joy, as the engine kicked into life brought about an instant smile from dad. Despair, certainly meant a curse. Each failure encouraged a louder and more elaborate swear word. To tease out the most outrageous curse I had merely to give too much choke and flood the engine; a dangerous game to play as an out-of-breath father, regardless of fault, inevitably blamed me. Retribution was swift and thankfully, on most occasions, only verbal. Any sign of corporal punishment led me to threaten dad with a repeat of his swear words to mum.

Dad had an amazing influence on me, even without any biological connection. He had a tremendous work ethic and consequently would never do a job slowly if it could be done swiftly and efficiently. With one exception, decorating. Decorating was dad's Achilles' heel. He could literally take years to fully refurbish even the smallest room. The fault lay in his perfectionism, which often caused him to half-do, and then undo what he had started, until in his mind the job was perfect. Sadly, this meant that mum could never allow him to start. Consequently, the internals within our house were inevitably run down to a state of dilapidation. Thankfully, he employed a professional painter and decorator to undertake the exterior.

A good example of his enthusiastic speed caught him out one day. My father kept in the garage, paraffin, stored in an old sherry bottle, presumably to top up the greenhouse heater. He used the bottle one day and carelessly left it in the kitchen. Mum, inadvertently returned the bottle to the cocktail cabinet. Sometime later dad opened the cocktail cabinet and poured himself a glass of 'sherry' and proceeded to down the contents in one swallow. Never have you heard such a fuss. Dad quickly worked out what had happened and after seriously reprimanding my mother, promptly telephoned Doctor Ford.

After dad had embarrassedly explained the error, the doctor responded, 'Don't worry Albert, you will be fine.' As an afterthought, he added, 'Whatever you do, don't smoke for at least forty-eight hours.' As a lifelong smoker, mum and I had a miserable two days suffering dad's bad temper. Doctor Ford later confided in me that it would have made little or no difference had dad smoked or not. The good doctor had hoped that a rest from the deadly weed might encourage Albert to give up. A forlorn hope indeed.

Coincidentally, Doctor Ford played a part in the next Albert saga. I came home from college on one dark winter's night to find dad collapsed on the stairs. Mum immediately phoned the doctor and by the time he arrived we had managed to get dad to bed. 'It could be your heart, Albert,' the doctor said, 'take these pills and I will look in and see how you are in the morning.' No paramedics in the Sixties! Before I retired that night dad called me into their bedroom. "Son, you need to know where I keep the money, I may not last the night," he said, melodramatically, in a faint whisper. Dad was always one to make a crisis out of a drama. He did not believe in banks, building societies, insurance companies or any financial institutions. Now with hindsight, I can see how right he was. Dad preferred cash, and would never carry less than £1,000 in his wallet. "You will find £500 up the chimney in this room, £400 under the cocktail cabinet, £400 in the loft." Dad went on to list different places in the house where he had hidden varying amounts of cash. The total came to well over £5,000, which was a great deal of money in those days when you could buy an average family home for less than that amount.

Next day I left early for college when dad was still in bed sleeping soundly. When I returned home that evening I found him seated in the dining room and happily attending to the shop accounts. "Hello John," he said with a smile, "the doctor said it was not my heart, I just got overheated: sat too close to the fire last night. By the way, regarding the cash, I have moved it all!" What a pity, as I had frittered away the best part of the day working out how I was going to spend the money.

Dad's great passion was the cinema and especially cowboy films. Throughout my childhood I was fed a regular diet of western movies and John Wayne was unquestionably his favourite film star. If the weather was bad on a Saturday afternoon, we would make for any one of a dozen cinemas in Brighton, Worthing, Littlehampton or Horsham to follow the cavalry over the hill. Mum did not share our passion, yet did accompany us on the regular trips. In the Fifties not only did we see the main feature in glorious Technicolor, but also an Edgar Wallis thriller in black and white, *Look at Life* (a documentary about a topical subject such as the hovercraft), *Pathé News*, a Bugs Bunny cartoon, Pearl & Dean advertisements and a trailer of the forthcoming films. All this could last up to four hours before they played *Perfidia* between shows.

The problem was that dad took no interest in timing and we could easily arrive ten or fifteen minutes before the end of the feature film. Any normal human being would wait until the start of the next show before entering the darkened auditorium. Not dad, 'I've paid, in we go,' he would state excitedly, and we then stumbled around in the dark to find our seats. Inevitably, we would discover 'who had done it' and then sit for four hours to reach the point we came in. Dad would jump up and the three of us repeated the stumbling as we struggled to find the exit, not to see the end again. I suppose it was a small price to pay for a good afternoon's entertainment, with ice cream, popcorn and, more than likely, a fish and chip supper thrown in for good measure.

Dad based much of his persona on John Wayne: roughly the same age, height and build and both chain smokers. I suspect they also shared the same weird sense of humour and eccentricity. My favourite story about 'The Duke', John Wayne, was a practical joke he played on an unsuspecting member of the public. John Wayne was driving through the suburbs of LA with his close friend and acting associate Ward Bond. Anyone who has driven from, say, Pasadena to Santa Monica, will know how each road, house and shopping mall all appears the same, mile after mile, after mile.

The Duke instructed Ward who was driving to pull up at the next Pizza Parlour to purchase a large, boxed pizza. Ward duly obliged. 'Are you hungry Duke?' 'Nope, drive on Ward.' He then told Ward to take the next left, then the second right and pull up at the property with the lollipop fence. The Duke stepped out of the car and armed with the food walked up the drive, rang the doorbell and waited. Soon a middle-aged woman answered the door. 'How-dee-do ma'am I have brought your Pizza delivery.' stated the Duke and promptly handed the box to the astonished lady. Eyes and mouth wide open, the lady exclaimed, 'You are John Wayne!' 'Sure am ma'am, enjoy.' The Duke then hurried back down the path, jumped into the car and told Ward to drive on. Now well underway, Ward queried the strange occurrence, 'Why on earth did you do that Duke?' 'Well Ward, when the lady tells her friends and family that John Wayne delivered her a Pizza, do you really think anyone will believe her?'

My parents' shop, The Chocolate Box, was situated in Lower Street in the very heart of Pulborough. Albert and Nora, ably assisted by Irene, and often reluctantly, me, dispensed sweets, ice creams, tobacco, toys, newspapers, magazines and most importantly, village gossip, to all and sundry including two well-known comedians: the shy and polite Norman Wisdom and the larger-than-life Jimmy Edwards both of whom lived just outside the village. Dad loved to while away the time with these two megastars often to the neglect of other customers and the distinct annoyance of my mum; herself an easy target for the sales representatives who called periodically to take orders for shop stock she didn't need, and ultimately could not sell. All discarded items would eventually find a home in the upper room: the Aladdin's Cave later to become a must-visit for my boys Mark and Andrew, although not before they had consumed vast quantities of confectionery courtesy of soft-hearted Albert.

One day when Albert was out Nora excelled herself and purchased two dozen toy boomerangs from a dapper salesman. Inevitably, upon my dad's return the usual row ensued: 'Nora this is just too bad, they will never sell and how do you know they will actually work?' After the shop closed dad and I armed with two boomerangs tried them out on the local recreation ground. "I just knew they wouldn't come back John, another complete waste of money!" dad cried almost triumphantly before hurrying back home to inflict another wigging on my poor mother.

The faulty boomerangs were consigned to the upper room and soon forgotten; until Charlie Drake recorded a little comedy number *My Boomerang Won't Come Back* which quickly found its way into the hit parade. Dad, never one to miss an opportunity, dug out the rogue boomerangs and placed them on display in the toy section of the shop, not forgetting to double the original asking price. Next he found a felt-tipped pen and a large sheet of white card and very neatly composed the following advertisement which he positioned pride of place in the centre of the shop window: 'BOOMERANGS FOR SALE – GUARANTEED NOT TO COME BACK – Only 5/- each. Hurry as supplies are very limited'. Within a week they were all sold.

Dad was taken into hospital with severe chest pains and subsequently diagnosed with terminal lung cancer. The surgeon called me in and showed me the X-ray, which clearly displayed that one lung was virtually eaten away by the terrible disease and the other had developed a sinister shadow. "It is too late to operate Mr Madell, your father has only a few months left. Shall I tell him or will you?" he said bluntly.

After consulting with my mum, I elected to tell dad his fate. "You know The Duke had the big 'C' dad. Well, you likewise," I found myself saying. "But John Wayne died from lung cancer," dad exclaimed. "Yes he did dad, and so will you." There is no easy way of telling a parent such devastating news, and I was making a real fist of it. We looked at each other long and hard and finally dad broke the silence: "I so wanted to get to know your son Paul." Paul was two at the time. "How long have I got son?" "A few months dad," I said, trying to be positive.

Dad, through sheer grit and determination lasted another eighteen months and did get to spend quality time with his grandson Paul, before he died in May 1984.

My Boomerang Won't Come Back
Performer: Charlie Drake
Composer: Drake
Number 14:   October 1961

Chapter 4 – Hurst

Psalm 22:16
An evil gang is round me; like a pack of dogs they close in on me; they tear at my hands and feet.

Late one afternoon a middle-aged couple approached me on the promenade and eagerly informed me that a couple of drunken yobs were becoming increasingly abusive to those in their vicinity on the beach. In fact they were only about thirty yards from my office and I was surprised that I hadn't noticed them myself. By the time I had informed them they were in an alcohol-free zone they had already consumed a dozen bottles from a Stella twenty-pack. Unable to persuade them to pack up and leave the beach, I collected both the dead bottles together with the remaining full ones and invited them back to my office if they wished to recover their property. The two men, both over six feet and in their early twenties became verbally abusive and I was relieved to see Dave my colleague quickly approaching. "Don't mess with these two comedians John; I have already called the Old Bill," Dave said, and turning to the men added, "Best sod off lads before you get arrested." However, calling the police and expecting them to appear is, frankly, worlds apart.

Back at the office I had separated the dead and live bottles and bagged up the live ones. I said, "It's your last chance; you can take the bag and immediately leave the beach area; alternatively, wait for the police to arrive." Reasoning with two drunks is about as productive as pissing in the wind and these two were on the edge of turning ugly. The tattooed one said to his mate, "Shall I hit him or will you?" I really needed the police backup to arrive.

I soon found to my delight that I was to become as happy at The Weald School, as I had been unhappy at Arundale School. The Weald School, built in 1956, was still finding its identity when I entered the gates three years later. The school, located in Billingshurst five miles from my home, was co-educational with a capacity for eight hundred students. The Headmaster, Mr V. V. Gee, was a no-nonsense man who appeared to me to be older than

God; in reality, I guess he was in his mid-fifties. His nickname was, not surprisingly, 'Dobbin'.

Dobbin was a frightening figure who without hesitation would lift a pupil off the ground and none too gently 'place him' against the wall, if he happened to be walking on the wrong side of the corridor. The very last place on earth you would wish to be was outside his office awaiting interrogation about some minor misdemeanour. Caning was the normal form of punishment; come to think of it, the only form of punishment. Dobbin's single deference to political correctness, if indeed it existed in the Fifties, was to delegate the task of caning the girls to the most senior female member of staff.

On the first day of term the new intake were ushered into the junior playground and called out alphabetically to form seven lines, the A-stream, B-stream and so on. I found myself standing next to Denis Evans and Brian Macey, two of my new class mates. Facing us was the Headmaster, and seven adults whom we assumed were to be allotted as our class teachers. While waiting patiently the three of us simultaneously noticed a young, petite, slim and beautiful lady. "Cor, I do hope we get her," Brian said with great enthusiasm. "Fat chance, I bet we end up with the mean-looking git in the checked jacket," Denis responded glumly. Denis, like me, was from Pulborough; Brian lived in the tiny village of Coolham located about four miles east of Billingshurst where his dad was the local butcher, and from that day the three of us became firm friends.

"Follow me," the young lady called out to our line in a low sexy voice, "my name is Miss Davis and I will be your form teacher this year. I teach art and crafts, therefore your room will be the school art room on the first floor. I am sure we shall all get on together really well." "We've hit the jackpot boys, come on!" I said excitedly. We nicknamed Miss Davis 'Dolly', and thereafter she became almost universally known as Dolly Davis. We entered a light, airy, brightly decorated room and soon learnt from Dolly that she was twenty-two years of age and straight out of teachers' training college; it was not only our first day at The Weald but also her first day in school as a full-time teacher, which instantly gave us a common bond. Imagine a cross between Audrey Hepburn and Jean Simmons with an added pinch of sex appeal; that was Dolly.

Surprisingly, she soon became equally popular with the girls in the class as with the boys and not just because she was a really nice person; Dolly gave the girls fashion and makeup tips and very quickly became their role model. For the boys her popularity was born out of lust, promoted by the odd glimpse of thigh or cleavage.

The trick for us was to stand alongside and a fraction behind our seated teacher when she was checking and passing judgement on our individual offerings. Peering over her shoulder there was a reasonable chance, if she was wearing a loose blouse, of spotting her bosom. In fact she sometimes had a very slight nervous tremor which had the effect of giving her pert tits a complete life of their very own. Not surprisingly, as the term wore on, her new male colleagues regularly seemed to pop into our classroom for the most tenuous of reasons, perhaps just to borrow a marker pen or a sheet of card, so I guess it was not just us lads who were besotted by the delectable Dolly.

The highlight of my time at The Weald happened on the final day of the 1959 autumn term when the last two lessons of the day were designated for the class Christmas party. Dolly was wearing a short low-cut dress for the occasion and looked the bee's knees. She asked me to help her pour the lemonade and I naturally took up my 'peering' position above and alongside our class teacher. Not only was the dress low-cut but so too was the matching bra; with her usual slight tremor she suddenly coughed and her left tit popped right out revealing to me full sight of her nipple. Dolly glanced up and, aware of her indiscretion, smiled, shrugged and within a trice adjusted her dress.

Without doubt it was an intimate moment between me and my beautiful teacher. Rather than rush back and report to my mates I privately savoured the moment and never did let on that Christmas had indeed come early for me that year. It was a moment that became indelibly printed on my twelve-year-old memory and needless to say, remains with me to this day. Never again did I take up pole position behind Dolly; what was the point now that I had witnessed all her charm!

The school day started at 8.50am with registration in our form room before we rushed down to the hall for assembly. This usually consisted of a hymn, a bible reading and prayers before the Headmaster's announcements which might include reading a letter sent by one of the junior officers aboard the school ship, the Border Reiver, or his observations on good, bad or indifferent behaviour, or perhaps congratulating a school team on a recent success. Once every term General Renton, chair of the school governors, joined Dobbin on stage and mumbled a few irrelevances before touring the campus. The General was nicknamed the 'One-Armed Bandit' due to the fact that he had lost an arm on active service during the First World War. The whole proceedings lasted twenty minutes before we filed off to our first lesson of the day. I presume the same ritual was repeated in every secondary school up and down the country.

When, finally, Dobbin was reckless enough to make me a prefect I took a turn or two in reading the lesson from the lectern, which in front of such a large audience I found a little daunting. Other than those experiences I can only really recall a handful of assemblies over my five years at The Weald.

One unforgettable occasion was when my mate Brian Macey decided, in his wisdom, to alter the words of the hymn *Stand up! Stand up for Jesus!* to 'Sit down, sit down, for Jesus, as the buggers at the back can't see'; neither did Brian see Mr Corby our science teacher standing right behind him, and who promptly hauled him out of the hall by the ear for a good caning.

Without doubt the most memorable assembly occurred on 4 November, 1960. Seated on the stage that Friday morning were Dobbin and the One-Armed Bandit, together with a rather attractive and immaculately dressed lady in her fifties. At the end of prayers, the two men stood up and shook hands with the female and Dobbin addressed the school: 'Staff and pupils, I am delighted to introduce you all to our guest on stage this morning who has kindly agreed to join the School Board of Governors. Please, by way of a Weald welcome put your hands together to appropriately greet Lady Shakerley.' Dear old naïve Dobbin really had picked the week of all weeks to make this grand introduction; a time when every paper, radio and TV news channel was eagerly, and widely, reporting the item that would kick start the Sixties' sexual revolution: *Lady Chatterley's Lover.*

The trial of Penguin Books Ltd over the publication of D. H. Lawrence's novel took place over six days, ending on 2 November 1960. The book was alleged to be an obscene publication as it described, in great detail, sexual encounters between Lady Chatterley and a gamekeeper; however, Penguin Books won the day and straight away published the novel, priced then at the equivalent of 18p – the first run of 200,000 copies sold out immediately.

There was total uproar in the school hall that morning. Never had an honoured guest experienced such a rousing welcome; applause, cheering, laughter and wolf whistles, from not only the pupils but also the twenty-five-strong teaching staff who were all in attendance. The bedlam continued for a full five minutes. The Head's complexion turned from a bewildered white, to an angry grey; the old general collapsed back into his chair wiping his brow with his good arm; his face gradually turned purple and I really thought he was going to have a heart attack. Mr Stone the deputy head saved further embarrassment by jumping on the stage, calling for order and dismissing the assembly.

When my class filed off into one of the huts adjacent to the hall for a General Studies lesson with the bearded and likeable teacher, Gerry Elliott, the hilarity continued. Dear Gerry sat at the front of the class with tears streaming down his face, his merriment was totally out of control. Nothing was achieved in that fifty-minute period for as soon as Gerry tried to speak he broke into uncontrolled laughter. I'm not sure what was funnier, the actual event or our teacher's subsequent reaction.

Oddly enough, I did know Lady Shakerley as she often popped into The Chocolate Box where I worked serving on the sweet counter most Saturday mornings, but I did not know her name until that fateful Friday. Two or three years had passed when I found myself alone in the shop with her on a quiet midweek-day during the summer recess. I casually mentioned the fact that I attended The Weald School and had indeed witnessed her introduction by the Headmaster on that memorable day in the assembly hall. Her eyes sparkled as she said to me, "That was, without doubt, one of the funniest moments of my life; it was absolute agony trying to supress my laughter. I just knew in advance that as soon as my name was announced all those present would be highly amused, so I suggested to Mr Gee it might be prudent not to introduce me by my title. Sadly, he failed to comply with my recommendation. Incidentally, did you laugh John?" "Maybe I did, just a tad, Lady Chatterley," I replied with a wry smile.

One day in the science class Mr Corby the teacher announced that his watch had stopped. My friend Terry Roberts, seated next to me, raised his hand. "I have a watch sir and the time is half past monkey's arse and a quarter to his balls." After the laughter died down a long silence prevailed. Handing Terry a blank piece of paper and pen Corby bellowed, "Write your answer down in very neat capital letters Roberts." Terry sheepishly did as he was instructed. Corby then added his comments. "Now Roberts, proceed to the Headmaster's office; knock on his door, enter and hand him the note, then wait for his reaction, and if you are able to walk Roberts, return without delay to this class."

Fifteen minutes later a red-eyed Terry returned. "How many strokes of the cane did you receive Roberts?" Corby enquired. "Sir, it was six of the best," Terry whimpered. "Not enough Roberts, not enough by far!" Corby then gave Terry another couple of strokes in front of the whole class. Terry was a little short for his age, yet swarthy and solidly built. He played right-half to my left-half in the school football team; deep-lying and tenacious in the tackle, he allowed me to push forward to make the occasional shot on goal. At the end of the lesson Terry said, "I will get even with those sadistic bastards John, you just wait and see."

The school-leaving age back then was fifteen. Terry hated school and at the first opportunity gained an apprenticeship at Hamilton Cole, a television and radio shop in Pulborough, and was set to start the day after his birthday in early November. His very last day at school was in fact November 5, Guy Fawkes Day. On that afternoon Terry crept under Dobbin's office window, which was located on the ground floor overlooking the drive. At the time Dobbin was enjoying his afternoon tea and biscuits with none other than the hated Corby. With great precision Terry lobbed a giant banger through the half-opened window; it landed on Dobbin's desk and promptly exploded.

Knowing the plan, a number of classmates and I had strategically hidden beside the wooden huts opposite the Head's office to witness the event. Dobbin immediately poked his head out of the window to spot Terry hot-footing it up the drive. Although both Dobbin and Corby gave chase, the middle-aged men were very unlikely to catch up with Terry: The Weald School's then champion runner. Needless to say, Terry declined the opportunity to return for Prize-Giving Day to collect his medal for winning the West Sussex Combined Schools Cross-Country Run.

Terry remained at Hamilton Cole for forty years, eventually acquiring the business; building and diversifying the now-sizable company into a commercially viable prospect for acquisition, before finally selling on to secure his early retirement.

Although Terry had no time for our Headmaster, I did. As demonstrated, Dobbin was a strict disciplinarian, consequently there was little or no disruption during the lessons. Those students who wanted to learn had every chance of gaining good GCE results. By and large the standard of teaching was good and this again was down to the Head's ability to recruit a strong team. Most of us believed that he had a good working relationship with his staff and we, the pupils, were most fortunate to receive a stimulating education in a happy atmosphere. Best of all, Dobbin had a zero tolerance to bullying.

In my first year I vividly remember a morning assembly when standing on stage was a third-year boy by the name of Duke with a sign hanging around his neck: 'Bully'. After prayers Dobbin announced that bullying had been detected in the junior playground and the culprit Duke would receive six strokes of the cane immediately after assembly. He added: 'What's more the punishment will not be lightly administered'. Ouch!

It is true to say that bullying cannot be stamped out altogether, and this applies in all walks of life. On a few occasions I did find myself on the receiving end at The Weald; however, it was not on the scale that my best school friend Denis Evans had to endure. Denis was small and well-built, and by far the best footballer in the school. Yet the real reason Denis was singled out was that he found great delight in subtly 'Taking the Mickey' out of the yobs to make them look small. Denis was a gold medal 'piss-taker'. Hanging out with Denis could be a risky business.

John Madell aged twelve years

In the first half of our second year we were experiencing big trouble with the fourth-year leavers, mainly from 4C: the bottom stream who were destined to dig the roads, work in the fields or similar dead-end jobs. The odd punch on the arm passing in the corridor, a trip from behind, a menacing stare, or a whispered threat would turn into a beating in the toilets or maybe a cigarette burn administered to the back of the hand. In our hour of need the saviour arrived: sitting suited and booted in the front row waiting for the Register to be called, was David Hurst.

Hurst attended a leading public school until his father hit upon hard times and was forced for financial reasons to switch his son to The Weald. Hurst was huge for his age, six feet tall and two hundred pounds. Having been in the private education sector myself I knew Hurst would need a friend to show him the ropes. Denis and I adopted Hurst who turned out to be a real nice guy, sadly without a brain in his head and no sporting ability that we could detect. In fact in a yes-no answer test in maths Hurst achieved an astonishing mark of nil out of twenty! The teacher, Fletcher, sarcastically worked out the odds of even guessing every question wrong were thousands to one against. So Hurst, with his Savile Row suit, posh voice and ungainly gait, ventured out into the big world of The Weald campus.

It was not long before we met up with the bad guys in the corridor and one Goozy Greenman inflicted a backhander to Denis's ear. Without hesitation, Hurst grabbed Goozy by the throat and expressed displeasure in his best Eton accent: "You leave my little friend alone you nasty yob." Then he casually pushed the astonished hard-man to one side and wandered on. Hurst had made his mark on the self-appointed leader of the bully-boys and I knew Goozy would not let this slight on his status go lightly.

Vying for leadership were Strippo Stivinsky, Gus and Fuller. Gus, who was in my scout patrol, warned me, 'The posh git is dead', and by association Denis, Brian and I needed watch out. The following day before assembly the three of us had a meeting with Hurst to discuss tactical defence. Hurst seemed totally undeterred and stated that if push came to shove he would sort out all four of them. He added as a postscript that if we found ourselves in trouble: "Don't worry lads, just whistle. Remember, just whistle."

Trouble came soon enough, at lunchtime in the boys' toilets. My head was smashed against the wall just as I was having a pee and Brian, who was standing next to me, received a kick up the arse. Denis wisely nipped into a cubicle knowing he stood no chance. Two punches grounded Brian and just as I was staring at Gus's right fist, in burst Hurst. So abrupt was his entry that he took the door clean off its hinges smashing into Goozy, pressing his face against the wall. One punch from Hurst knocked Fuller clean out. Just as Strippo attempted to make a run for it I administered a neat trip and down he went banging his head on the floor. Meanwhile, Hurst wrestled Gus to the ground and proceeded to wipe his head in the urinal which Brian and I had just peed in. "You can come out now Denis and enjoy the fun," Hurst cried.

At this very moment Cheeseman the school caretaker entered the room, most probably saving Gus from drowning. When Cheeseman saw the state of the toilet door he went absolutely mad and immediately marched us all to the Headmaster's office. Denis claimed his innocence: "But, Mr Cheeseman I wasn't there." "Well you are now," the middle-aged caretaker tersely replied.

We all stood right outside the Head's door glaring at one another; the yobs were seen first. Through the door we could clearly hear the dialogue. It turned out that Strippo and Goozy had been expelled from their previous school. Dobbin, in considering his options, told them that should he care to expel the duo then the authorities would undoubtedly send them to an Approved School. In his wisdom Dobbin decided that provided they paid to replace the damaged door, then he would merely suspend them all for a week. Not, of course, before he administered his trusty cane. Twenty-four strokes seemed to take forever, especially as we were anticipating the same fate. The downcast yobs marched out; we filed in. Dobbin tore into us, first threatening to invite our fathers to the school; followed by the prospect of all sorts of unpleasant punishment. "However, in view of your previous good record I'm going to let you off this time. Do not let me see you in this office again, you are dismissed."

As we hastened toward the door he called, "Madell, come back in and shut the door." Oh no, just as I thought I'd got off, was I back in the sticky stuff? Dobbin stood up and said, smiling, "Well John, today it looks like the good guys won and the bad guys lost; you may go." What a lovely man!

You can imagine it took no time at all for Hurst to reach cult status, and basking in his reflected glory Denis was insufferable. Denis took every opportunity to taunt and goad the yobs, now powerless to respond. The spring term came to its end and we returned for the summer term after the Easter holiday. No sign of Hurst. Denis and I rushed off to find our popular form teacher Charlie Redman. "Sir, where is David Hurst?" Denis enquired. "Hurst? Oh, his father has come into an inheritance and David has returned to Eton," Charlie said. True enough, we never saw Hurst again. Denis's wheeze to put it out that Hurst had chickenpox and would not be at school for a couple of weeks, merely delayed the inevitable.

Denis, Terry and I were picked to play football for the school's First Eleven. This was most unusual, as no second-year pupil had ever been selected to play with the fourth and fifth-years, let alone three picked for one game. Denis decided that our elevation was down to our outstanding ability and this was our first stepping stone towards a career in the professional game. He took great pleasure informing all and sundry of his first-team status. Terry and I were not so sure though. True, Denis was easily good enough to play first-team football; Terry and I, not so.

The match was scheduled as an afternoon game away to St Thomas More School, which meant time off lessons, and training with the First Team. Thomas More was a Catholic Approved School run by Jesuit priests for bad boys from South London. This fixture gave us the perfect opportunity to ingratiate ourselves with our older peers most of whom were prefects. They were all well aware of the trouble we had endured at the hands of the yobs and were sympathetic to the problems we had to face without our guardian Hurst. They informed us that all four yobs had received letters home from Dobbin making it crystal clear that one more incident would lead to expulsion.

Changing into our football kit in the dressing room Mr Baker the PE teacher explained that the last time we had played Thomas More, The Weald had won by eight goals to nil. "I have therefore decided to introduce Evans, Roberts and Madell to even things up today," Baker casually stated. In other words, we were there to weaken the team! Denis's face was a picture: you would think he had just chewed a wasp. We won by five goals to two. Even before their defeat, the lads from Thomas More had appeared oppressed and downtrodden, and we felt for their plight. As we changed after the game Terry declared that he would never be a naughty boy again. I suspect that vow lasted all of twenty-four hours.

As the summer term neared its conclusion I became increasingly wary of our adversaries. All four were leaving at the end of term and the threat of expulsion was fast becoming diluted. Intimidating stares told me that trouble was not far away; as Nat King Cole sang, *Let's Face the Music and Dance*, or should it be 'Run'?

On the penultimate day of term Denis, Brian and I were passing time after lunch playing football with a lightweight ball in the senior playground. The area was marked out as four tarmac tennis courts, surrounded by an eight-foot-high wire mesh fence with a four-foot-wide gap at the entrance leading back to the main teaching block. It was a hot day and most of the school were scattered over the extensive playing fields; we were on our own. Or were we? Four menacing figures were leaning against the inside of the fence next to the only exit. This was payback time; the three of us were cornered with no escape route other than a vague chance of climbing the fence. That was not to be as the yobs had read our thoughts and were now spread out and strolling towards us. Surreal, just like a scene from an old western movie that was very familiar to me.

Attack is always the best form of defence; with this in mind I removed my belt which had a large brass buckle, wrapped the strap around my wrist and ran straight at Strippo who in my opinion was one of the softer targets in the gang. Swinging the belt around my head I caught him with a well-aimed blow to the side of his cheek. The buckle pin opened up a three-inch wound and down went Strippo in agony. Strippo now had a better reason for his nickname. Amazingly, there was no reaction from the other three yobs. I yelled to Denis and Brian to run. They needed no further encouragement and had already brushed past our opponents and were through the gap in the fence, closely followed by me.

Within seconds we were in the relative safety of the teaching block and kept on running, stopping only to collect our belongings from the cloakroom; up the drive, down the road to the station and straight on the first train home. I don't remember what Denis or Brian did next. For myself, I skipped the last day of term hoping never to see my adversaries again, of course there was little hope of that as Gus lived in Pulborough. To be fair, when I saw Gus again he never referred to our past skirmishes and over latter years we became friends. Sadly, Gus died from a heart attack in 2006; the industrious labouring man worked himself into an early grave.

Meanwhile, back on the Littlehampton beach there was no sign of police backup. Unlike the playground confrontation I was in no position to pre-empt the situation and therefore waited for the threatened blow. I just had to work out which one was going to perform the deed. I said, "Well lads I've been hit before and no doubt I shall be hit again. Do your worst." Perhaps they realised through their drunken haze that it was no contest. One of them replied, "Best leave him; he's an old man." With that they walked off down the promenade straight into the arms of two police patrol officers.

Rather than detain the pair the police took them to the railway station and made them catch the train back home to Pulborough, effectively running the two thugs out of town. Purely out of curiosity I asked Dan, one of the police officers, if he had taken their names. Dan said, "They are well known to the police, Chatfield and Greenman." Small world. What comes around goes around, methinks.

Catch Us If You Can
Performers: The Dave Clark Five
Composers: Clark and Davidson
Number 5:   July 1965

Chapter 5 – Denis

Ecclesiastes 3:1
Everything that happens in this world happens at the time God chooses.

The greensward runs from the Windmill Theatre car park to East Beach Café car park, an area approximately two thirds of a mile long by two hundred yards wide sandwiched between the promenade and South Terrace. The green was originally sand dunes, levelled and seeded in the 1860s, a promenade walkway created and timber groynes built to dissipate the waves. It incorporates crazy golf, a putting green, a designated barbeque area and a children's playground, punctuated half-way along by a large coach park at Banjo Road. It is also ideal for dog walkers, games such as rounders, cricket and football. During high summer weekends the occasional official event will take place: a rock concert, a circus and go-kart-racing spring to mind. In short, a very popular attractive amenity much used by all and sundry.

Wandering across the green one afternoon a football struck me on the back of the head and knocked off my cap. I looked round to see four young teenage boys laughing at me and politely requesting the return of the ball. I could see the funny side, happily kicked the ball back and sat on the promenade wall to mentally join in the fun. At that age, together with my mates Denis, Brian and a few others, we could easily while away seven or eight hours on long hot summers days playing football on the local recreation ground, dreaming of gracing the Wembley Stadium turf. Half a century later these Littlehampton boys were no different and having a great time in the sun.

Sadly, my football career did not take me to Wembley. Nearing the end of the 1965/66 season in West Sussex League Division Five (Northern Section), the Pulborough second team was bottom of the league and away to Stedham. They were just one place above us and to avoid finishing last, we needed a win. Not that we could be relegated as we were in the lowest division, yet we certainly did not want to collect the wooden spoon. Ever present at left-back I guess I could shoulder some of the blame for our lack of success.

When we arrived at Stedham Football Ground that sunny afternoon in April we were a man short. That man was our centre-forward. Our twelfth man who would normally run the line was a full-back. I volunteered to play up front and our reserve slotted into the left-back position.

Minus two goals after half an hour, our heads were down, until our keeper cleared the ball in my direction; I was standing just inside our half, the lone forward marked by two defenders. The obvious course of action was to run toward the high ball, trap it, and turn. In one exceptional movement, worthy of Denis Law, I had turned both defenders and found myself on a breakaway in the opponents' half. Running with the ball at top speed – well, my top speed – within a very few seconds I reached the edge of the penalty area and with only the advancing goalkeeper to beat, I had what seemed to be an age to decide on how to finish; would it be a deft lob, a sidestep and a low-positioned shot, or merely blast the ball into the corner? By now I was nearly on the penalty spot where the keeper was standing spreadeagled to narrow the angle. Decision made, I pushed the ball through his legs into the centre of the goal: 1-2. Before Stedham could restart the referee blew the half-time whistle.

Oranges sucked dry, the second half kicked-off. With ten minutes gone we were once again on the back foot with play mainly in our half until awarded a generous free kick approximately ten yards from the left side of their penalty area. I normally took throw-ins, free kicks and corners, mainly to justify my place in the team. Being twenty-five yards out, the assumption was that I would chip the ball towards the far post in the hope that one of my teammates might connect and head the ball goalwards, and with that in mind both teams lined up accordingly. In the mid-Sixties the balls were still leather, laced and considerably heavier than they are today. Football boots were designed to cope with the weight and consequently had hard toes. As I ran up to the ball I made a split-second decision to aim at the undefended near post and struck the ball with my reinforced left toe, derisively known as a toe punt. The ball hit the underside of the bar before nestling in the corner of the net: 2-2.

The Stedham team were by now deflated and with fifteen minutes remaining I was certain that we could go on to win. Our winger, John 'Little Otter' Stewart (so named for his swimming prowess and being the younger brother of Michael 'Big Otter'

Stewart) picked the ball up on the halfway line and tore down the left side. I was the only other forward and ten yards behind in the inside-right position. Fast approaching the corner Otter had already passed two defenders and was clearly planning on making the cross. I was still too far behind to receive the centre ball. No problem, Otter was right-footed and I knew he would check back and cross with his right peg. This would give me enough time to find the perfect near post position. With the sun gleaming on his pebble glasses Otter did just that, sidestepping their full-back and delivered a floating cross. Diving past Stedham's centre-half and captain, with the flick of my head I directed the ball into the right-hand top corner of the goal. Final score: 2-3.

Thanks mainly to me, Pulborough were not going to end the season bottom of the league. Geoff Hurst was soon to experience the elation I was feeling that afternoon when three months later he also scored a hat-trick, not on a Sussex field, but to secure the World Cup for England on the hallowed Wembley turf.

The Pulborough Football Club selection committee met on a Monday night in the Red Lion's function room to pick the teams for the coming Saturday fixtures. The First Team were home to Slindon in the semi-final of the Divisional Cup. The Seconds were away to Fittleworth. The team sheets were already posted on the board outside the pub when I arrived that night for a pint. In fact I didn't even bother to look as I was always left-back; however, a friend did look and called me back, saying with a hint of glee: "John you've lost your place in the team." Sure enough last week's Twelfth Man had replaced me, and to add insult to injury I had not even made the reserve spot. I was terribly upset and wished I had not volunteered to play centre-forward against Stedham. "I thought you said you played a blinder?" he laughed.

"Clearly that was not the case," I had to reply. Landlord Les Morrison poured me a pint and congratulated me on my hat-trick: "Changed your name to Pele then John?" "A fat lot of good it did me Les, I've been dropped," I exclaimed. Les looked puzzled as he moved to the public bar to serve another customer. When Les finally returned to the saloon bar he suggested I look again on the notice board: "You are not dropped John, you are playing centre-forward for the First Team in the big match!"

This was a big match indeed; Pulborough had not made the final of the cup for at least ten years. I shined my boots so hard that I could see my reflection. With number nine on my back and a home crowd of three hundred villagers I knew we had a great chance of winning the semi-final tie. Slindon were lower in the First Division than us and we had already beaten them in the league at home less than a month previously. The pace appeared lightning-quick to me and I seriously wished I had not smoked a cigarette in the dressing room just before the game commenced. The first-half play was evenly balanced when the whistle blew for the break. In truth I had played badly, hardly touched the ball, and it came as no surprise when Tony the club captain called me over and advised me that I would play the second half at left-back.

Tony, in his late twenties, was a good footballer who had once represented the Army in his National Service days. Slindon's right-winger was a 'tricky bollocks' and more or less tied me in knots for most of the second half. Tony once again approached and curtly said, "Shit John, if you can't tackle him at least take him out; know what I mean?" I knew what he meant. Two minutes later I did exactly what my captain had instructed me to do: with a thigh-high hack I finished his trickery for the afternoon. There was one problem: the referee deemed the foul to be inside the penalty area. With ten minutes to go Slindon scored from the spot. Although Pulborough had more of the play and much the better chances we lost 0-1, and it was my fault. As the final whistle blew I sank to my knees on the wet and windswept pitch. When Tony trotted over and placed his hand on my shoulder I thought the old warhorse was about to whisper a few comforting words to lift my dulled spirits; wrong: "Yours was easily the worst performance I have witnessed in my eight years as captain. Now do something right for the first time this afternoon and take the nets down you useless sod!"

Sheepishly I called at the Red Lion the following Monday night to check who the Second Team were playing on the last day of the season, only to find I had been selected as Twelfth Man. I never played for Pulborough again.

Since about the age of ten, association football has played a big part in my life be it playing, watching, or collecting autographs, programmes and various memorabilia. Regardless of life's highs and lows, football has for me been a stabiliser and even a brief escape from reality. It is easy to forget the defeat and relegation, as somehow victory and promotion will always have greater clarity in the memory bank.

Even after a heavy home defeat there is always next week. It is hard to convey to the uninitiated the raw emotion football can kindle; it was probably best summed up by the late, great Liverpool manager Bill Shankly: 'Football is not just a case of life and death; it is far more important than that'.

On my eleventh birthday my father took me to see Brighton and Hove Albion play Charlton Athletic at the Goldstone Ground in Hove for the opening home game of the 1958/59 season. Having gained promotion from Division Three South it was Albion's second game in Division Two. The previous Saturday the team had been defeated 9-0 away to Middlesbrough with five of the goals scored by a certain Brian Clough. Wedged in a twenty-eight-thousand-strong crowd behind the South Stand goal I could see precious little other than Eric Gill the Brighton goalkeeper's backside. Regardless, armed with a blue and white scarf knitted by mum and a Second World War air raid rattle painted blue and white by dad, I was intoxicated by the atmosphere generated by the partisan crowd. The free-flowing game ended in a 2-2 draw and I instantly became a passionate Albion fan. From that day on I made the fifty-mile round-trip whenever I could.

There was always great rivalry between football fans at The Weald School, where they were predominately Portsmouth supporters; not so my two best classmates: Denis Evans and I were fanatical Albion fans, and Brian Macey, a Fulham supporter. The three of us fell into a Saturday routine, playing for the school in the morning and then catching the train, one week to see the Albion and the next weekend to see Fulham. From September 1959 through to April 1962 we rarely missed a trip to London to witness Division One games or to Brighton for Division Two matches. The trip to Hove was comparatively easy: from Billingshurst Station to Littlehampton; switch to the coast train bound for Brighton alighting at Hove station, then a five-minute walk to the Goldstone ground, took an hour. The trip to London was more like two-and-a-quarter hours.

After the morning game at school we normally returned to Pulborough to have a bite to eat at Denis's house with Ken his younger brother, who from time to time might join in on our adventures. Their house was right next door to the station and we usually caught the fast train to Victoria, jumped on the underground and made one change before arriving at Putney Bridge. From Putney, Craven Cottage the home of Fulham Football Club, was approximately a one-mile walk west alongside the River Thames. I guess I preferred the trip to the south coast to cheer on my favourite team; yet somehow travelling to London at the age of twelve, thirteen, or fourteen years to watch all the top teams was perhaps equally good, if not, sometimes, even more exciting. To spice up the afternoons we took to collecting the footballers' autographs.

Once we learnt the ropes we became most adept at maximising our collection both before and after the games. To secure the coveted signature there were only a very few opportunities to catch the celebrity at the right moment. In the case of professional footballers we found these were when they arrived on the coach, when they left the ground or when they inspected the pitch to select their footwear. Better still, if they were likely to catch a train, we hot-footed to the appropriate mainline station. The home team players were easy, as we normally collared them when they left the ground after the game and soon reached the stage where we had secured all their signatures.

Fulham's top player and captain was Johnny Haynes, then the England captain and the first £100-a-week player. Haynes arrived on match day in his Jaguar and one of the ground staff parked the car for him, returning it to the main entrance after the game. The Fulham players normally left the ground about one hour after the end of the game to walk either to the underground or home. Haynes waited outside for his car, and whilst waiting, lined up the autograph hunters and signed in turn. He only provided one autograph for each of the twenty or so eager fans. If a boy returned to the back of the queue he knew instantly, and reprimanded the culprit for being greedy.

Eventually, Denis, Brian and I became familiar to the great man whom we addressed as 'Mr Haynes' and he, amazingly, took the trouble to ask our names, and even more surprisingly, he remembered them. I think it would be most unusual for the current England captain to take the same trouble, and much less likely for the fans to gain such easy access to the current hero. Johnny Haynes played for Fulham for seventeen years and earned fifty-four caps for England. His special gift was to perfect the long pass with his exquisite left foot and deliver the ball inch-perfect to a colleague at a time when the old-fashioned balls were heavy and inconsistent in weight. Fulham were perennially fighting a relegation battle and had Haynes played for one of the top teams like Manchester United, Wolves or Spurs, then there is no doubt that he would have won every honour that football had to offer. Yet he remained a loyal servant to the one club and was liked and highly respected by his peers. To Denis, me, and especially Brian, Johnny Haynes was a god. When Haynes died in 2005, Brian's wife, Glynis, told me that her husband actually shed a tear.

Johnny Haynes

Ernest autograph hunting can be great fun and most challenging. We often sneaked on board the team coach to acquire as many signatures as possible before the driver threw us off. On one occasion, outside Craven Cottage, the West Bromwich Albion coach drove off with Denis still on board. When discovered a quarter of a mile down the road, Denis was kicked off accompanied by cheers and applause from the players. Yet some players would just not sign however hard we tried. Denis and I walked alongside Bill Foulkes and Noel Cantwell of Man. U. all the way from Craven Cottage to Putney Bridge station with no success. Jimmy Greaves of Spurs so exasperated Denis that he tapped on the window of his train compartment and gestured 'big-head' much to the amusement of the other Spurs players! Most were OK and seemed to like the recognition that fame had brought their way. On good days at the mainline stations catering for northern journeys such as St Pancras or King's Cross we acquired the signatures of whole teams including Wolves, Liverpool, Sheffield United, Leicester City and Manchester City. Back at Brighton and Hove Albion we made friends with the trainer Joe Wilson who nagged some players into coming out of the dressing room just to sign our books and pictures. Sometimes good old Joe would even take away our programmes and source the signatures on our behalf.

One Saturday in the summer during the football closed-season the three of us decided to take the train to Victoria and ended up in Battersea Park, which had good amenities including a permanently sited fun fair, and is located just south of the Thames. As soon as we arrived we made for the amusements, which turned out too pricey for our lowly budget. Pooling our meagre funds we could afford, at best, only a couple of rides apiece. Disconsolate, we wandered over to the football pitches where only one was still marked out with goalposts intact. Frustratingly, we had not brought a ball with us and decided instead to sit on the bank and eat our packed lunches. Nevertheless it was a beautiful June day and we tucked into the sandwiches and cake our mums had provided.

Four men turned up and started to kick around in one of the goalmouths. "They are not very good, are they?" Denis commented. Denis was a brilliant footballer and had his own party piece. With the ball placed on the penalty spot, Denis could hit the bar or either post at will, with a nine out of ten success rate. "How much money have we got?" Denis enquired. Brian, who was holding the pot, replied "About thirty bob." "Go and challenge them, John;" Denis instructed, "tell them what I can do." I did just that; they laughed and told me to piss off. I responded as follows:

"I bet you £1 that my little friend can hit the bar and both posts with just three shots." "It's a bet," the fat one replied. I called Denis over and quietly said, "Sorry Denis, no margin for error, can you do it?" Denis smiled, "Don't you worry John, pressure is my middle name, just pass me the ball."

As a warmup Denis juggled the ball in the air for a couple of minutes alternating both feet, knees and head as only Denis could; big head! Finally he placed the ball on the penalty spot. One minute later Tubby was handing over a £1 note. Denis then bravely said, "Double or quits on the three of us beating you in a match. The first team to score five goals wins." "Three boys against four men, you have no chance; line up and prepare to be slaughtered," Tubby scoffed. Well, Denis could run rings round most and score with ease. Brian was the school goalkeeper and a fearless shot-stopper. For my part, I was reasonably adept at tackling and distribution. Tubby was right: it was no contest; we won 5-0. In less than half an hour we had turned £1.50 into £4.50 and returned to the fun fair determined to sample all the rides.

It is amazing to look back and realise how much freedom we village lads had back in the early Sixties. At thirteen years of age we could leave home at eight thirty on a Saturday morning and not return until ten at night, and in the interim, dash all over London and think nothing of it. I am sure we gained a great deal of self-reliance and confidence through our adventures.

Waiting for the trains at Pulborough station we occasionally spent time with an elderly porter by the name of Charlie Balcombe. Charlie was a great old character who had plenty of 'war stories' to while away the time. One Saturday morning Denis and I were standing with Charlie when the main London to Chichester train pulled in and out stepped Katy Boyle. Katy was one of the first TV stars to make her name through game and panel shows, then in her early thirties, very attractive and glamorous. When Charlie rushed over to attend to her cases she asked him to call a cab and said that she was due to play golf that afternoon at the West Sussex Golf Club situated two miles south of Pulborough. Charlie duly found a taxi and called over to the female star, "Would you like your hockey knockers on the back seat or in the boot Mrs?" Charlie was not impressed with the size of his tip, I can't think why!

I lost touch with my old friends a few short years after we left school. Both Denis and Brian left at the age of fifteen, joined

Sainsbury's and moved to London. After two-thirds of a lifetime we all finally met again in May 2010 and, fifty years on, the three of us once again visit Brighton and Fulham together whenever the opportunity presents itself.

John, Denis and Brian, outside Craven Cottage, 2015

Since our reunion, I have spent many hours with Denis and only now do I fully appreciate the tragedy that so quickly unfolded for him in 1963. Denis and I were jogging along at The Weald at the beginning of our fifth and final academic year when his mother Dot Evans was taken seriously ill. By half term, breast cancer had stolen away her life at the age of forty-three.

Within two weeks of that devastating event Denis's dad, Bert Evans, and his younger brother Ken had moved to Kent to live with sister, Val, and her husband John. Bert was a signalman with Southern Rail and consequently able to do his job anywhere within the South of England. John Finch, the manager of Sainsbury's store in Chatham, arranged for Denis to be interviewed for a position as a shop apprentice with the company. Needless to say, Denis, a highly intelligent young man, passed with flying colours and began his career with Sainsbury's almost immediately. Accommodation was arranged and Denis was housed in a company hostel above Sainsbury's shop in Pinner High Street. Clearly, John had pulled out all the stops as his young brother-in-law ended up sharing a room with Brian Macey, by then a year into his butcher's apprenticeship.

For Denis, his immediate future was a fait accompli. Less than twenty days after losing his beloved mum, the fifteen-year-old was parted from his Dad, younger brother, the only home he had known, and the familiar surroundings of The Weald School to find himself in West London which was absolutely nothing like the rural village in which he had grown up. Clearly, his world had been turned upside down and perhaps the only saving grace was the company of his old school chum Brian Macey.

I am not sure, however, that either Brian or I did anywhere near enough to support our old mate in the depths of his despair. Brian, by the time Denis arrived at the hostel in Pinner, had fully established his role with his employers, found new friends and a position in goal with a local football team. No longer just the boy from a tiny Sussex village, and growing in self-confidence, perhaps Brian was subconsciously reluctant to fully include Denis within his new lifestyle and comprehensively show him the ropes. Over those first weeks and months Denis felt a lost soul in an alien world.

Could I have done more to mitigate the circumstances that Denis found himself in the autumn of President Kennedy's assassination? The answer, more than likely, is yes. There was a spare room at my home. Both my mum and dad liked Denis and, knowing their kind-hearted nature, I have no doubt they would have taken my friend under their wing until at least the completion of his education in the summer of 1964. Regrettably, they were not given that opportunity as neither I, nor anyone else in the village, asked them. As we lived in a comparatively close-knit community and The Chocolate Box, my parents' shop, was in the heart of Pulborough, the Evans family's dilemma would have been a hot topic of conversation.

In the circumstances, John Finch did his level best to sort out the conundrum that faced him. What defence can I offer? Although Denis was just a year younger than me, I was very much into discovering girls and consequently less interested in my mates. Moreover, coinciding with Mrs Evans' demise I contracted chicken-pox and was out of the loop for a couple of weeks. By the time I was fully aware of all the ramifications impacting on my old friend, his immediate future was a done deal. In short, Denis had left Pulborough for good. Sadly, the clock cannot be turned back and weak excuses became irrelevant a very long time ago.

This was not the first time that disaster had struck Denis. In 1955, he was playing with his older brother, Stan, and a number of other young friends in the sand pits adjacent to the Pulborough railway goods yard when a section of the pit collapsed, trapping Stan. Try as they might, the lads were unable to pull Denis's brother clear and when a rescue team arrived Stan was pronounced dead at the scene; he was just eleven years old.

In 1969 I received a call from Brian advising me that an accidental blow to Denis's head had caused a blood clot in his brain and our friend was lying unconscious in Maida Vale Hospital in North London with a 50/50 chance of survival. When I arrived at the hospital the next day Denis was half propped up in bed and totally unaware of my presence. After an hour-long one-way conversation I left his bedside. Shortly after my visit Denis was transferred to Russell Square to have the clot removed; the operation was a great success and within eighteen months he had made a full recovery.

Denis stayed with Sainsbury's for thirteen years until he was head-hunted by Texas Homecare whose rapid expansion had caused them to recruit tried and trusted retail executives to manage their DIY stores. Denis soon climbed the promotion ladder and eventually became Group Marketing Manager. Today, now retired, Denis lives with Barbara, his partner of twenty-four years, in the centre of St Albans. Twice married and divorced, with a son, Lee, and two daughters, Deanne and Hayley, five grand-children and three great-grand-children; he remains closely in touch with his sister Val and brother, Ken.

Spookily, Denis has continued to collect footballers' autographs and has amassed an enviable catalogue, just as I have also continued to collect antique football programmes. Both of us, since the age of eleven, have relentlessly pursued our parallel hobbies without the other's knowledge; until recently, when we discovered our lifelong obsessions, which were no doubt born out of our youthful adventures together.

Goin' Back
Performer: Dusty Springfield
Composer: Goffin and King
Number 12:   August 1964

Chapter 6 – Maiken

Isaiah 59:19
From east to west everyone will fear him and his great power. He will come like a rushing river, like a strong wind.

As Foreshore Inspector, 50% of my watch covers Arun Parade and the river walk adjacent to the Arun on the east bank; a pleasant duty to stroll on a summer's morning, check the lifebelts and oversee any early launches from the public ramp situated opposite the Lifeboat Station. At this time of day there is usually plenty of maritime activity in evidence: fishermen preparing their boats to host parties of expectant day-trippers, kids hanging over the railings dangling bait for hungry crabs and both dry/wet fish shops opening for the lunchtime trade. On the far bank lie the Yacht Club, the Surviving Island and the Marina. Beyond, there is a clear view of the second tee of the Littlehampton Golf Club, which is built on top of the ruins of the old fort originally constructed to protect the harbour mouth from a potential French invasion.

The Arun, which holds a strange fascination for me, has its source somewhere between Rudgwick and Horsham. It meets the River Rother just south of Stopham Bridge at which point it becomes tidal. One mile south-east of Stopham is my childhood home village; Pulborough was founded at the time the Romans forded the river to facilitate the construction of the Londinium (London) to Noviomagus Reginorum (Chichester) road. Half a mile south of Pulborough at the hamlet of Hardham the Romans built a staging post, the first on Stane Street. It is estimated that the camp was established within ten years of the conquest of southern Britain by Aulas Plautius in 43 AD and remained in occupation for a hundred years, when it was then moved to a better site on Pulborough Ridge. For protection, a hill-fort was built on a man-made hump at what is now known as Park Mount. The camp was also used for the manufacture of pottery, where Belgic folk imitated plates and other vessels imported from the continent, mostly grey wares, with some red and black; maybe, the first examples of 'Made in Taiwan'! Certainly no imitation is the

Saxon Church of St Botolph at Hardham; significant for the earliest complete series of wall paintings in England, and a real gem. The Church was built (circa 1050) by Godwine, lord of the manor in the time of Edward the Confessor. A very special place for me: it was my first place of worship in the Fifties, and on Midsummer's Day 2013 it is where I married my second wife Jan.

When the railway arrived in Pulborough in the 1850s it made both the coast and London commutable. Indeed, my father caught the 7.29am train to Victoria to go to work, returning home around 7pm every weekday from 1943 to 1959. As kids we fished in the river for chub and bass, but normally only succeeded in landing eels that inevitably swallowed the hook. Our favourite spot was where the Rother and Arun meet; there, a small patch of sand that created a tiny beach from which to swim, more or less where the tidal ebb peters out. Provided the midges and horseflies were kind this was a great place for twelve-year-old boys to idle away the odd summer's afternoon.

In 2008, two good friends, Colin Bailey and Dave Brown, and I set out to walk the Arun from this very spot to the pier at Littlehampton. The distance, as the crow flies is fifteen miles; yet walking the riverbank, probably more like twenty-five, passing on the way: Hardham Waterworks, Pulborough Brooks, Amberley Castle, the Chalk Pits Museum, South Stoke church, the Black Rabbit pub, Ford Open Prison and Littlehampton Marina.

Dave Brown, Colin Bailey and John Madell at Amberley 2008

The Arun is the fastest-flowing river in the country and probably the most dangerous. Sadly, a number of my old school friends and acquaintances have drowned over the years. Beware:

the Arun, beautiful though she is, takes no prisoners. Hence the need for lifeguards in the summer months to oversee the estuary; and more specifically, to watch over first beach and the harbour mouth to prevent swimmers from venturing near the ebb and flow at that point.

The lifeguards work alongside me on the foreshore, two during the week, four at weekends and during the school holidays. A prerequisite to undertake the job is speed and stamina when swimming in the sea. Only one in four applicants makes the grade and like me they become trained first-aiders; although, primarily the job is preventative. The Arun estuary, effectively the harbour mouth, is only thirty-five yards wide. At times the river is like a raging torrent caused by the very wide Weald floodplain narrowing to canalisation and then colliding with the ebbing tide and a high south-westerly wind. Result: extreme turbulence and irresistible undercurrents. Even the lifeguards will only train with the aid of a rope in the harbour mouth. Huge warning notices adorn the pier and the first groynes advising the public of the danger, yet bewilderingly swimmers still venture into the sea at this point, and when they do the lifeguards politely request them to move to a safe area of the beach.

I will attempt to explain tidal movement. The tides are harmonic, vertical movements of water on earth caused by the gravitational attraction of, primarily, the moon and sun; with the moon extending a greater tidal attraction than the sun. As the earth rotates, two tidal bulges sweep around the earth's surface from east to west creating a twice-daily cycle of high and low tide within the period of the lunar day, which is 24 hours and 50 minutes long.

The height of the tide varies from day to day as a result of changes in the angle of the moon and its orbital position around the earth. The sun plays its part when the moon is either new, or full, then the combined gravitational effects of the moon and sun complement one another. At those times, approximately twice a month, high tides are at their highest and low tides at their lowest; these are known as spring tides. Conversely, when the sun and moon are at right angles to each other, the sun's influence moderates the stronger lunar effect and gives rise to a low high-tide and a high low-tide; these are called neap tides. For anyone wondering why Easter is on a different spring weekend every year: the reason is that the Catholic Church has set the date of Easter as the Sunday following the paschal full moon, which falls on or after the vernal (spring) equinox. Therefore Easter dates will vary from 22 March up to 25 April. (Read this paragraph again, a couple of times, to get the hang of it!)

It was on 17 August as I was walking back across second and third beaches – so christened as they are divided by breakwaters and provide a useful reference to the most popular area for the day-trippers to convene – that I was greeted over the public loudspeakers to a hearty rendition of *Happy Birthday To You* from my young colleagues. It was my own silly fault; I had provided them all with cream cakes for elevenses. Not content with that level of embarrassment on a hot and busy day, they seamlessly continued with *When I'm Sixty Four*, undoubtedly prompted by my colleague Dave. Our Tannoy announcements can carry on the wind for two or three miles. It occurred to me that the 'Suits in The Kremlin' (Arun District Council Head Office) would not be impressed.

At that precise moment I heard a grinding noise emanating from the mouth of the estuary; the sort of sound that can put one's teeth on edge. A large cargo ship entering the port had drifted onto the east wall of the harbour. On closer inspection I could see Johnny, our harbour pilot, peering over the side of the MV Mungo looking somewhat perplexed as the vessel appeared to be straddled over the eastern training wall, and was now blocking most of the entrance to the Harbour. As the tide went out we could clearly see the seriousness of the situation. There were real fears that by low tide the fully-laden ship's back might break, leaving nothing to support most of the hull, which jutted above East Beach at a steep angle.

Hundreds of people gathered on the beach and pier to watch the spectacle, with the Shoreham lifeboat, Littlehampton Coastguards and Littlehampton Harbour Board officials in attendance. The Mungo was refloated with the help of a tug at 2am, shortly before high water, with no pollution and no damage; the cargo was offloaded that afternoon. Apparently, and thankfully for Johnny, the steering had failed. No-one was injured and the whole incident was well covered by our local TV stations.

Maiken Hilding Larsson had a great impact on me, far greater than I could see at the time. I would like to say that I first became acquainted with her in July 1964; in reality, I had casually met her in September 1962, nearly two years earlier. My school had an exchange partnership with a school in Valby, a suburb of Copenhagen, Denmark. The Danish students were visiting at the beginning of the 1962/63 academic year. Each student was allocated a family to stay with. They took part in some of the school curriculum, had away-days to places of interest and generally integrated into the community for the duration of their two-week stay.

A coach trip had been organised to visit Stonehenge, spare places were available and I had elected to go. At the end of an unremarkable day, and anyone who has visited the giant stone circle will understand what I mean by unremarkable, I was dropped off by Pulborough Church, along with a blonde Danish girl. Her name was Maiken; she was staying with the Daily family in The Spinney. We walked home together and both agreed that there must be more interesting sites to be seen in the South of England. We parted company, and that was that.

In the summer of 1963 I returned to the Boys' Club behind the Village Hall, only this time to attend the youth club, which had been set up on a Wednesday night. Perhaps fifteen to twenty of us met to chat, smoke and play records on a Dansette. The building was an old wartime asbestos Nissen hut and a totally unsuitable venue for a youth club; however, as luck would have it, Mr Allfrey the local builder offered us the use of an old house in Lower Street. The house, which had been empty for many years, was due for demolition as permission had been granted to erect three blocks of flats on the three-acre site.

Skeyne House was originally owned by the Church and once housed a retired Bishop of Chichester. The five-bedroomed property was set back from the main road and surrounded on three sides by a ten-foot-high wall with the garden stretching down to the north-east bank of the Arun. Within the walls to the west there was a separate stable/garage block. A large imposing property built in the late nineteenth century; it was the perfect venue for a youth club.

Skeyne House, 1963 *Janet Madell*

The only neighbour was Tom Allfrey and his family, and Tom took it upon himself to be president of the newly formed Skeyne House Youth Club. Tom recruited a local policeman, Alan Flexman, to help run the club, and Bob Pyggot the oldest member of the club, became club captain. All three did a superb job. Electricity and water was soon switched on and we all set about cleaning out the rooms and clearing the overgrown garden.

The garage block became a workshop for the biking fraternity and very soon we painted every ground floor room of the house. The kitchen and the pantry became the coffee bar and a jukebox was installed in the main lounge. Gradually, bits of furniture were acquired; old leather chairs, stools, a table for the coffee bar and a

TV for upstairs. By the autumn of 1963 Skeyne House had become our second home, and sanctuary.

The club was open six days a week. It was always closed on Saturday because on Saturday night there was a regular dance and a not-to-be-missed punch-up at the Village Hall.

Word spread far and wide and very soon the house, at times, became overrun. Rival gangs descended upon Pulborough from the neighbouring villages of Petworth, Billingshurst, Storrington and West Chiltington. One hard gang superseded the next hard gang and so on – until the Smiths arrived: four brothers of gypsy descent, Jim, John, Pete and Samson. After Jim Smith brutally, yet fairly, beat up Herb Hatchard, an uneasy peace descended on the house. From then on the Smiths became the unelected vigilante police force for the club. There was no trouble when the Smiths were around. Indeed, even the presence of just one of the brothers was enough to deter all bar the brave or foolish. The recriminations would be swift and sharp, and most certainly painful, for any interloper who upset the Smiths' tranquillity.

On one such occasion the Billingshurst gang led by Pansy Potter were chased down to the riverbank. Faced with the option of a stand-up fight with all four Smiths, or the river, the seven- or eight-strong gang decided their best bet, with the advantage of low tide, was to wade across the river to the far bank. A sight to behold indeed; the Billingshurst mob were unlikely to win the Skeyne House popularity contest! By way of compensation for missing out on the anticipated carnage, the Smiths vandalized motorbikes the timid gang had left behind in the drive. Generally, a peace did settle over the club, and thankfully more girls joined, not that there was an official membership list. My band The Skeynes played once a fortnight in the main lounge, and by and large, a good time was had by one and all.

By June of 1964 I was going steady with Maxine, a delightful redhead from West Chiltington. The last bus back to West Chiltington would leave just after 10pm. As I was walking her to the bus stop she complained to me that one or two of the local boys had been bothering her on the upstairs deck. Not wishing to have to accompany her on the bus and then walk four miles back home I had a brainwave: John Smith more often than not caught the same bus after club and, as luck would have it, he was waiting at the stop that night. I took John to one side and politely addressed him as follows: "John, I'm afraid that just occasionally some undesirables ride on the upper deck on this last bus. Would you do me a great favour and see that no-one bothers Maxine tonight?" "Delighted; no problem," John responded. The next time I saw Maxine I asked her if all had been well on the bus that night. "Yes all was OK," she replied, "John Smith was a perfect gentleman, which was strange, as he was one of the lads I was complaining about!" From then on John, and indeed all the Smith brothers were always very friendly, kind and polite to me. I suspect playing in the local band, gave me a degree of street-cred. Whatever the reason, the right friends to have, I think.

On popular nights there could be up to one hundred people at the club, coming from as far away as Worthing, Littlehampton, Horsham and Crawley. Clearly there was a great need for more organisation and management. That management came in the guise of Eric Baker Fazackerly, a twenty-two-year-old chef employed at the local Arun Hotel. Eric, a Liverpudlian, lived in at the Arun, which was less than a five-minute walk from Skeyne House. To describe Eric as a loveable rogue is an understatement; with the gift of the gab and not-so-accidental malapropisms he would hold court whilst running the coffee bar after he had finished cooking the evening meals at the hotel. Eric regaled us with fantastic stories about the Beatles and all the other Mersey groups, who of course, knew him intimately.

Eric was as skinny as he was tall: six feet five inches, and chain-smoked Senior Service cigarettes. He collected the nightly 6*d* entrance fee and also made a handsome profit from the fruit machine, pin tables, juke-box, drinks and confectionery sold in the coffee bar. I would be most surprised if any of the profit found its way back into the club coffers. Yet Eric was good at organisation and we all loved him, in a cautious kind of way. He bravely called in the Smith brothers' father, Jim senior, to lay down the parameters for his sons' involvement at the club.

Eric soon acquired a motorboat, no doubt funded by his ill-gotten gains, which he moored at the bottom of the garden. I enjoyed many a trip with him down the river to Amberley on sunny weekend afternoons, armed with Cokes, crisps and Mars bars 'borrowed' from the coffee-bar store. On one such outing we came across a swan caught up in a fisherman's line. Eric captured the swan and took the bird back to the clubhouse. I held the poor creature down while Eric attempted to remove the offending line. Sadly, the line had wound deep into the swan's leg.

Eric instructed me to hold the swan tightly and then rushed off to the Arun Hotel. Ten minutes later he returned with a set of chef's knives, and without further ado amputated the swan's leg. He then bound up the now flipperless leg, and returned the swan to the river. Once in the water, rather than swimming away from us, the swan merely swam around in circles. At this point Eric called the Royal Society for the Prevention of Cruelty to Animals and the swan was taken into care. Three weeks later Eric received a letter confirming that the swan had survived its ordeal and would soon be ready for release back onto the Arun. Moreover, Eric's congratulations for his efforts came with a certificate of commendation from the Society, which he proudly pinned to the coffee-bar wall.

Eric acquired a projector and screen and promptly knocked a hole in the wall separating the old pantry from the dining room, which we used as a games room. Gleefully drawing the dining room curtains and placing the screen in the bay window, Eric rushed into the pantry and set up the old-fashioned projector. After winding a celluloid film into the projector, those of us present were amazed that within minutes we were watching a Tom and Jerry cartoon. Eric charged an additional 6d on Monday nights for access to the weekly film-show which proved very popular with the membership. Either Fifties, American B-movies or horror films were eagerly lapped up by one and all.

On one memorable night, when Eric showed an X-rated blue film, the smoked-filled room was tightly packed, with standing room only. As the club age group ranged from fourteen to nineteen, the mind boggled: what if Alan Flexman, or indeed anyone in authority, had found out? It would have been a racing certainty that Skeyne House would have been instantly closed and boarded up; fortunately, no-one did find out.

Amazingly, there was never any evidence of drugs or alcohol being consumed on the premises, but shagging, illegal gambling, wild-west-style fights and Swedish sex magazines were commonplace. I have often wondered what other forms of degradation may have occurred had the membership actually consumed illicit substances. There was even a fruit machine that paid a 30/- jackpot, even more, when rolled on its side! I remember dear old Alan Flexman pleading with Eric to get rid of it; Eric refused. When Alan said he would have to resign, Eric found a compromise: the offending machine was hidden in a cupboard only to be played by the older members; a forlorn hope indeed.

Encouraged, by the commercial success of the film nights, Eric hit on the idea of coach outings to see the top rock bands live. We went to see the Stones and Hollies perform in Guildford, and Johnny Kidd and the Pirates with Billy J. Kramer and the Dakotas in concert at the Brighton Dome. Great nights out, well done Eric!

It was 7.30pm on Sunday, 26 July 1964 when, as usual, I called for my friend Colin at his house in Rectory Close to walk together the few hundred yards to the club. Colin was still playing bass guitar in The Skeynes and on the way to the club we chatted about the forthcoming rehearsal on the following Tuesday. As usual, Colin had not done his homework on the three new numbers we had agreed to practice. I told Colin that both Tango and Jim, the other members of the band, were tiring of his apparent complacency. Colin was a long-time friend and I did not want the conflict that his inevitable sacking from the band would cause. I knew I was wasting my breath so when we arrived at the club I went straight to the coffee bar to join the regular card school.

"Have you seen the foreign bird in the lounge, John?" Terry Walker (always known as Stick) remarked as I sat down, "She's a cracking blonde." Well, I was very happy with Maxine and therefore not particularly interested and, if the standard of Stick's own past girlfriends was to anything go by, I was taking his judgement with a pinch of salt. As it happened, Maxine had gone on holiday to Butlins with her parents and would be away for the next two weeks.

Neither winning nor losing at cards, I drifted into the lounge where the jukebox was playing the Zombies' *She's Not There*. But she was there: sitting on a sofa with Ann Daily, and Ann's boyfriend Glenn Lewis, was without doubt, the most beautiful girl I had ever seen: tall and slim, with curves just right, and short platinum-blonde hair. I was sure she half-smiled at me. Colin joined me as I leant against the jukebox. "She's not half bad," Colin whispered in my ear, as ever the master of the understatement. "Nobody has the guts to ask her for a dance. I bet you a packet of fags she won't dance with you John" he added. "Well Colin, you have a bet," I said instantly. The smile had just told me I was about to win a pack of ten Guards filter-tipped cigarettes.

I casually slotted a shilling into the jukebox and selected three slow numbers. Up came Billy Fury's *It's Only Make Believe*. Now acutely aware that Colin was telling Herb and Terry that he was about to win a bet, I suddenly felt my mouth go dry and my confidence wane. No worries, within ten seconds we were dancing and two minutes later I was holding her really close. She smelt divine, and despite the loud music and her Scandinavian accent the conversation flowed. It had been a smart move to select three smooches, and courtesy of Jim Reeves and Roy Orbison we stuck together like glue, until Colin intervened: tapping me on my shoulder he presented me with the cigarettes and loudly said, "Well done John, you have won the bet fair and square." "What does he mean by that?" quizzed Maiken and promptly sat back down on the sofa next to Ann. "Great, thanks a bunch Colin," I growled. As I returned to the card school, I knew Colin's band days were now well and truly numbered.

At the time I was working in Horsham as a clerk for the National Federation of Building Trades Employers and on the Thursday of that same week I was aimlessly window-shopping on my lunch break. To my utter amazement standing next to me was Maiken. She was alone; I said hello and apologised for the misunderstanding on Sunday night. "Don't worry, Ann told me you have a steady girlfriend. I thought the bet was funny anyway. So when do you see your girlfriend?" Maiken asked. "Oh, Maxine is on holiday until the ninth of August," I replied. Maiken grinned, "Well I go home on the eleventh; perhaps we can see each other in the meantime?" Was I mistaken, or had she just asked me to invite her on a date? I was totally lost for words. She continued, "You don't remember our coach trip to Stonehenge? I really hoped after we walked home together that day, we would meet up again." Ah! the penny suddenly dropped; she was *that* girl, and she had turned into a real beauty. Regaining what calm I could, I asked, "Maiken would you like to meet me at the club tomorrow night?" "That will be great, I will see you tomorrow at seven-thirty," she responded as she walked away in the direction of the train station.

I rushed home from work the following day, jumped into the bath and splashed on some of dad's cologne. There was no such luxury as after-shave or deodorant in 1964. On with my Ben Sherman button-down shirt, ice-blue drainpipe jeans, three-inch-Cuban-heeled Chelsea boots, striped Italian jacket (with a cardboard-backed hankie in the top pocket as a finishing touch), and combed my mop-top Beatle-style hair in front of mum's long mirror; I thought, no wonder she fancies you!

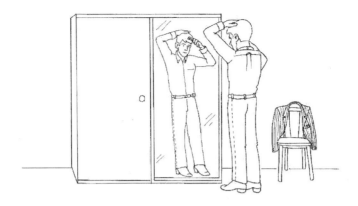

I arrived at the club spot-on seven-thirty. "Thank goodness you are here John," Glenn said and continued, "as beautiful as she is, she has become Ann's shadow, and I can't afford two women." "Where are they?" I said. "Don't worry they will be here in ten minutes; they are sprucing themselves up for us. As soon as they arrive we will split them up. You look after Maiken, while I take Ann for a drink in the Red Lion." That sounded a very good plan to me.

Being the start of the August Bank Holiday the club was not particularly busy that night. When Maiken arrived we walked down to the Arun and talked some, followed by Cokes in the coffee bar. Dusk had fallen by the time she selected a few records on the jukebox, the first being Dusty Springfield's *I Just Don't Know What To Do With Myself*. As we danced closely she whispered, "Until tonight I just did not know what to do with myself, but I do now!" When her selection had finished I suggested that on such a warm night we should take a breath of fresh air outside.

Although there was no moon, there seemed to be at least a thousand stars. We stood behind a fir tree and leant up against the old stable block, and kissed. I didn't think it was possible: Maiken actually tasted as good as she looked. It was the first time I had experienced a French kiss. As her tongue licked the top of my mouth, my breath was literally taken away. Her body slowly swayed against my groin, very, very gradually speeding up. I pulled her blouse out of her skirt and undid her bra. Her breasts were firm and her nipples erect. "*There* you are Maiken," said Ann, appearing from nowhere, "it's time to go home; you know my dad expects me, and you, in by ten-thirty." "Do me a favour Glenn…" I pleaded. "Can't be helped John, her parents are very strict you know," replied Glenn bluntly.

The next few days were, and still are, a blur. A walk in the country, trips to the pictures, tea with my mum and dad and inevitably, more nights at the club. Then, all too soon, the day came when it was time for my blonde to return to Denmark.

I took the day off work to accompany Maiken on part of her journey: the train from Pulborough to Victoria station, then the underground to Liverpool Street Station where she would catch another train to Harwich to meet the Esbjerg boat. I carried her case onto the train and kissed her goodbye. I stood on the platform, a smile, a wave and the train pulled away. Soon she was out of view. I felt the life-blood drain from me. Fighting the tears, I shuffled back to the underground. Six days short of my seventeenth birthday and I could truly say: 'I just don't know what to do with myself'!

We wrote every week, and I visited Denmark the following Easter. Indeed, we met up every year until 1969. Yet, somehow we never rediscovered the magic of '64. Maybe, being the same age, I was too young for Maiken. In the teens I am sure girls grow up faster than boys. I tried so hard to hang on in there. I returned to full-time education; in the back of my mind I figured that a qualified John Madell would become a successful businessman and one day be able to win the hand of the beautiful Maiken; however, this was not to be.

On a cold winter's morning in early 1970 I rested my elbows on the old Swan Bridge, and with a heavy heart, dropped Maiken's picture, which had been tucked in my wallet for over five years, into the Arun and watched it swallowed by the grey and murky water.

Accompanied by my young son Paul, I met up with Maiken again in 1986 and spent a pleasant afternoon in her summer home on the north coast of Zealand, together with her husband and two children. In 2005 I saw Ann Daily, now Lewis, in Pulborough and enquired after Maiken. "John, about eight or nine years ago I sent you a message via your mum to let you know that Maiken had died from cancer," Ann said sadly. I never received the message; I guess that mum, by then on her deathbed, could not bring herself to pass the note onto me.

Rarely a day goes by when I do not momentarily dream of my beautiful 'Little Mermaid' from *Wonderful, Wonderful Copenhagen*.

She's Not There

Performers: The Zombies
Composer: Argent
Number 12:   August 1964

Chapter 7 - Bob

Psalm 81:2
Start the music and beat the tambourines; play pleasant music on the harps
and the lyres.

Pier Road, Littlehampton, straddles the east bank of the harbour, where up to fifty swans can usually be found waiting to be fed by the customers of the two takeaway fish and chip shops on the opposite side of the narrow road. The road eventually leads into South Street and the main town centre located about a quarter of a mile to the north. On the west side of South Street is situated The George Inn, part of the Wetherspoon chain of public houses. Back in the Sixties the shop housed Jones and Tomlin's furniture store, and above on the first floor was the Top Hat Club.

The Top Hat was the first music venue opened by the Beat, Ballad and Blues Management Company. The location was a former restaurant and could be accessed via a narrow staircase leading from the sidewalk. At the top of the stairs, to the left, could be found a bamboo-framed coffee bar boasting an expresso machine and a Fifties Wurlitzer jukebox; to the right was the main auditorium; the dance floor was part toughened glass with lights beneath, and at the far end was the stage. The Top Hat was the 'in' place for teenagers to meet and was always packed at weekends when top local groups performed the latest hit tunes.

The club was run by Bob Gately, a somewhat shady character of Jewish origin, then in his mid-forties, with a goatee beard and a reluctance to pay the performers the agreed fee. Right-hand man was Tinny Wells, also in his forties, bald, rather rotund and always ready and able to undertake any of Bob's necessary dirty work. Sitting on a stool at the coffee bar listening to these two chatting was like being party to an old-fashioned comedy music hall act:

Tinny: 'Bob, Bob! the customers want their money back.'
Bob: 'Why Tinny?'
Tinny: 'The group hasn't turned up, Bob.'
Bob: 'Well Tinny, tell them they are out of luck and can't fucking have it back; give them a Coke voucher instead!'

The sessions were regularly DJ'd by Chris Valens who went on to run The Chris Lynn Entertainment Agency and subsequently became a good friend. In addition to local talent Bob also booked top national bands including The Hollies, The Swinging Blue Jeans, The Barron Knights, The Searchers, Brian Poole and The Tremeloes, and even Gene Vincent from the States. The club ran for ten years until it closed in 1969.

Passing the old club site always brings back happy memories of 1964 when I hopped on the back of Jim Chatfield's 650 Norton parked in the driveway of Skeyne House Youth Club, to attempt a ton over Arundel rough and reach the smoke-filled venue in what seemed no time at all. Little did I know at the time that within three years I too would be performing on the cramped stage.

With few, if any, fire regulations then, I suspect that the club was nothing short of a firetrap. With highly inflammable sofas and chairs immediately below; one totally inadequate fire exit to the rear, and the narrow staircase at the front so tight that it was a struggle to pass anyone already on it. Curiously, although the scene of many punch-ups and brawls, the club had no drinks licence; but this was easily overcome by an ultra-violet pass-out stamp on the back of the hand to facilitate a visit to either the Dolphin opposite, or the White Hart next door but one. The only band entrance was via the back alley where we parked the Transit van, offloaded the equipment and carried the drums, guitars and amps up the rickety staircase to the rear door, which backed onto the stage. The best place, in fact the only place, to store the cases was in the doorway, which provided the only fire escape!

I bought my first three rock 'n' roll records in the Fifties: *Rock Around the Clock*, *Heartbreak Hotel* and *Great Balls of Fire*. From that time on I developed a life-long love of beat music, which eventually led me to acquire my first drum kit. Some of the guys at the local youth club were attempting to form a band, or as it was known in the early days of the Beatles and the Mersey-beat sound, a 'Beat Group'. The year was 1963 and I was just sixteen.

The majority of my friends and contemporaries had motorbikes or motor scooters. Their reasons were partly for transport out of the village, partly for the speed; but I suspect the real incentive was image. I had sitting in my Post Office account the princely sum of £100, saved up over many years: Christmas and birthday presents donated by relatives, together with a handsome win at bingo, played when on vacation with mum and dad at Bembridge Holiday Camp on the Isle of White. At sixteen I was old enough to ride a motorbike and what's more, I could afford one. 'You have no chance, John; only over my dead body.' Dad stated when I floated the idea. When my dad said no, he always meant no.

"We have a lead guitar in Jim; Colin has just bought a bass, and I can play rhythm and sing; we now desperately need a drummer to complete the line-up," said my friend Tango. Keith Russell was the only drummer in the locality and he played with the Triffics based in Petworth. The Triffics were in big demand and there was no chance Keith would join a start-up band. This was my cue; prompted by my three years of ballet training and with £100 burning a hole in my pocket, I quickly volunteered to be the band's drummer. The next weekend Tango and I caught the train to Horsham and headed for Latimer's music shop. Lew Latimer showed me an Edgeware kit manufactured by Boosey and Hawkes, which I duly purchased. Despite protestations from my father: 'Mark my words son: this is a nine days' wonder', the deal was done. Once home I proudly erected the kit in the front room; then, and only then did the realisation hit me: I had not a clue how to play the drums.

I never had any doubts that I would learn the art of percussion. I thought that my fellow band members and I were only a few short months away from fame and fortune; however, first things first. I am frequently asked: 'How did you learn to drum?' First stop: I purchased a drum tutor manual. The snag with a teaching manual, probably written in the Fifties, was that to decipher the damned thing one needed to read music. Not just read, but drum read! This will take years, I thought, and the band had the chance of our first booking in less than two months.

The next obvious choice was a live tutor. I found a little old man living in a ground-floor flat in Shakespeare Road, Worthing, who chain-smoked Woodbines and charged me 5/- a lesson; unfortunately, he did not know his paradiddle from diddly-squat. Now with two blanks drawn, my next port of call was to ask an accomplished drummer how he became proficient. There was a band that regularly played on a Friday night at the Horsham Boys' Club and the lead singer and guitarist, Pete Reynolds, was always happy to talk music during the breaks, and his brother Barry played the drums. I explained my dilemma to Barry: "What can I do to learn to play the drums in a hurry?" I tentatively asked. "Simple, just watch me and copy what I do," a smiling Barry said, "and when you go home, play along with your favourite records; you'll soon catch on." Barry was absolutely right; from then on I subjected my parents, neighbours and passers-by to hours of torture. Gradually, I was able to co-ordinate my hands and feet and hold the beat, gingerly adding a hand-to-hand run around the kit and the odd press roll.

Mrs Kelly, the Principal of Arundale School, kindly let Tango, Jim, Colin and I use the school cellar for rehearsals, and slowly but surely we strung together a dozen numbers. On Saturday nights a dance was held at the local village hall. The regular band was a quintet made up of middle-aged men playing Forties and Fifties tunes, normally in Strict Tempo time. Mrs Jenner, a near neighbour who looked after the catering, arranged for us to play the last hour, eleven until midnight for the grand fee of £1. On Saturday, 30 January 1964 my 'professional' music career began. The first number we played that night was a minor hit for Joe Brown and The Bruvvers: *What a Crazy World*. How appropriate, I had indeed joined the crazy world of popular music.

The Skeynes in 1964.   *Graham Allfrey*
(*Left to right*) Colin Bailey, John (Tango) Tangstram, John Madell, Nancy Roberts, John Bowyer, Jimmy Chatfield

We played either at Pulborough Village Hall or the local youth club Skeyne House, and appropriately decided to name the band

'The Skeynes'. As we had no way of transporting the equipment we rarely played elsewhere. I recall it was a superhuman effort to acquire enough material to play for two and a half or three hours and repeats were not uncommon. John Bowyer from Horsham joined the band and soon after, Colin was sacked. Colin never really bothered to learn to play bass, and Jim recruited Viv his cousin as replacement. Viv had recently left Screaming Lord Sutch and the Savages; yes, the Lord Sutch who later founded the Monster Raving Loony Party. By July 1965 Tango was poached to play with the Triffics and a few months later Jim emigrated to Canada. After an eventful eighteen months The Skeynes were no more.

My next band came via Tango. The manager of the Triffics was looking to form another group for his youngest son Bernie; it was born as The Inventive Mr Jeff. The backbone of the band was Roger on bass, Ally on rhythm guitar and vocals, and me on drums. We were very soon playing all over the south of England thanks to our manager 'Harris', his mini-bus and contacts. The three of us stayed together until 1971 with various good, bad and indifferent musicians coming and going, including the forementioned Pete Reynolds, who, it must be said, was very good.

Our best venues were the Armed Forces' bases in Hampshire and Wiltshire where we played, normally on a Wednesday night, and were always well paid. The band was based in the little market town of Petworth, where 'Harris' owned the Queen's Head pub. Harris's real name was Gerald Humphries. Ally nicknamed him Harris because he was always harassed. He was forever jumping up and down when we were doing a sound check: 'Too loud, too shrill, too sharp!' he would cry. We were, I am sure, committing the said misdemeanours but took no notice of old Harris; yet with hindsight I am certain he was absolutely right. To travel from Petworth sixty miles to Salisbury or Tisbury for a midweek gig was no mean feat. We would meet at the pub at 5.30pm, load up the equipment, and jump in the van, simultaneously consuming hot pies or fish and chips provided by Mrs Humphries.

On one occasion I suffered Montezuma's revenge, better known as severe stomach cramps. By the time we reached the Tidworth army camp in Salisbury I was in agony. As soon as we stopped at the gate I jumped out of the van and rushed into the guardhouse. "Where are your loos?" I pleaded. "Straight down the corridor," a voice replied. Being mid-winter it was dark, and with no lights on in the toilets I pushed open the door of the first cubicle, and with a feeling of enormous relief, sat down.

A couple of minutes later the rest of the band also found the loos, and the light switch. It turned out that the cubicle I had selected in so much haste only had a half-door; I was in the guardhouse's observation toilet. The boys had great fun leaning on the door and, perhaps appropriately, 'taking the piss'. Strangely there was no urinal and soon they found their way into the other cubicles. Immediately after they had disappeared, I heard a stamping of feet, which became louder by the second and was clearly headed in my direction. The guard was changing and into the loos came four female squaddies! The penny finally dropped: we were in an all-female army camp, hence no urinals, and I was still sitting with my trousers around my ankles in the observation toilet. Well, I can only leave to the reader's imagination the comments and heckles I received from the army personnel, very much encouraged by my fellow band members.

This was without doubt the most embarrassing moment of my life. Harris inadvertently came to my rescue in a typical panic: "Come on lads, we are late and must find the service club to offload the gear," he shouted down the corridor. Eventually, I was alone in the loo and at last able to adjust my dress; thank goodness that was over. Within an hour we had set up and as the curtain opened we kicked into our first number. To my horror the same four 'ladies' were now in civvies and standing right in front of the stage. Worse still, they were pointing at me, giggling, and calling over a half-dozen more friends to join in the fun. When the evening finally came to an end, in more ways than one, I am sure you can imagine how relieved I really was!

If the Triffics were playing on the same night as us, Harris invariably drove them, his first love, to their gig. In which case Mick Pretty our arrogant vocalist, about five years our senior, undertook the driving duty; which, more often than not, proved to be a harrowing experience. Mick had very poor eyesight and to guide his way on narrow and poorly lit country roads he straddled the central white line. When challenged by an oncoming car Mick would swerve toward the kerb and comment, 'He wanted a lot of bloody room.' What's more, Mick suffered with piles and a double hernia. These, on occasions, caused him to be gruff and bad-tempered, and we played on his discomfort finding great amusement in the surgical truss he had to wear from time to time.

On one trip we teased him all the way to the venue. A soul number we played that night included the words, 'Woo, woo, poppa was a tramp'. This phrase came at the end of the chorus when the instruments would stop, leaving an unaccompanied Mick to sing out the line, loud and clear. Poor old Mick must have been very upset with our joshing and clearly had his mind on his medical problems, as in the very last chorus, instead of singing the appropriate words, and with his subconscious working overtime, Mick sang: 'Woo, woo, poppa was a TRUSS'! Although the audience probably did not notice the error, the band did, and we all collapsed with laughter, bringing the number to an abrupt end.

Mick only lasted with the band a year and little more was heard of him until Roger was informed of his untimely death. While on holiday in Cornwall he was having his photograph taken on a cliff top. Tragically, Mick took one too many steps backwards and disappeared over the edge.

Midweek gigs were difficult as there were few motorways, bypasses or late-night service stations in the Sixties and the prospect of an early start for the day job was always in the back of our minds. As the band's popularity increased so did the size of the venues and consequently the equipment; by now there was only room for two or three at most in the van, which required the other two members to travel separately.

One Wednesday we played the Cobweb Club in Weymouth. Accompanied by Roger, I took the van and drove the hundred or so miles west. Ally and John Katon (Katy) travelled in Roger's Mini. After the gig Ally and Katy took charge of the van and I returned with Roger in the car. Ten miles out of Weymouth, Ally noticed that the fuel gauge registered zero and decided to pull into the first petrol station, which was by then closed, and wait until morning to fill up. Ally and Katy spent six very uncomfortable hours, no doubt cursing me for leaving the tank empty, until the station finally opened. Ally instructed the attendant to fill the van's fuel tank. The attendant stopped when the pump indicator showed half a gallon. 'Well, fill her up!' Ally shouted. The attendant responded, 'It is full; in fact I filled your van up around six-thirty last night.' The attendant was right; I had stopped there on the way to the gig, but inexplicably, the gauge had failed. Ally and Katy had spent six hours in a freezing van for no reason, and Roger and I laughed about it for weeks.

More equipment required more muscle, it was therefore time to employ a couple of roadies. Bob and Phil were friends of Ally and Roger and were very happy to accompany us to the gigs, shift the gear, do a sound check and so forth, in return for a few beers. The going rate was three pints each. Bob generally helped me by erecting and dismantling my drum kit. Bob was a hard man: a builder's labourer aged twenty-four, six feet tall, one hundred and ninety pounds, greased-back hair, and a broken nose. Bob was very handy in a fight, which, more often than not, he instigated.

One summer's weekend we were booked to play at a society wedding. The National Hunt jockey Terry Biddlecombe was marrying a minor Royal and the reception was at a large mansion on the outskirts of Petersfield in Hampshire. We pulled up in the van at the front of the house. I told Bob I thought we were expected to set up in a marquee, which might be in the garden at the rear of the house. Bob disappeared to look around the back and I waited in the van. A few moments later the bride and groom together with all the guests spilled out onto the front lawn for a photo shoot. Bob appeared from the far end of the house some hundred yards away, on the other side of the assembled throng, and yelled out at the top of his voice, "Oi, oi John!" at the very second the main wedding photograph was being taken. All the posing guests swung round towards Bob who once again shouted to me, "John, you were right: the beer tent is round back." I often wonder if the wedding photographer kept the picture with his intended subjects in profile.

The marquee was huge, accommodating over two hundred guests and two raised wooden stages. We set up the equipment and were then directed by the butler to our dressing room, which we understood to be on the 'second floor of the east wing, fourth room on the left'. We entered the room to find the curtains closed. All I could see was a very large room with a four-poster bed, two old oak wardrobes, a table, comfy chairs and a basin in the corner. Bob said he was desperate for the loo and disappeared into the corridor. Seconds later he returned having been unsuccessful in his search. "I can't wait!" he said, and proceeded to piss in the basin, just as Phil decided to use the bed as a trampoline. Well, the bed came alive; a grey-haired figure arose and with a booming voice that even Lady Bracknell would have been proud of, announced: "I would rather you did not do that, you horrid man." Whether she was referring to Bob or Phil I shall never know. I later learnt we should have been on the *first* floor and had unwittingly entered the room of an eccentric old aunt.

With the speeches over, we were called to play. The main band was the Nashville Teens who'd had two or three top-ten hits, the most notable being *Tobacco Road*. Ally foolishly chose to close our first set with *Tobacco Road*. This was outside the unwritten rules of band etiquette, and totally unacceptable behaviour on our part. The Nashville Teens immediately followed on and quite rightly announced: "This is how *Tobacco Road* should be played." And it was.

As the night wore on I was surprised to see Princess Margaret and Lord Snowdon dancing a waltz to one of our slower numbers. Were The Inventive Mr Jeff now by Royal 'appointment'? When the 'Teens' and we finally finished playing at 2am, the remainder of the party moved to the cellar where a disco had been set up. When we packed up and left at dawn the champagne was still flowing. Arriving back in Petworth, and totally shattered, I opened the rear of the van to find a shiny new set of luggage wheels stencilled 'Property of the Nashville Teens', and a top hat that belonged to the bride's father perched on the head of a spaced-out Bob who had a wide grin across his silly inebriated face.

Coincidentally, nearly half a century later, Pete Harris the Nashville Teens' bass guitarist sat in with one of my later bands for a few gigs. I never mentioned the wheels to him though!

One night we were 'headlining' at The Crown, Midhurst with a rock 'n' roll band and a disco. To spice up our performance Bob had set up strobe lighting and a dry-ice machine to be introduced towards the end of the set. To round off proceedings Bob had placed a small amount of gunpowder in a tobacco tin, which he carefully placed on top of an old grand piano sited to one side of the stage. As our act progressed I could spot the shadowy figure of Bob rushing back and forth from one side of the stage to the other, working the dry-ice machine and the strobe in time to the music.

Dressed in our kaftans and bandanas we were five years ahead of the glam-rock era. Apart from being suffocated by the mist and blinded by the flashing light, all went well, until halfway through our penultimate number, when Bob lit a match to set off his homemade firework. The explosion not only blew the lid off the grand piano but also projected Bob headlong into Ally and Roger, catapulting all three from the stage into the audience, bringing the performance to a very abrupt end, and setting off the fire alarm for good measure.

Apart from burnt fingers and a bump on his head Bob was OK, which is more than can be said for the piano. We fixed the lid back on and covered the hole caused by the explosion with a strategically placed flower vase found in the kitchen. Repairs completed, we began to pack up the gear. I noticed Bob was not in the best of temper when I asked, "Where are my cymbals?" "How the fuck should I know," he replied. "Well did you pack them in the van Bob?" I asked gingerly. "No," Bob tersely responded. "Maybe the other band has nicked them," Ally suggested. "Stop the bastards!" Bob cried, as he flew out of the front door with both me and the other band members in hot pursuit.

The rock 'n' roll combo were just closing the doors of their van. Bob promptly pushed their drummer to one side and opened the door to find my crash and ride cymbals tucked down the side of an amplifier. Bob retrieved the cymbals and, one in each hand, landed simultaneous blows to both their lead singer, and drummer.

I had never perceived my percussion instruments to be dangerous weapons; I was wrong as by now both culprits were spread out on the pavement bleeding profusely. To Bob's credit he warned the other two members of the rock band to stand well back. I think his precise words were, 'Just you take one step closer and I will fucking kill you.' Not surprisingly, they both froze. Bob then triumphantly handed me the pair of cymbals as if he was presenting me the Jules Rimet Trophy, the World Cup. I would have been eternally grateful had it not been for a large dent in the ride cymbal which never sounded quite the same again.

Once a month, on a Thursday night, we played the Worthing Assembly Hall with a full-to-capacity audience of one thousand; sadly, the crowds came, not to see my band, but rather, a chart-topping act. We were employed for the princely sum of £15 to warm up and then down, the audience. Our illustrious colleagues on stage included: John Mayall's Blues Breakers with Eric Clapton, Peter Frampton's The Herd, Zoot Money's Big Roll Band, Desmond Dekker and The Aces and Eddy Grant's Equals to name just a few. We played from eight to nine and then for a half an hour after the main band had finished their set.

On one Thursday night a man's black face peered around the door of our dressing room. "Which one is the drummer?" he enquired. I put up my hand. "Our drummer has been delayed in Scotland and won't make the gig. Please sit in with us tonight?" "No," I instantly replied. Desmond Dekker had topped the charts that very week with their recording of *The Israelites*. The hall would be packed, and The Aces were predominately a reggae band. Reggae was a very new style of music, born in Jamaica and distinguished by a laid-back offbeat. This was a rhythm I had not yet attempted to play, mainly due to the fact it was exclusively the domain of black musicians. *The Israelites* was very much a breakthrough track and opened up reggae to the mainstream. The market for this style of music was later successfully developed by the great Bob Marley.

Despite my protestations the man persisted: "How much are you being paid tonight?" he questioned. "£15," I replied. "If you play with The Aces tonight we will give you another £15." As I was only earning £10 a week as a claims clerk at Sun Alliance and London Insurance Company, it was too good an offer to turn down. "OK" I said, and when he promptly handed me three crisp £5 notes, there was no turning back. I later learned that their fee for the night was £300 and their contract required a drummer on stage. After my band had completed the first set I remained on stage and was quickly joined by five others of Jamaican origin. Off we went with me playing a straight rhythm to their music. The crowd seemed happy enough and the ordeal eventually came to an end, but not before my fellow band members, who were standing in the wings, had taunted me relentlessly about my white skin as opposed to The Aces who were all black.

A little while later we were booked to play with The Equals who also had a number one. Most of the top acts at that time were, just a few months or a year earlier, unknown, and then, literally overnight, catapulted to stardom; The Equals were no different; and were a nice bunch of guys from South London. Our PA system was playing up that night during the sound check. Eddy Grant their lead singer told us not to worry; we were welcome to use their equipment. This was unusual, as most bands do not generally like their equipment tampered with by others, and especially just before they were due on stage. It was a very generous gesture.

We played really well with a superior sound system and The Equals were great. The audience just erupted when they played *Baby Come Back*. We all had a laugh and a beer together afterwards before we packed away the gear. One problem, a big problem: Bob packed The Equals' PA into our van. Not surprisingly The Equals were seriously upset, especially Eddy Grant, and a bit of pushing and shoving ensued in the back alley. I tried to calm the mood and apologised profusely. I was about to explain that the band knew nothing of the error and it was down to our roadies, and then wisely thought better of it. Eddy Grant might hate me, but that was preferable to Bob's likely reaction had I opened my big mouth.

I was beginning to think that Bob was fast becoming a liability, yet, cometh the hour, cometh the man. Whilst driving home from a gig one night a black Ford Consul overtook us in a built-up area just north-east of Petersfield; the Ford must have been travelling at sixty in a thirty limit. I commented to Bob and Roger that the excessive speed could well cause an accident. Unfortunately, I was very soon to be proved prophetically correct. Less than five minutes later we rounded a corner to find that the black Ford had crashed head-on into another car. Both cars were joined together in the middle of the road. The occupants of the Ford, two men in their late twenties, were unconscious. A woman, the lone occupant of the other car, was screaming and clearly in great distress. The engine of the Ford was on fire and fuel was leaking all over the road; it was quite obvious that we had to extract the car passengers before one of the cars exploded.

With no time to lose we tackled the Ford first; both passenger doors were jammed and would not budge. In a flash, Bob smashed the passenger-side window with his elbow, leant in and wound down what remained of it; then with superhuman effort ripped the door off with his bare hands. Bob pulled the passenger out and passed him to Roger and me, and we hurriedly dragged the man to the side of the road and laid him down. Bob pulled out the driver and we repeated the manoeuvre. Both men were now safely away from the cars. The woman on the other hand had the engine of her car sitting on her lap, and was therefore completely trapped.

Led by Bob we tore the cars apart and pushed the still-smouldering Ford at least fifty yards down the road, which was most fortunately on a downward incline. Just as well we did, for as we ran back the petrol tank exploded. Miraculously, the fire did not spread to the other car. By now, other people had arrived on the scene and a couple were doing their best to comfort the trapped lady. The services soon appeared; the Fire Brigade extinguished the fire and then cut the lady from the wreckage of her car. Still conscious and clearly in great pain, she was rushed by ambulance to hospital, but sadly died the next day. The two men were also taken to hospital and made a full recovery. There is no doubt that Bob's determination and great strength saved their lives. I also had no doubt that the driver of the Ford had killed the poor woman, and said as much when called to be a witness at the Coroner's Court.

Big Bertha, 1970.
(*Left to right*) Roger Cross, John Madell, John (Katy) Katon, Alan (Ally) Jones

By 1970 we had changed our name to Big Bertha after the giant First World War gun, which we considered depicted the heavy style we were playing. We had recruited John Katon (Katy) on lead guitar from The Triffics, whom we had superseded in the pecking order. Simon Renouf had replaced Harris as our manager and he immediately moved the band onto the London Club circuit. Regular articles were appearing about our progress in both *Melody Maker* and the *New Musical Express*. We cut a record: *When Rosalind Moves Me*, and both Ringo Starr and George Harrison were present when we made our debut at the Pheasant Tree Club in the Kings Road, Chelsea. Were we a whisper away from at last breaking into the big time?

We then auditioned for Mecca at their theatre in Piccadilly; I knew we had done well that day because Olivia Newton-John told me so. She was appearing nightly there with her vocal group 'Tomorrow' and had witnessed our performance that afternoon.

Mecca offered the band a six-month contract to play the American Forces' bases in Germany. Moreover, Justin Hayward of the Moody Blues, who also ran Threshold Records, liked *When Rosalind Moves Me* and told us to look him up after our European tour. John Peel promised us a slot in one of his late-night Radio One shows. Clearly all was going to plan, we resigned our day jobs, kitted out 'Brown Bertha' the band van, and cancelled all our forthcoming UK gigs. We were well prepared and raring to go; until the Black Panther movement spooked the US Military, who promptly decided that heavy rock was subversive and cancelled all live music acts booked to perform on their property. Big Bertha well and truly fell into this category and three days before we were due to catch the ferry at Dover our contract was cancelled, along with those of half a dozen other English bands.

Not only were we without our day jobs, we were also without any bookings and now in competition with the other bands returning from the continent. The band folded; Ally moved to London and formed Montana Red, and Katy had a nervous breakdown. Roger and I, unbelievably, joined a Trad Jazz band which proved to be a short-lived move. I guess all good things come to an end.

So You Want To Be A Rock 'N' Roll Star
Performers: The Byrds
Composers: McGuinn and Hillman
Released: February 1967

Chapter 8 – Janine

Proverbs 24:5
Being wise is better than being strong; yes, knowledge is more important than strength.

Today, sitting here in my office, I have a fantastic view of a rough sea. Gale-force winds have caused a mass desertion from the beach and promenade, but the sun shines and the sky is blue, reflecting on the sea with a multitude of white horses racing toward the shore on a spring high tide. Huge waves break over the West Works at the entrance to the harbour. The only noticeable sign of life is a trio of kite surfers intermittently leaping the surf one hundred yards off East Beach. The idyllic vista is abruptly interrupted by Tyndall's voice as he attempts to conduct a search for shoplifters on Shopwatch Radio.

Each business has an intercom linked to fifty other members of the Littlehampton trading community. The network is co-ordinated by Tyndall, a semi-retired shop owner. Littlehampton Police Station is also a member, which can prove useful, when manned. The idea is for each member to advise the network of the location of any ne'er-do-wells and to call for assistance if in trouble. Thereby, each member is in theory looking out for his neighbour. As the town centre is over half a mile away, the Foreshore Office generally looks after itself and should we be in difficulty I normally dial the three nines.

On this particular occasion a couple of Eastern European women had stolen clothing from Peacocks and were heading towards the seafront. Armed with a full description I advised Tyndall that I would attempt to intercept on my beach buggy. Tyndall agreed to hop on his bike and meet me outside the O2 Club. Two minutes later we had the culprits cornered and waited for the police patrol car. As soon as the police arrived we identified the women who were promptly detained, and when the police found the booty in their possession, arrested. Old Tyndall was tickled pink that his beloved radio network had proved so efficient. I thought for one awful moment he was going to kiss me!

Recently, the local police sergeant decided in his wisdom to allocate each member of Shopwatch with a phonetic alphabet call sign. For example the Train Station would be known on air as Tango Sierra, the Police as Papa Uniform and so on. When the call sign list was distributed we found to our great amusement that the Foreshore Office had been dubbed Foxtrot Oscar. Dave was in his element signing off with great glee, 'This is Foxtrot Oscar Foxtrotting Oscar, goodnight!' It did not take Tyndall long to figure out the error and promptly changed us to Foxtrot 1.

In 1967, about the time I was dating Janine, I was stopped and abducted by the police. I had dropped Janine at her parents' house in Salvington and returned to Worthing town centre to pick up Charlie, a friend I had promised to give a lift home to Sompting. It was around ten and Charlie said he would buy me a pint for my trouble. I parked behind the Dome Theatre where Charlie was waiting for me and we quickly walked towards the Thieves Kitchen, when from nowhere, a squad car appeared. Two burly cops jumped out, grabbed us and pushed us into the rear of the car. The car sped up the road and we pulled up outside the Spaniard public house. "Right, in you go," the tall constable said. Charlie instantly responded, "Thanks for the lift mate, but this is the wrong pub; it was the Thieves we wanted." That was not a wise response and we were both frogmarched into the centre of the crowded bar. The publican was sitting on a chair holding a damp flannel to his bruised and bleeding forehead. Apparently, a couple of jokers had removed the signature Spanish guitar from the wall, hit the governor over the head and helped themselves to the takings. "We have got the two bastards, sir, and here they are." The bewildered publican looked at us for just a couple of seconds. "It's not them, nothing like them," he said, before, semi-conscious, he slumped back into his chair. "Are you sure? These two were running in the opposite direction," the cop said. "No we were not; we were hurrying to order a drink before last orders," Charlie said indignantly. "I am certain it was not those two men, officer," the publican repeated. The tall policeman said to us disparagingly, "Well think yourselves lucky, you can piss off."

Before Charlie could protest, I pushed him out of the door and back in the direction of the Thieves. "I am not standing for that John, false arrest, bloody cheek, I'll get even." We just managed a drink before time was called. Charlie was still furious as we made our way back to the car park. "Quick, run for it John, follow me!"

said Charlie as he grabbed my arm and pointed to the police car parked forty yards away. As soon as we were on our toes the police car gave chase, siren and all. We darted into the nearest back alley. "What are you up to Charlie?" I said breathlessly. "Don't worry John, stick with me; now, walk slowly back up the alley." As I followed Charlie up the alley I thought, what are we doing?

I recalled that a few months previously Charlie and I had been cornered in the very same alley, located close to the La Casita coffee bar, by three Italians who, alarmingly, pulled blades on us. On that occasion we only escaped in one piece by wrapping our coats around our arms and charging them. Slashed jackets, thankfully, not cut throats. That memory evaporated the moment we arrived back on the main street as we were arrested again, this time by a different pair of policemen.

We were driven back to the Spaniard and as before marched in. The pub was by now deserted except for the disoriented landlord. Still looking sorry for himself he looked up and shook his head. "What is the matter with you? I told you less than an hour ago that it was not these two," he complained to the now confused policemen. Then, gesturing for us to join him at the bar, he said, "Want a drink lads? I am sorry for your trouble", and promptly poured a couple of large scotches. When we looked round the police had disappeared. I could see Charlie's game; he had indeed reaped his revenge on the hapless Worthing police force.

A week or two passed and once again I was with Charlie, this time in the Ocean Club, a smoky dive just off Worthing seafront. The local hard case had teamed up with us and appeared to know Charlie quite well. When we left to drive home he cadged a lift. This time we were in Charlie's old estate car. I was in the front passenger seat when 'our friend' wound down the nearside rear window. Charlie was a farmer and keen on game shooting in his spare time. To my horror, our uninvited passenger had found Charlie's shotgun wrapped in a blanket behind the back seat complete with a box of cartridges. Before our protests could register, both barrels were loaded and poked out of the window. Blam, blam! The blast took out a pillar-box-red phone booth. "Wow, did you see? I fucking blew it away," the nutter exclaimed.

Charlie sped away and after a mile or so turned into a quiet side road. He stopped the car, jumped out and dragged the culprit out of his seat, and to my amazement beat the hell out of the hard man, leaving him lying in the gutter. He then drove to his farm and hid the shotgun in an old barn. When he dropped me off twenty minutes later I had decided that in future I would give Charlie a wide berth and stick to Janine for my entertainment.

Jan was eighteen years of age and waiting on her A-level results with expectations of booking a place on a teacher training course at Homerton College, Cambridge. Her brother was something of a swot and already studying at Cambridge University. Normally I called for Jan between seven and seven-thirty at her parents' house. Her home was a large, imposing five-bedroomed house set back from the road, with an in-and-out driveway, and well camouflaged from the road by beech trees. The house and extensive grounds would eventually make way for a dozen detached houses.

Her father was always most genial, whereas one look from mother could easily wilt the flowers in the well-stocked garden. On my second visit her mum asked what I thought about Janine's intention to train to be a teacher. I answered with what I considered to be a witty reply: "You know what they say: those who can, do; those who can't, teach." Her response was, to say the least, icy. Later that evening I casually mentioned the conversation to Jan. "I bet she was not amused John; she is a primary school head teacher and dad is Head of Education for West Sussex." Oops! Even though my ill-conceived remark did not ingratiate me, I continued to call for Jan and make small talk with her parents.

One evening I was invited in for tea and biscuits while we all watched *University Challenge*. Jan's brother was at home and this round was of particular interest as his College was competing. For those not familiar with the programme, each is a contest between two teams from rival universities. The teams consist of four undergraduates, one of whom is appointed captain. Speed is of the essence; the first individual to 'buzz' must immediately give an answer, which if correct, earns ten points for the team and gains three further questions, each worth five points. The team with the highest score at the end of the half-hour programme wins through to the next round, and so on until two teams eventually reach the grand final.

In the Sixties the show was hosted by Bamber Gascoigne, a rather curt, but obviously intellectual chap, then in his mid-thirties. He was slightly pompous and prone to become annoyed and tetchy with team members – but I found him nowhere near as boorish as I now find Jeremy Paxman who has been quizmaster since the show was revived by the BBC in 1994 – it is very easy to be clever when you have in your hand both the questions and answers.

On that particular evening, surrounded by Jan's egghead family, and much to their amazement, I was able to provide the correct answers to the questions, ahead of the contestants. By the advert break I had on average, seven out of ten correct answers when Jan walked in. "I'm ready to go John, coming?" Before I had time to respond, her father said, "Sit down Janine, John is stopping for the second half of this programme, you listen: amazingly, his general knowledge is just remarkable!" With false modesty I said, "Well I just happened to get a few of the questions right, I am sure that I shall be clueless after the commercial break." With Jan sitting next to me I made an even bigger effort in the second half, and my performance did improve considerably. Even her mother was complimentary about my quick-fire response to the majority of the questions. As we headed for the door I could see Jan was beaming with delight, which I thought boded well for the rest of the evening.

The reason for my Mensa-like performance was purely down to my family living fifteen miles north of Worthing. My father, a Londoner, had adjusted our TV aerial to pick up London ITV. On the coast, however, the height of the South Downs prevented any reception other than from the Isle of White providing Southern ITV. *University Challenge* had been broadcast twenty-four hours earlier and, coincidentally, I had viewed it at my home. With the answers still fresh in my brain I was able to respond to the majority of the questions. I never let on and in future I made sure that I avoided like the plague calling for Jan again on that day of the week and at that time of the evening.

Two months later I was sitting in the Carousel Club in Copenhagen talking to Dave Davies of The Kinks. England had just won the World Cup and British pop music, largely thanks to The Beatles, had conquered the universe. A great time to be British; as a nation we were oozing with confidence and the 'baby boomer' generation were facing a golden future.

It was my second visit to the Danish capital and once again I was staying with Sven-Eric Hansen and his family. Sven and I became pen friends through school exchange trips. By now Sven had undertaken a marine apprenticeship in the dockyard. While he was at work I spent my time exploring the Copenhagen city centre and Malmo in nearby Sweden, often accompanied by Maiken. After an idyllic month idling my time, I had to make a choice: to stay in Denmark, find employment and accommodation, or return home. Like all things in life there were pros and cons, not least the language difficulty. I made the decision on Copenhagen railway station by the toss of a coin, and went home.

The city of Copenhagen was twenty years ahead of London: spotlessly clean, with paved walkways, shopping malls, draft lager, efficient tramways, canal transport and thousands of bikes; much like Amsterdam, without the seediness. The jewel in the crown was the Tivoli Gardens for heady late-night strolls through the sophisticated funfair. The downside: freezing cold in the winter and absolutely every item twice the price of the UK equivalent; however, this was August and the Carousel Club had a relaxed ambience, great bands and a sprung dance floor.

Strangely, back then there were very few English tourists to be found in Scandinavia; consequently Dave from London and I, both with Danish girls in tow, struck up a casual friendship and met perhaps twice a week at the club. Dave's band, The Kinks, which was fronted by his brother Ray, had notched up a dozen Top Ten hits including three number ones, and were second only to The Beatles and The Rolling Stones in rock-star pecking order. Needless to say Dave was recognised wherever he was out in public.

By mid-September I was back in the UK and once again dating Janine who, not surprisingly, was miffed by my absence throughout the long hot summer. To appease her I suggested a day out in London, which she readily agreed to. I parked on the third floor of the NCP car park and we spent a lovely day visiting the National Gallery, walking the Mall to Buckingham Palace and then back through Hyde Park and Oxford Street, ending up in Piccadilly Circus.

Sitting on the steps adjacent to The Statue of Eros I heard a male voice call my name. I looked round to see Dave Davies approaching us. "John, what are you doing here? I thought you decided that your future lay in Denmark," he exclaimed. I rather sheepishly mumbled, "Oh, I decided to come home." Quickly changing the subject I introduced him to Jan. Dave, who also had an English girl with him, suggested we go and eat somewhere. After a pizza and Cokes we parted company and Jan and I took in the latest Bond film before returning to my car. It was my first car, and my pride and joy: a Morris 1000 convertible with a black body and a dark red hood. We all fall in love with our first car don't we? It sounds better than it was in reality; the hood was held together with tape; the windscreen wipers had a knob for manual use in case the motor failed, as did the semaphore-style indicators, which performed much like railway signals. Never mind, it only cost £100 and was all mine.

Walking hand in hand back to the car park, I was now smugly basking in Dave Davies' reflected glory. "I had no idea that you knew The Kinks, John, I just can't wait to tell my girlfriends," exclaimed Jan. "Oh, us rock 'n' rollers stick together, girl," I grinned, becoming more insufferable by the minute. Indeed, I was really heading for a fall, and it was just around the corner; unlike my Morris 1000, which was nowhere to be seen on the third floor of the NCP car park we had just entered. "John, are you sure this is the right car park?" said Jan. "Don't be silly, it had 'NCP' in ten-foot letters at the entrance; someone must have nicked it," I answered, gruffly, as by now I was desperately searching the ground floor for an attendant.

"Your car can't have been stolen, unless you left the ticket in it," said the little black man in the pay box. "No I have it here, see," I said and waved the offending ticket in front of his quizzical face. "Well there is your answer man, your ticket is from another NCP car park; it is blue and mine are yellow, your car has not been stolen, you have parked it elsewhere." Well that's a relief brother, but where?" I questioned. "Well in the blue car park of course!" The little man was beginning to frustrate me: "I understand that, but where is the blue car park?" "I don't know, it could be any one of five in and around the West End." Taking Jan by the hand, I gave up the discussion and headed back towards Trafalgar Square.

Two hours later, after searching a further three car parks, we found my car. Being a country lad, how was I to know there was more than one NCP car park in London? Anyway, I was definitely no longer one of the 'in crowd' in Jan's eyes, just a stupid idiot with no sense of direction. A week or two later she went off to teacher training college and I never saw her again, much to her mother's delight, I have no doubt.

Days
Performers: The Kinks
Composer: R. Davis
Number 12:   July 1968

Chapter 9 – Elizabeth

Jeremiah 3:15
I will give you rulers who obey me, and they will rule you with wisdom and understanding.

Since Roman times Littlehampton's economy has been based largely on the area's ability to generate wealth from the sea and river. It was officially designated a port by William I in 1071, a mere five years after he had conquered England. Under the feudal system William designated Roger de Montgomery, who thereby became the first Earl of Arundel, to rule the town and surrounding area, indeed much of West Sussex. The subsequent building of Arundel Castle immediately demoted Littlehampton into second place to Arundel located four miles upstream.

In all probability the original point for the disembarkation of cargo prior to the construction of the castle was at Ford, for ease of access and due to the changing position of the river mouth. By the end of the seventeenth century access to this area of the river was becoming obstructed through tidal erosion, and silt and shingle deposits. Gradually over the next one hundred and thirty years Littlehampton superseded Arundel, commercially. Simply, it was far easier to offload cargo near the harbour mouth than horse-tow the shipping upriver to Arundel. This is probably the only time that Arundel has lost out to its near neighbour.

The castle is one of the most visited attractions in the South East. Curiously, the only original feature is the Norman keep, as the vast majority of the castle was built in the late nineteenth century. Arundel also boasts the Catholic Cathedral and a picturesque cricket ground where the Duke of Norfolk's XI play touring elevens, including international teams. The Duke of Norfolk flies the Union Jack from the castle keep when in residence. His official duty as Earl Marshal, is to arrange the reigning monarch's state occasions: weddings, coronations and funerals. Most reigning kings and queens have stayed at, or at least visited, the castle over the past thousand years including HM Queen Elizabeth II.

Throughout the nineteenth century Littlehampton wharf grew and by the 1880s two thousand vessels a year were visiting the port; its thriving shipbuilding industry, with chandlers and public houses servicing salty dogs, significantly swelling the town's population. Today, the port hosts in the region of one hundred visiting commercial ships every year, often ably guided through the narrow harbour mouth by Johnny, the resident pilot. Mostly the traffic is leisure vessels moored at the Marina situated on the west bank. Once inside the harbour, there are pontoons complete with power, light and drinking water adjacent to the Harbour Office.

From the mid-eighteenth century, visits to the seaside became fashionable for the gentry. When the railway station was built in 1863 the town was opened up to the masses; from then, until the present day, Littlehampton has become a popular destination for day-trippers and holidaymakers.

I spent two very happy years at Worthing College of Further Education and conversely, two miserable years at Crawley College of Technology. I did, however, pass twenty-four three-hour examinations to gain both the Ordinary and then the Higher National Diploma in Business Studies. Why? When I failed the Eleven Plus, I must have had a subconscious masochistic desire never to fail another exam again, and consequently ended up on a route that would more than prove the point. I'm not sure that I had a burning desire for knowledge; I think my interests were more akin to rock 'n' roll. If I could avoid a 'real job' then I would be available to play in the band and just maybe, find that elusive path to fame and fortune.

Harold Wilson, in the days of a proper socialist Labour government, allowed me to study and be grant-aided. Yes indeed, they paid me along with thousands of others to further our education. Not a great deal of money: a few pounds a week, travel vouchers, free books, and the tuition fee. Add these benefits to my other forms of income and I was quids in. I had little concern for my grades provided I passed the exams and handed in a half-decent thesis per course as our lecturer's reports, together with the term's work, counted towards fifteen percent of the marks. I guess my youth made me happy at Worthing; by the time I found myself at Crawley I was four years older having spent two years at Sun Alliance and London Insurance Company; maybe knowledge is more easily absorbed by a young mind.

I decided to stay at Sun Alliance after a two-month vacation job. I worked in the claims department, which I found fascinating, not least the rather clumsy fraudulent claims I came across from time to time. Sun Alliance and London was an amalgamation of a dozen other smaller companies that had been acquired by the holding company since the war yet, to maximise revenue, appeared to the public to have retained their independence.

My department looked after all the group claims. One particular gentleman of Indian origin had insured his property with all the companies and set about claiming the same identical loss twelve times over. Needless to say, he was invited by my boss to collect his claims cheque from the office, along with the police who promptly arrested the fraudulent individual. Handcuffed and disconsolate, he was led away and the whole office broke into spontaneous applause and cheering. On another occasion an insured claimant pulled his loo-chain (the old-fashioned high-level variety) and the cistern promptly collapsed. He claimed the price of a new toilet most eloquently, adding as a postscript, 'I await a reply at your convenience'!

The job of claims clerk had some magic moments, until I decided to have a long hard look at my colleagues. They were, by and large, decent enough guys who had become entrapped by circumstance: wife, kids and mortgage, with no way out, until receipt of the gold watch and pension. I thought, surely I can do better than this?

The man sitting opposite began to irritate me; it can so easily happen in a confined space over hours, days and weeks. In his forties, he was an ugly beggar, with pebble glasses and big ears, and he had a very bad habit of picking his nose with the end of his ballpoint pen, usually after lunch. I did my best to ignore him, but I became fixated upon this horrid habit. This ritual went on for week after week and to obviate the problem I saved up my photocopying and left my desk as soon it began. Day after day this occurred and I grimaced at the thought of it. I even requested a move, to no avail.

One day, I was stuck on a prolonged telephone call and was unable to make my usual exit. Call completed, I just blew and shouted, "If you carry on with that filthy habit your head will cave in!" Well you could have cut the atmosphere with a knife. The gnome swiftly left the room, and my section leader promptly marched me to the comptroller's office where I was given a severe lecture on how to be a team player. Today, it would be called a verbal warning. Oddly enough, over the next few days, one by one, my colleagues congratulated me for speaking up, and it goes without saying, the gnome gave up his revolting pastime, and it was time for me to move on.

When I bumped into my former Worthing College Head of Department, McGregor, he told me he had moved to Crawley College and invited me to continue my full-time studies with him; I thought this a good option and promptly resigned my job in insurance. Worthing College has happy memories for me, most of my classmates were a delight, and the lecturers were old eccentrics and highly inspirational. As a bonus I met David Brown at Worthing, and he turned into a life-long friend. The campus was very dated and sad, yet cosy and safe. We seemed to spend most of our time either in the refectory, the Kenya coffee shop or one of the four local pubs, and only on the odd occasion ventured downtown, or perhaps to the beach if the weather was kind.

The key to a successful student lifestyle is money for the little essentials in life: transport, cigarettes, alcohol and girls, though not necessarily in that order. My parents were happy to feed me and provide a roof over my head. Thereafter, quite rightly, all else was down to me. Since I was thirteen I had worked in my parents' shop and the strawberry fields that surrounded Pulborough village. By the time I left school, work had become a way of life. To enhance my meagre grant I found a variety of jobs. For two weeks prior to Christmas I worked as a postman from 6am to 6pm.

In the summer vacation I signed on with the Horsham Urban District Council. I arrived each morning at the depot and waited to be deployed either to a dustcart, road-gritting gang, or more likely, the town centre road-sweeping crew. Anyone clocking in after time was condemned to eight hours of recycling, which consisted of baling paper with Bill the transvestite. Without going into detail, Bill had some rather anti-social habits prompted by discarded girlie magazines.

Another hazard of this department was outbreaks of skin rashes and dermatitis. It would be overstating my enthusiasm to say I was happy to be allocated regular road-sweeping duties under the watchful gaze of Blackie, the foreman. Blackie was a veteran of World War II and seemed very pleased just to have survived his six-year tour. He taught me an important lesson: man can only enjoy three meals a day, sleep for eight hours a night in one bed and wear one set of clothes at a time. As many people in the world are not able to enjoy the basic necessities of life we should be happy, content and thankful. Blackie taught me to count my blessings and I am very grateful for his simple words of wisdom.

The four-strong gang also included Reg Carstairs and Stinky Hewitt. Dear Reg was a large man in his late twenties, very well spoken, but sadly, not the full shilling. Fifty-year-old Stinky, unshaven and dishevelled, lived up to his nickname. In fact I never discovered his Christian name, and avoided at all costs being downwind of him. By the time we had 'swept' our way to the high street the time was eight-thirty, just as the dolly birds were making their way to the shops and offices. I hardly need to say that while working alongside such illustrious new-found colleagues, I did my best to keep my head down and vigorously pushed my broom with the forlorn hope of not being recognised; the job did my 'street cred' no favours!

On very hot days I found myself transferred to road repairs, which proved to be an interesting distraction. The work was undertaken as follows: a section of road was speedily repaired and tarred; a lorry followed on and tipped grit over the tar; then two of us evenly distributed the grit on the new surface, and a heavy roller immediately compressed it into the still-hot tar. The next operation was for us to sweep up and then shovel any loose material back onto the lorry. The procedures were repeated as the repairs progressed along the road. As the work occupied one entire side of the road, it was necessary to have traffic control in operation: nothing sophisticated, just a simple Stop/Go sign. Mad Jack, a regular council worker, operated the sign.

During the progress of repairs on one stretch of road, there was only a narrow passing-space, with the lorry on one side and a flint wall the other. A Colonel Blimp type, driving a Rolls Royce, suggested to Mad Jack that the lorry needed moving to allow enough room for him to pass. Jack told him, 'There is enough room for a bleedin' Sherman tank; get a move on guv, you're holding up the traffic.' Blimp did proceed and wedged his very expensive car between the wall and the lorry. Totally trapped, he couldn't get out of either door and decided to communicate his plight by opening the roof light, just as I was shovelling the excess grit rather too enthusiastically. Blimp was showered with still-hot blackened white pebbles. A terrible row ensued and the depot manager was called. Somehow I managed to wheedle out of blame, unlike Mad Jack who was promptly transferred to the low-loader dustcart; demotion indeed.

Curiously, my most lucrative job was organising and delivering Sunday newspapers. This required me to be at Pulborough station at 6.45am to collect the newspapers, drive home, sort into rounds, distribute to four paperboys, deliver some myself, collect the money and bundle the returns. I finished all this around noon. This was no mean feat when you take into account that I had probably worked in the shop Saturday morning, played football in the afternoon and drummed in the evening. On more than one occasion I did not bother to go to bed; I simply headed for the station after offloading my drum kit. My approximate annual tax-free income was as follows:

Government education grant:	£300
Band income:	£125
Sunday papers:	£400
Post Office:	£30
Horsham Council:	£88
Shop work: (Keep only)	Nil
TOTAL	£943

This was certainly more than the average wage in the mid- to late Sixties. Ironically, when I finally left full-time education in 1970 and reluctantly took up a permanent position as office manager for Gripperrods International, I was financially worse off. With hindsight, I should have then and there started my own business; however, at the time I felt obliged, and under pressure from my parents, to find a 'proper job' where I could make use of my qualifications.

The Crawley College main building is to Sixties' architecture what King Herod was to babysitting, a total disaster; nine storeys of concrete and glass with no redeeming features. The Business Studies Department was on the ninth floor accessed by stairs, lift or paternoster. I have nothing good to say about Crawley College. The kindest word I could find for my fellow students was bland; and the lecturers, with the exception of Stan Hall, were appalling. I arrived, attended lectures, and returned home; occasionally I turned out for the college football team – and that was it. There were, however, two unusual occurrences during my time at Crawley.

The Queen paid a visit to the town and one of her duties that day was to open a new wing at the college; not unreasonably, all lectures were cancelled after 12 noon. Rather than witness the event I decided to catch the first available train back to Pulborough. When I arrived at the station I found I had a twenty-minute wait for the next train. I bought a paper, went to the toilet, sat on the loo and read the paper.

When I finally vacated the gents, the Royal Train had just pulled into the station, and the Queen was at that very moment exiting from the main entrance. I would have bumped straight into Her Majesty had it not been for a security guard who quickly blocked me. Elizabeth the Second, by the Grace of God, of the United Kingdom of Great Britain and Northern Ireland, and of her other Realms and Territories Queen, Head of the Commonwealth, Defender of the Faith was less than one yard away from me; so, so close, I could have touched her. We looked one another in the eye, and then she was gone.

The other strange occurrence happened in February 1970 when simultaneously, a flu epidemic knocked out half the staff together with a quarter of the students, and a power failure took out both the lifts and the paternoster. After climbing the nine storeys on the Monday morning McGregor called me into his office. He said, "John I need your help; I have a skeleton staff and am teaching myself. I know it's a big ask, but starting right now, could you take over and lecture the first-year Business Studies class until the crisis is over?" "No problem sir, which number class room?" was my immediate reply; McGregor had always been fair with me and I was pleased to help, indeed, flattered to be asked. Having spent so much of my life attending lectures, I found it amazingly easy to conduct them. Maybe I had stumbled upon a career that might fit with my lifestyle?

On my last day in full-time education Stan Hall took me to one side and said, "John, ninety-nine per cent of the staff and students here are losers, please don't even consider a career in teaching as I'm certain you can make it in business; you have got what it takes. As you know I ran my own successful business and I am telling you that you can do the same. Go and find a skill, or some sort of trade to harness your natural business acumen to, and then you may well find the elusive key to wealth. Remember just one thing: money can at times be easy to make; equally, very hard to hold on to."

I was very moved by Stan's encouraging words; not only was he a great lecturer and an astute businessman, he had also had a distinguished military career. In World War II he parachuted into Arnhem for Operation Market Garden, a significant event in British history made famous by the film *A Bridge Too Far*. Stan claimed that upon landing he dug a big hole and hid for four days. The truth was very different: he had in fact fought a bloody battle, losing both the bridge and his left eye, before briefly being taken prisoner by the Germans. Stan was a war hero and a man to take notice of. Abandoning the chance to remain at the college as a junior lecturer I set out to follow his words of wisdom.

Killer Queen
Performers: Queen
Composer: Mercury
Number 2:   October 1974

Chapter 10 – Jamie

Proverbs 14:10
Your joy is your own; your bitterness is your own.
No one can share them with you.

Banjo Road is situated bang in the middle of the greensward, halfway between Harbour Park and East Beach Café. Banjo Road coach park holds up to twenty-two coaches or buses and it is the Foreshore Inspector's responsibility to close the gate at 6pm. If the barrier is left open all sorts of gypsies, didicoys and itinerant travellers have been known to set up camp in the coach park or on the green, and in so doing sometimes create mess and havoc for both the local community and visitors alike. Even with a court order it can sometimes take weeks to remove them.

On weekdays during term-time coaches generally bring down school parties for an educational day by the sea. The primary school children visit the Lifeboats, the Look & Sea Centre and explore the beach, followed by a fifteen-minute talk from Dave or me. From time to time I involve the Lifeguards when they are on duty. We explain the tides and the hazards of the river and the sea, and let the kids have a go on the walkie-talkie, which always proves popular. At weekends the visitors who arrive by coach are generally from South London, on club, pub or church outings.

When the coach park is full there is an overflow option next door to the Swimming & Sports Centre.

On a busy weekend or bank holiday there can be literally thousands of day-trippers also arriving by car or train from as far away as a fifty miles. The ethnic minority, or on occasions, majority, spills out onto the green, shelters, beach and the amusement park often attired in traditional dress, armed with ghetto blasters and exotic barbecue food; always good-natured and determined to enjoy a great day out at the seaside.

The Foreshore Inspector's job at these busy times is primarily one of controlling the crowds in a sensitive manner and helping our visitors to have a happy, safe and informative time. As we are first-aiders the Foreshore Office, which also houses a defibrillator, is the designated first-aid post, and my colleague and I have treated up to a dozen people in one day. By and large we treat cut feet, weaver fish and wasp stings, and occasionally, hypothermia, when visitors stay in the water too long; normally only teenagers fall into this trap. Hypothermia is usually easily cured by wrapping the shivering individual in a foil blanket, and if necessary, offering them a hot shower in the boat-house. First aid is what it says on the tin. For anything more serious we dial 999 and call the paramedics who always respond immediately to our request for assistance. The heat will often bring on a faint in the elderly; if this is the case we take no chances and call for backup as heart failure could be imminent. I had one lady suffer an epileptic fit only a few feet from the office; interestingly, there is not a lot one can do other than to make sure the tongue is not swallowed. In this instance I located her pills and placed one under her tongue; within two or three minutes she recovered, and after a ten-minute rest and a cup of tea, was back to normal.

Lost kids are something of a headache and most especially when we are busy. Regardless of whatever else is happening, they immediately become the number one priority. There is no specified drill when a child or individual is reported missing. A typical response is as follows: one Foreshore Inspector will stay in the office to co-ordinate the search; once the child's description/details have been determined, the other will start to look in the obvious places. If, for example, I am in the office at the time of the first report, Dave may be up to a mile away; in that case I will call him on the intercom with the child's details and last known location. Then in the same way I call all the lifeguards to report to me in the office and allocate them areas to search.

Normally at the weekend there are four lifeguards on duty: men and women in their late teens or early twenties, often university undergraduates earning holiday money. These 'guys' are always superfit and intelligent; I keep one, normally female, by my side to be available to deal with the by-now-hysterical parent(s) and undertake any first-aid requests that may occur during this time. The second guard will take the beach buggy and patrol the promenade and greensward; the third checks out both the gents' and ladies' toilets situated a few yards behind our office, and the fourth alerts Gary and his Harbour Park staff.

Nine times out of ten my team locates the child within ten minutes of being advised of the disappearance. We use a secret formula, which is simply that the child will go the way the wind is blowing. We use it like this: Dave makes his way to the location on the beach where the child was last seen. He then assesses the speed and direction of the wind and calculates how long the child has been missing, which may well differ from the time they were actually reported lost. Using this he works out where he suspects the child is likely to be. I know this method is hit and miss, but it has always proved the best bet.

Age, siblings and clothing are other factors. Sometimes a child wanders off when its parents fall asleep on the beach. If the family has been in Harbour Park just before settling on the beach, then there is a good chance with a child over five years, he or she will have returned to the fun of the amusements. When the child is only in swimwear and was last seen at the waterside, I immediately call out the lifeboat to patrol the waters nearby. If the Coastguard, located next door to the Foreshore Office, is on duty I inform them of the problem.

Should the child not be found within twenty minutes then I consult with Dave and the Senior Coastguard on duty; we then decide whether to inform the police. We are always conscious of the fact that our community suffered a horrendous child abduction in the not-too-distant past. Seven-year-old Sarah Payne was snatched and murdered by Roy Whiting who lived at the time on South Terrace which is less than one hundred yards from the seafront. Consequently, if the police are called they usually appear very quickly and always treat our report seriously; normally they clear the immediate beach area, and cordon off the promenade between the pier and East Beach Café.

Whether to inform the police is a dilemma for my team as history tells us that the child is very likely to be found within the hour. One young lad, just short of his fourth birthday, walked well over a mile in an easterly direction to beyond the last beach hut and crossed the main road; he was found in the Swimming & Sports Centre car park fifty minutes after he was reported missing. If in doubt we always call the police and live with the consequences, which include total disruption to our patch, and the task of calming demented parents.

To place this problem in perspective: on average each season we have around fifty reported cases, of which no more than half a dozen will involve the police. All children reported lost thus far have been found within a reasonable timescale.

Notwithstanding all this kerfuffle we often have to deal with kids who have lost their parents! They are brought to our office by well-meaning members of the public who are most concerned by a young child in distress. Sometimes the child may be so young they have yet to learn to speak, which can make life tricky. In such cases I generally ask a female lifeguard to entertain the child while we make enquiries as to the parents' whereabouts.

The best case, or should I say the worst case, was that of a three-year-old girl whose parents, as it turned out, had caught the coach back to Streatham without their daughter. I announced the surname over the loudspeaker system and an aunt of the girl turned up to collect her. The lady had heard me as she was queuing to board another coach back to Streatham. I was able to verify with the coach driver the legitimacy of the relationship and, thankfully, the problem was quickly resolved. Normally, I resist the temptation to make such a public announcement in the case of a lost parent as it may inadvertently prompt a total stranger to lay claim to the child. Anything involving children is, to say the very least, delicate.

A Foreshore Inspector's 'FAQs' include: 'Where are the toilets?', 'Where is the cash machine?', and "Where has the sea gone?' (When the tide is high – twenty feet, or more – the sea at low tide retreats well over one hundred yards.) Understandably, people who visit the coast infrequently, have little or no concept of tides, currents, winds and the effects of the moon in relation to sea levels. We are always happy to explain the variations in water levels and give an approximate time for the next high tide. We keep a supply of tide tables that we are happy to hand out when requested in return for a small donation in the Lifeboat collection box.

In summer, at high tide, we are often treated to a full-immersion Baptism service. These usually involve a Free or Baptist Church, generally with members of West African origin, who turn the event into a celebration of singing, music and prayer, attracting a big crowd of onlookers. In August, it is not unusual for Littlehampton to become, for a few sunny hours, totally cosmopolitan with every colour and creed represented, creating a magical carnival atmosphere. Dave might occasionally comment, 'You would never know we are in England'.

On one occasion, seeing a couple of black men pulling an inflatable out of the sea, Dave whispered in my ear, 'Here John, don't you think those two have travelled a mighty long way to get here, quite a paddle from Africa?' I find it very difficult to understand political correctness. We are all different and as a child I was often teased about my buck teeth and my Irish descent. If you are black, white, yellow, or a mixture – what does it matter? We are what we are! With that in mind I will introduce James Peter Madell.

Almost five years after Jean and I married, Jamie was born on the 28 April 1978. Due to serious financial restraints, and with children Mark and Andrew from Jean's first marriage to provide for, we delayed starting a family of our own until I had established my career path. At last confident that we could afford another mouth to feed we were delighted to learn of the forthcoming happy event; however, life rarely works out exactly as planned or anticipated – I guess it might be boring if it did.

When Jean was taken into labour I drove her over to Zachary Merton Hospital in Rustington arriving around 4pm. I had just started to refit the kitchen and knew I would have to complete the project within the next seven days. In the Seventies it was the norm for new mums to spend at least five days resting up after the birth.

After admission very little happened and by 8pm I was in need of refreshment. Jean told me to go and find a café or pub expecting a long wait 'from here to maternity'. As ever, I did what my wife instructed and soon found myself leaning on the bar of The Windmill Inn in Rustington. One hour, two pints and a very large pork pie later I was back at the hospital only to find that she had been taken to the delivery room.

My understanding of the 'father's job' was to walk up and down the corridor outside chain-smoking, until the magic moment when he would be summoned to his wife's side to inspect the now-clean-and-shining new addition to his family. I am sure that was the case until the mid-Seventies, when some bright spark recommended that every father should now expect to enjoy the most intimate experience of the new arrival's first sight of the world. A new era had dawned and I found myself pushing Jean's left leg whilst she cursed me far more effectively than any of my roof tilers had ever achieved. Why did I have two pints? I asked myself. By the time the maternity experience had completed its cycle, I knew for sure that I could never, never ever consume another pork pie as long as I may live!

I left mother and son sleeping soundly and returned home just after 1am. I woke up at 7am to press on with the kitchen refurbishment, taking time out to phone my colleague Trevor to inform him of the happy event, and to say that I would not be back at work until after the May bank holiday. Satisfied with my progress at home I drove back to the hospital arriving just after lunch.

As I walked briskly up the corridor, approaching me from the other direction was my father-in-law Ron. By the time we met in the middle I could see he was clearly in a distressed state. "What is the matter Dad?" I heard my voice echo off the grey walls. Ron tried to speak; yet nothing came out, until, with tears in his eyes, he half mumbled, "I am sorry, so sorry." Leaving the distraught man behind I ran the rest of the way to the ward to find Jean quietly sobbing into the pillow. "Jean, what on earth has happened? I have just seen your dad who could make absolutely no sense whatsoever." At last Jean sat up in bed and whispered, "They have just this minute told Dad and I that they think our new baby boy is mentally handicapped! Just look at him John, you can see by his round face and flat nose he is a Mongol." Jamie was lying in the cot next to the bed, and sure enough those were his features; however, to me all babies look the same and I said as much. "They have to do a test to see if he has an extra chromosome which will prove that he is Down's syndrome; that's the posh way of saying Mongol," Jean said.

Just at that moment a doctor arrived and informed us thus: "Your son has all the classic features of Down's and I fully expect this to be confirmed when we receive the test results in forty-eight hours' time. I think it best that we do not encourage him to eat as they normally have trouble feeding immediately after birth and we expect your baby boy will fade away, which I am sure will be the best result for all concerned."

Eventually, I returned home that day totally drained emotionally, forgetting the kitchen was in disarray. Trevor, my work colleague who lived a couple of streets away, called round to report on the job front and enquire how things were at the hospital. When I told him the news, his reaction was amazing: "John it's Friday night we have all the May bank-holiday weekend to finish your kitchen. Let's start right now; best thing to do, it will take your mind off your problem." That indeed is just what we did; Trevor and I completed the project by late Monday. The only time I laid down my tools was to visit the hospital; I will never forget the kindness and support that Trevor gave me in my hour of need.

The tests did prove positive; we did have a handicapped child. Yet, Jamie was not going to fade away and took food normally, even though Jean was unable to breastfeed. Soon they were both home and the two of us, together with Mark and Andrew, slowly came to terms with the new arrival.

When Jamie was a mere three weeks old I found myself alone in the house with him one Saturday afternoon. Looking down at him in his cot, I thought of the animal kingdom where the parent often ends the life of the runt of the pack, for both the youngster's sake and the good of the family. I thought of the words the doctor uttered that traumatic day at the hospital. It would be so easy to place a pillow over his tiny face and end his life right there and then. No one other than me would know as the child was not expected to survive anyway. How will he manage his life with such a handicap? Will our marriage survive this challenge? (Fact: two out of three marriages break up soon after the addition of a severely handicapped child). If I do the deed, will I manage to keep the knowledge that I had murdered my baby boy to myself until my dying day? Would I regret the deed? I really don't remember how long these thoughts passed through my head; I just know that eventually I marginally concluded that the matter was best left in the hands of God.

We joined the Down's Syndrome Association (then in its infancy) to learn as much as we could about this genetic disorder. Coincidentally, my work colleague Charles, had twin Down's boys born in 1971, and I subsequently learned from him a great many of the practicalities in bringing up an infant with the condition.

Jean, to her great credit, tirelessly worked on Jamie to stimulate body movement and keep his tongue in his mouth. Down's are naturally floppy and tend to hold their tongue on the bottom lip; hour after hour she massaged his arms and legs, and discouraged the lazy tongue.

Jean Madell, 1976

Jamie's sleeping patterns were not normal and most nights he woke up hourly. I often used to bed-down next to his cot and as soon as he cried I sang to him, which with my 'dulcet tones', was more than enough to discourage anyone from waking up.

It was soon time for Jamie to go to school. Durrington was the obvious choice as we lived only a short walk away. Both Andrew and Mark had attended the school a decade previously, and Jean herself had first walked through the gates as a pupil in 1953. The local Educational Physiologist, Mr Cook, took the bold decision to place Jamie in mainstream education long before the Warnock Commission made just that recommendation for all slow learners. Mr Cook spent many hours assessing Jamie who usually sat on his knee in the back garden as they scoffed tea and biscuits liberally provided by Jean. Jamie used to stroke his bald head and call him

'Cooker'! Sadly, the experiment did not work and Jamie lasted just one term before being transferred to the George Pringle School (for special needs) also in Durrington. Clearly the mainstream school was not geared to a special case like Jamie; the reception teacher was understandably overwhelmed by Jamie's demands, along with those of thirty other normal five-year-olds. After the first month the headmaster added a full-time teaching assistant to the class, and although a progressive move, she too was not trained to deal with a Down's syndrome child.

The unsung and biggest knock-on effect of mental handicap is the impact it has on the siblings in the family. Inevitably, they take a back seat, as well-meaning family and friends tend to concentrate their attention on the 'special' child. Often, the handicapped child becomes subconsciously jealous of the progress made by a younger brother or sister. We found that Jamie was inclined to bully his younger brother Paul. Jamie being three years older and physically stronger, Paul was unable to be himself and develop normally. It was as if Jamie wanted to get inside him, and *be* Paul.

Back in the Seventies, society was not as liberally minded towards minority groups as it is today. Like blacks and homosexuals, mentally handicapped people were singled out for persecution and ridicule. This became an issue for Jamie as some members of the family found just being with Jamie a great challenge, especially in public. Andrew was the exception and seemed to take the unsolicited attention in his stride. I believe finger-pointing and strange looks when walking through the town with Jamie was very hard for Jean who is naturally shy, and she was undoubtedly not helped by her introverted tendencies. I was like Andrew: not bothered by some people's ignorance. Yet, as Jamie grew up he became more self-aware and quizzed me why some people were overtly 'in his face'. All I could say to Jamie was that when some people saw him in public, to them it was like seeing a pop star or famous footballer in the street. Rightly or wrongly Jamie was more than happy with this explanation, and to this day I am pleased to say he sees himself as a very special person.

Jamie did all right at George Pringle under the stern gaze of his teacher Mrs Pitt. Coincidentally, her husband taught me Economic History at Worthing College. However, it became clear that for Paul to blossom he had to be out of Jamie's reach. Once again we consulted 'Cooker' and within a few weeks Jean and I were taking a tour of St Cuthman's school at Stedham, which is situated on the northern boundary of West Sussex.

We were both very much impressed with the boarding establishment ably run by the headmaster Howard Rooks and his wife Dale. Aged eight, Jamie became a weekly boarder. Miss Fake, an elderly spinster who looked after the younger boarders, was brilliant and very soon Jamie made friends and settled into life in this old rambling country house. Jamie spent eight very happy and productive years at St Cuthman's, and I was soon invited to join the governing body as a Parent Governor and took on the not inconsiderable responsibility of the maintenance and development of the campus.

The Governors' meetings were, I suspect, a throwback to a bygone age. The body was generally made up of the great and good of the county, consisting of: the chairman Alan Bloomfield, a retired ICI director; the local Roman Catholic priest; the Bishop of Chichester; Lady Bolton; a wine importer called Eggor; Paul Mellings who ran a dental practice in Midhurst; the Clerk from County Hall; the Head, and me. We met for lunch at 1pm in the Head's dining-room and enjoyed three courses accompanied by a few sample bottles of Eggor's wine. The meetings started at 2.30pm and finished at 5.30pm. We all had allocated jobs such as teaching appointments, curriculum, staff, and finance. No Governor interfered with another's delegated specialist subject and the whole process ran like a well-oiled clock. Anything remotely controversial would be referred to a steering committee consisting of the Chair, the Head and the County Hall Clerk.

For five or six years the school became a 'home from home' for me to retreat to away from work. Apart from the Governors' meetings, I also met with the County's property manager to agree items for improvement; saw Jamie, attended the various fundraising events, and rounded up my band for the odd Friday night dance party. My fellow Governors were a great bunch: full of fun and all happy to give of their time freely in the best interests of the School and the welfare of its pupils. (Including the priest who often partook of one-too-many glasses of wine at lunchtime, and then told unbelievably blue jokes!)

Immediately after one lunch Alan Bloomfield called for the school chef Brian, and poured down great compliments on his catering ability. "Brian, you excelled yourself last weekend; the meal you prepared for the school fete guests was sublime," said

Alan in his best Mr Grace 'you've all done very well' tone. Indeed, I attended the lunch (and had the 'onerous' task of looking after the attractive actress Geraldine James who opened the event) and the food was way better than the very average fare Brian generally served. All present gave the school chef a round of applause. Rather than smile and nod to the Governing body for the generous reception, Brian appeared embarrassed and somewhat sheepish. "Well sir, I was not on duty last Saturday, in fact I was away visiting family; Mrs Bridge from the village club stood in for me." The subsequent silence was golden.

'If it ain't broke don't fix it'. The 'powers that be' had no concept of this wise saying, and after five or six years of happy governing a wind of change blew through St Cuthman's Victorian manor house school. Rather than inviting, and co-opting the local wealthy or well-appointed members of the community to serve, a directive arrived from County Hall (originating, no doubt, from central government) informing our body that in future all were to be appointed by election only. The makeup of our small, but highly effective group changed radically over the next twelve months.

I survived because very few parents were interested in becoming a Parent Governor; indeed the new system required an additional Parent Governor to join the body. Even the Head would not necessarily have to remain on the board. From the original body only four survived. We were joined by a number of left-wing ladies with sensible shoes. Howard the Headmaster became the Headteacher. I now had two of these apparently Brylcreemed ladies 'helping' me run the campus. There was no more wine at lunch as old Eggor was, very sadly, the first to go.

The dialogue within the meetings became hugely politically correct, to such an extent that it became impossible to talk openly and passionately about the school that we so cherished. Both Howard's and my contributions to the meetings became minimal, and dear old Alan was totally sunk both by the revised agenda and the new incumbents. To add to my misery, the aftermath of the Dunblane school massacre created a whole new slant on site security. My role as campus manager could easily have become an unpaid full-time job. New build and renovation immediately took a back seat to locks and passes which became an essential addition to school life; the bogeyman must be kept out at all cost. Whatever system we considered introducing could never have been totally effective, because the school, which was remotely situated in fifty acres and surrounded by green fields, simply could not be secured. I stepped down in 1998 after ten years' service. County Hall budget cuts finally led to the closure of St Cuthman's in 2004.

Armed with a very good education Jamie left St Cuthman's in 1995. The success of the school could not be measured by exam passes, (although, unbelievably, in latter years County Hall produced a results league table that somewhat inevitably, marked our school bottom.) St Cuthman's aimed to send out its students equipped to make their way in society. Jamie learnt how to read, write and keep his room tidy. Jamie and his old school mates know better than most how to conduct themselves with polite, consideration and respect for others. Moreover, acting, art and music have played a big part in his education. Jamie loves Dickens, especially *Oliver Twist*, and played a part in the school's production of *Down to Earth* which won first prize in the grand final of the Variety Club Theatrical Competition 1989 when performed at the Royalty Theatre in London on the 2 July 1989.

Next stop for Jamie was Yeovil College in Somerset; two more years of general education coupled with working on the farm and in the kitchens. Jamie shared a bungalow with two other students and learnt how to become more self-sufficient. The learning curve included setting the kitchen on fire! That said, the highlight of his two years in the West Country was the Dartmoor Ten Tors: Jamie completed the forty-five-mile route, twice, with the help and oversight of the Armed Forces.

At the age of nineteen Jamie moved to The Old Rectory, Singleton, where he lived for two years while completing his education at Chichester College. The charity Dignity, which runs The Old Rectory, also has half a dozen houses into which able clients may move when they are ready for greater independence.

Currently Jamie lives in Stockbridge Road sharing with four other people. Jamie is able to walk into Chichester alone or pop down to the Selsey Tram for a pint and collect his newspaper from the local shop. He worked in the restaurant at Sainsbury's for six years before moving to The Weald and Downland Open Air Museum at Singleton. Oddly, one of the jobs he undertook at Sainsbury's was to stand by the tea and coffee machine and assist the customers in its operation. I am sure that to some it was something of a shock to be instructed by a Down's syndrome man in the subtle art of self-service technology.

Not many of us can say that we have featured in a movie that had world-wide general release, can we? Yet Jamie can. In 1997 Jamie spent two days filming *Shooting Fish* in Dorking where he can be clearly seen congratulating the actors Dan Futterman and Stuart Townsend for saving their Manor House home. Spookily, the surroundings were not dissimilar to St Cuthman's. I understand that although Jamie did ask Kate Beckinsale, the leading lady, for her phone number he had to make do with an autographed photo.

In 1989 I purchased a bungalow on Pagham beach, which was a converted railway carriage. The carriage, originally built in 1870, was retired to the beach in 1923 when the first owner purchased it for £5, and a further £5 for the freehold plot of land. Sadly, I paid a tad more, and on and off for next twenty-odd years let it out, until my marriage broke down at which point I finally decided to move in permanently. The property represented a refuge to hurry back to from my job on the foreshore, where unknowingly, Dave provided me with great moral support during one of the toughest periods of my life.

Thankfully, life moves on and by 2013 I had met and become engaged to Janet MacDonald. Jan and I began to explore a way of subtly knitting together our two families before our forthcoming wedding in June of that year. As some time previously I had promised Jamie a 'bit of a do' for his thirty-fifth birthday, we hit upon a cunning plan to include as many as possible of our seven sons to celebrate the occasion in style. The vehicle we chose was to recreate *The Jolly Boys' Outing*, an old episode from *Only Fools and Horses*, the popular sit-com. In this episode Mike the pub landlord of The Nags Head in Peckham organised a coach trip to Margate for his regular customers. As Jamie has always been a big fan of Del Boy and Rodney, the two main characters in the long-running series, I knew he would jump at the chance of retracing their steps.

The plot, if you can call it that, entailed leaving the pub, stopping en route at the Halfway House pub, visiting the funfair, a nightclub, and then missing the last train home; leaving the group of family and friends with the no other choice than to find accommodation for the night. I hired a minibus and invited my available sons, Mark and Daniel, grandson Luke, Jan's boys, James and Ross, and Ross's father-in-law Denis and brother-in-law Dan. We met up at 1pm in The Nag's Head, Chichester for a quick drink, then drove to the Halfway House just outside Tonbridge, and by the time we arrived at the Blues-Brothers-themed B&B in Margate the party was in very good voice.

We all took on a character from the series and agreed that we would only address each other by our stage name; failure to do so would result in a 50p fine. Jamie naturally became Del; Daniel was Del's younger brother Rodney; I was Uncle Albert, and so on. Three hours after leaving Chichester we arrived in Margate with the pot totalling a massive £120 which provided an excellent starting sum for the pub-crawl kitty!

After dumping our kit in the B&B we hit the town, starting at the Dreamland amusement park where James (Trigger) seemed very happy to escort Jamie (Del) on every ride on offer, with the rest of us settling for the bumpers and shooting gallery for our entertainment. Next we found a pub close to the sea front, sporting a pool table in one corner, which kept the boys entertained for over an hour. I decided to keep the bar stool warm and was viewing the proceedings from afar when in staggered 'Napoleon'. A middle-aged man attired in a full military uniform including a three-sided hat leaned up against the bar and ordered a large gin and tonic. Planting his bum on the stool next to me, he was soon regaling me with some story about Waterloo and how his French army 'was robbed'. I decided it was best not to encourage the nutter so totally ignored him, and very soon he minced off to watch the boys playing pool.

On the way to the funfair my eighteen-year-old grandson Luke (Micky Pearce) had put his arm around my shoulder and assured me that I had nothing to worry about on our big night out as he would take it upon himself to watch my back. 'You enjoy yourself granddad I will look after you.' Luke had said with great confidence as is becoming to youth. The game of pool was well-advanced and Luke, having beaten the two Dans, was in the final with Ross. Napoleon, clearly without Josephine in tow, must have at some point counted to 'ninety-nine and changed hands', as by now his main point of interest was quite obviously Luke. My grandson, becomingly increasingly aware of his unwelcome admirer, quickly lost the final to Ross (Boycie) and joined me at the bar. Luke was clearly spooked by the effeminate weirdo and when, a minute later, Napoleon chose to nudge up to him on the adjoining stool, I decided it was time for me to step in: "Go and sit down with your dad Luke," I said before turning my attention to my unwanted drinking companion. Looking Napoleon straight in the eye and carefully choosing my words I whispered, "It is time for you to go home old fruit, you are upsetting my grandson." Without further ado he turned on his heels and disappeared into the night. As we walked up the street to the curry house, it was my turn to place my arm on Luke's shoulder and say, "Don't worry boy, this old man will look after you!"

Soon after Jamie had consumed Del Boy's favourite dish, lobster vindaloo (I suspect King Prawn Madras), we split up: Denis (Denzil), Mark (Mike) and me back to the B&B to watch Match of the Day, and the remainder of our party setting off to explore all the night-life attractions that Margate had to offer, which must have been considerable as by all accounts the younger members finally went to bed at 4am.

Next morning Denis and I met to enjoy a full English breakfast at 8am. There was no sign of the others though, and by checking-out time at 10am, the two of us had to roam around the house and wake up our hung-over family members. The journey home was largely conducted in silence; broken only by the odd groan and a forlorn request to stop the bus to be sick. Clearly, all had enjoyed a very jolly time.

When Jamie was dedicated at Durrington Free Church at the age of six months, the then minister Rodney Kingstone, prayed that God would bless Jamie and that he would reach his full potential. God has surely made good that prayer.

Blue Suede Shoes
Performer: Elvis Presley
Composer: Perkins
Number 9:   May 1956

(Jamie won a karaoke competition in Madeira performing this song)

John Madell and Dave Strong with the harbour mouth and West Works in the background

Littlehampton Harbour

East Beach Café

Part of The Longest Bench, Littlehampton

The River Arun towards Bury Hill

Church of St Botolph, Hardham, from the rear

Wedding group outside Hardham church, (21 June 2013)

David Sawyer

(*Front row*) Anne Paul, John Paul, Daniel Hooper, Lucia Hooper, Mick Walker, Jamie Madell, John Madell, Janet Madell, Sue MacDonald, Marion Dunn, Holly Madell, Daniel Madell, Debbie Brotherton, John Brotherton. (*Middle row*) Rebekah Madell, Gail LeGrove, Dawn Madell, Andrew Madell, Terry Redhead, Ross MacDonald, Amy MacDonald, Joan Brine, James MacDonald, Paul Madell, Soumely Madell. (*Back row*) Dennis Hooper, Peter LeGrove, Lloyd Gordon, Mark Madell, Luke Madell, Pete Redhead, Ian Dunn.

John Madell at Cranleigh British Legion, Christmas Eve, 2012

Janet Madell (2016)

Paul Millen

(Left to right) Mark, Andrew, Jamie, Paul and Daniel Madell (21 June 2013)

David Sawyer

Chapter 11 – Marley

At the start of the 2010 season the Littlehampton Harbour Board was without a Harbourmaster as the tall and amiable incumbent since 2001 had been placed on 'gardening leave' pending an investigation into alleged misconduct.

The Harbour Office is an impressive whitewashed building situated adjacent to the river walk, with vehicle access from Pier Road. The Harbour Board has responsibility for the mile-long stretch of the Arun from the road bridge to the harbour mouth. As the Board was short-staffed the Foreshore Office was commissioned to oversee the public slipway. The foreshore team members were given a short course in launching and the recovery of small crafts, primarily to ensure the safety of the boat crews and the general public. We were instructed to check the validity of those using the facility, and to send those without permits to the tourist information office to buy one; thereby maximising the harbour dues.

This was all well and good in principle, yet in practice proved highly problematic. The slipway is over half a mile from our beach office, and busy times, which generally coincided at both locations, required our presence at the office which doubles as a first-aid centre. Despite this, foreshore staff were required to man the slipway full-time in high season, and to facilitate this demand Arun Council sometimes allocated an additional Foreshore Officer to cover the ramp.

Arun Council also has responsibility for the Bognor Regis Foreshore Office, located on Bognor promenade approximately one hundred yards west of Butlins. Consequently our opposite numbers (also managed by the amiable Geoff Taylor) were occasionally seconded to the delights of the Littlehampton ramp. The position of the slipway ramp catches the predominant south-west wind; with the harbour mouth and river acting as a funnel, and with no shelter provided, the job soon became the most unwelcome ongoing duty. Behind the slipway stands the Lifeboat Station, which when open, can offer some limited cover within the boathouse.

The 'usual suspects' from Bognor were David Court, Mick Loveland and Stevie Potts; all fully trained, with bags of common sense and a pleasure to work alongside. David, an ex-Telecom engineer is hugely practical, totally reliable, and most importantly, very good company. Mick is an all-round good guy; as a retired senior manager with the London Ambulance Service he is more than able to deal with any crisis relating to first aid. Stevie is a former car salesman, single, with an eye for the ladies and chat-up lines that only he could get away with. Any of the trio was always very welcome in the Littlehampton office.

On busy weekends up to half a dozen vehicles together with trailers might, with luck, form a disorderly queue to await a launching slot. Feasibly, two boat-trailers can be backed down the ramp, and/or recovered simultaneously; however, the larger trailers need to back at an angle to avoid grounding on the ridge between the road and ramp. The regulars have developed the knack of negotiating this hazard quickly and efficiently; not so the weekenders. The impatient will, more often than not, break ranks, and without tight supervision any element of order quickly disappears; managing the ramp was a thankless task.

The Harbourmaster was eventually found guilty of gross misconduct and he was replaced by a lady with the title of Harbour Manager. Her well-meaning predecessor had donated a trip up the Arun as a raffle prize for a local school's fundraiser. Foolishly, he had overloaded the boat and had not issued lifejackets. Moreover he had pretended to have a health and safety meeting, and went as far as to write-up fake minutes for it. In reality, no meeting had ever taken place, and to compound his misdemeanour he had forged a signature at the bottom of the document. The final report of the tribunal said: 'The view of the respondent was that the claimant had blatantly ignored/disregarded all health and safety requirements of the board and, in doing so, put members of the public at serious risk.' Indeed a foolish man; yet, a really nice guy.

On Good Friday 2011 the Harbour Manager, Anne, an attractive middle-aged lady called for my assistance on the slipway where chaos was reigning. I found two cars parked on the south side of the ramp where the owners, seemingly oblivious to the obstruction they had caused, were refurbishing their boat. To the north side a Ford Transit was parked. The owner of a large powerboat was attempting to back his trailer down the ramp without the luxury of an angled run-up. Bang in front of the Lifeboat Station a brewery lorry had parked with the drayman unloading barrels to wheel into the adjacent angling club. Adding the finishing touch to this interesting scene was a combined-local-churches gathering outside the Look & Sea Centre; and as their numbers grew some members were spilling onto the slipway.

Anne and I agreed to hold up the powerboat launch whilst we moved the dray, van and the two cars. Although the car owners were reluctant to shift, I did manage to persuade them that it would not be unreasonable to park in the council car park situated behind the Lifeboat Station; however, the Transit van driver proved to be a different kettle of fish, which in this instance comprised the bass and skate that had just been loaded into the rear of his van. "Sir, would you please move your van from the launch ramp?" I politely requested. "I most certainly will, just as soon as the service has finished," he tersely responded. By now, the Christian throng was clearly set for a few hymns, a reading or two, and was now probably sixty-strong in numbers. "Sir, you can't park here, if you wish to join the service kindly park in the car park opposite first," I said pointing to the side of the boathouse. Immediately, the fisherman revved up without any attempt to move, and succeeding in disturbing *There is a Green Hill Far Away*. He then stepped out of the van muttering something about me being 'a git' and called in a loud voice to the minister, 'This jobsworth is making me move. I don't want to disturb your service vicar! Did you know the disciples were fishermen?' I very much doubt that this fact had escaped the Reverend.

Climbing back into the van my newfound adversary once again revved the engine and very slowly drove around the congregation and disappeared down the road tooting his horn as a passing, defiant gesture. Anne and I were now in full view of the disapproving worshippers and at last able to assist with the powerboat launch. Although the job was done all right; was it worth the hassle? The answer to that conundrum was to be found the following week in the letters page of the *Littlehampton Gazette* which bore a rather interesting headline: 'THE INSENSITIVE FORESHORE INSPECTOR'.

I have never really seen myself as an insensitive jobsworth git. I have nevertheless worked for two most unpleasant individuals back in the Seventies. After two years of being bullied by the Gripperrods Managing Director I decided to look elsewhere for employment. The Sales Director Richard Lynch-White was, like me, on the brink of jumping ship and thought I could do worse than joining the Marley Tile Company where he had worked in various middle-management roles before joining Gripperrods. He made a couple of telephone calls on my behalf and I was soon attending what turned out to be a successful interview at the Marley Storrington complex.

Owen Aisher (Senior) had founded The Marley Tile Company in 1924 as a concrete tile producer that manufactured, supplied and fixed roof tiles and accessories in Kent. By the early thirties his son, also Owen Aisher, had taken over running the business and within twenty years had turned the company into the leading supplier of building products in the UK. By the time I joined Marley it was a multi-national corporation still run hands-on by the founder's son.

Throughout the Seventies Owen Aisher turned up at Storrington once a month, en route from Sevenoaks to Portsmouth. After lunch in the canteen he travelled on to sail his yacht, usually with his great friend, the then Prime Minister, Edward Heath. Not surprisingly, Owen was knighted for his services to the building industry, charitable works, and no doubt financial support of the Conservative Party. Marley's growth and profitability peaked in the late Sixties and by the time I joined in 1972, was heading for a slow decline. Sir Owen, then in his mid-seventies, made the mistake of passing on the baton to his children; the saying: 'From rags to riches and back again in three generations' fitted Marley like a glove.

I spent exactly, to the day, ten happy years at Marley learning my trade as a roofing contractor, steadily moving up the ladder from Sales Representative, to Contracts Manager, to Area Manager and finally Regional Manager. Estimating, quoting, securing work, supplying, fixing roof tiles, invoicing and collecting money was a very demanding job; and not least was the supervision of sub-contract roof tilers to correctly install the product. In the mid- to late Seventies there were half a dozen of us working out of Storrington in the Group's contracting division, supplying and fixing, in addition to roof tiles: floor tiles, carpet, rainwater goods, plastic cladding and folding room-dividers. We had a great team and consistently produced the best figures within the Group; as a consequence, senior management, by and large, left us alone to such an extent that the autonomy we enjoyed eventually prompted me to set up my own business.

My first six months at Marley were spent training at various locations until I was appointed as flooring representative for East Sussex working out of Storrington. The five-week residential course could not have come at a worse time: the so-called Winter of Discontent, with numerous power cuts and industry on a three-day week. I had been married for less than three months and the course, and attendant national circumstances promised a miserable spell away from Jean and the boys. Nevertheless, the small hotel served excellent food and being situated next door to a real ale pub with a cosy open fire, alleviated the homesick feeling somewhat.

The course itself was demanding; very efficiently run and the senior staff who conducted some of the lectures were both well-informed and skilled in the art of lecturing. The sixteen course-members all seemed keen to learn, with the exception of David Aisher the grandson of the owner. David was a great guy, yet clearly not happy to be part of the family empire. The format was such that the top two students were awarded a pay rise and the bottom two sacked. David was exempted from this Dickensian management style, which was fortunate for him as he came last; good order demanded on this occasion for the company to reprieve the second-to-bottom student who was given a further three-month trial period.

Thankfully, I came second and qualified for the £100 rise. We were given product knowledge, sales technique, estimating skills, company history, and so on. Ted Ball, the course tutor, gave us an amusing and effective lesson on how to answer the phone. Armed with an old-fashioned black dummy-telephone Ted instructed us as follows: 'Ring, ring', he said 'ring, ring, smile; breathe in gentlemen and say, "Ball here, how can I help you?"' Every morning for five weeks Ted performed this ritual. Although painfully obvious, the technique worked; even to this day that is how I answer a business call. David Aisher, as ever cynical, the night before our final day boot-polished the earpiece. Poor old Ted, oblivious to the practical joke, spent the day with a black ear.

The job was high pressure, mainly due to the unreliability of the sub-contract labour and the unreasonable demands of the site managers; interference from above did not help to co-ordinate these two volatile ingredients. Hence only one in five contracting representatives lasted the six-month probation period. Anyone with two or more years had unquestionably made the grade.

Here are some of the ways my colleagues brought their Marley careers to an abrupt conclusion: one found dancing on the South Downs high on drugs; another hopelessly drunk and locked in the site's cement shed for his own safety; a third nailed to the rafters by an unhappy gang of roof tilers, and a fourth returned to the Teddington office in the back of a floor tiler's van suffering a complete breakdown after jumping from a scaffold.

Mostly, new recruits were sacked for incompetence or dishonesty, although some merely gave up in frustration. In the main the sub-contractors we employed worked for the company full-time and were usually reasonably compliant. When we became over-committed we were forced to recruit labour by whatever means we could; on occasions even tapping into our competitors' workforce. Sometimes we advertised in the local paper 'A pie-and-a-pint night' to be held in a backstreet pub. As most of the attendees were borderline illiterate, jailbirds or violent hard-men these evenings were generally a waste of time, although we did find the odd good tiler and, if nothing else, it was a great excuse for a piss-up on the company.

For self-protection against the violent element of the sub-contract workforce I took to keeping an iron bar under my office desk. One day I had to withhold a tiler's pay when I found his workmanship to be below standard; the week before I had warned him that if he didn't immediately rectify the defects then I would send another workman to do just that. When I notified him that the work had now been completed to specification and monies deducted from his next payment, he swiftly informed me that I would be dead within the hour. Sure enough, he turned up at my office and I chased him outside into the carpark waving the bar above my head. He cried out, "Please don't hit me, I was wrong and only came to apologise and ask for my job back." Needless to say, I told him to sling his hook.

The best form of recruitment was appointing trainees, or as they were once termed, apprentices. A long-time regular tiler, Terry Dodd, had a sure-fire winning formula for interviewing trainees. He maintained that the ideal candidate should have:

1.   LOVE and HATE tattooed on his fingers and 'Cut here' on his neck.
2.   A police record for grievous bodily harm.
3.   A Saturday night beer-intake of eight pints.

If they passed Terry's test then they would be, without doubt, silly enough to run up and down a ladder all day bumping roof tiles. Interestingly enough, I have employed hundreds of trainees over my long career in roofing and the most successful applicants were often rough diamonds: non-academics who failed at school yet were able to stick out the three-year tough training environment, and then had the good fortune to meet and marry a well-educated girl. The lady in question, probably a legal-secretary-type originally looking for a bit of rough, with the nous later to cajole her husband into becoming a highly skilled and productive tradesman. One or two who worked for me have eventually progressed to run their own businesses.

Dick Douglas was the second boss who, over the next two or three years, attempted to make my working life a misery. Marley's Southern Regional Manager was a humble little man, (with every reason to be so), approximately five feet five inches, with long thick sideburns and a big pointed nose. I guess he was about fifty when I first encountered him; the man could run his department only through fear and intimidation. Dick never hesitated to fire members of his team and was universally hated by all levels of staff throughout the company including directors, secretaries and the factory personnel; however, he was my boss and I had to deal with him at least twice a week. Someone would shout out, 'Hitler's on the phone for you', and instantly, the sky turned from blue to grey.

Throughout the early to mid-Seventies I managed, on average, twenty roof tilers, to help build Crawley New Town (often described as a 'garden city') mainly on council estates, providing homes for South London overspill and the immigrant community arriving from India and Pakistan via Gatwick Airport. The houses, built in blocks of between fifteen and thirty units, were often of a quick-build construction, which could be completed in less than three months from groundwork to second fix.

On one occasion Dick received a belated complaint from the main contractor about the quality of both tiles and tiling. Notwithstanding that I had already addressed and dealt with the problem, Dick ordered me to meet him on site. Early one morning we met with the builder's general manager and the council's Clerk of Works, with whom I had good working relationships. Armed with his binoculars Dick strode purposefully through the slush and ice toward the 'offending' block. On any one site there could be up to a dozen blocks in various degrees of completion and they all looked the same.

After much viewing and consideration Dick turned to the three of us and said, "The workmanship is a disgrace and Madell will strip off the tiles and retile the block." I tried to interrupt his, by now, long and inane ramblings but to no avail. Eventually I took him to one side by his arm and said, "Dick, the block you are so keen to condemn is not the block they are complaining about, the roof was passed fit to specification by the Clerk of Works two weeks ago. The offending block is behind you and I have already made it good to their satisfaction. So for fuck's sake shut up!"

Thankfully, our customers accepted our assurances that we would do better in the future and we parted company. Unperturbed by his foolish utterances he then insisted on addressing our on-site labour. I said, "Don't upset them; I'm short of men as it is." I called the men down from the scaffold and they formed a bedraggled semi-circle around Dick and me, and begrudgingly waited for the inevitable bollocking. Worked-up, red-faced and just as he was about to launch his tirade, Dick stepped back onto a piece of ice that was concealing a deep pool of mud. Doddy one of my old stagers half cried, "Don't…" too late; Dick was slowly sinking into Sussex clay and we all watched spellbound as his boots disappeared beneath the sea of mud and slush. "Pull me out, pull me out you shocking shower!" he ordered. This we did with no great hurry or enthusiasm and without further ado the boss beat a hasty retreat back to head office.

One evening I received a call from Dick. "Madell meet me outside The Star, Witley at nine tomorrow morning, together with a roof tiler and ladders, we have a leak to investigate." There was no mileage whatsoever in pointing out that Surrey was outside my area. Dodd, van, ladders and I waited patiently in The Star car park for our boss. "Follow me" cried Dick and within a couple of minutes we were driving into an estate of Swiss-chalet-type houses; all of them gable to gable roofs with steep pitches. As Doddy removed the ladders from the roof of the Transit van he commented, "Can't possibly leak; must be condensation at that steep pitch." "I will be the judge of that Dodd," barked Dick just as an attractive lady in her mid-thirties answered the door. Dick appeared to grow about six inches as he smarmily introduced himself to the lady: "My men will sort your problem out in a jiffy madam. Get on the roof Dodd; Madell, you check the loft."

As there was no loft ladder I took a pair of steps out of Dodd's van and climbed into the attic. Sure enough Dodd was right, the Cosywrap insulation felt was sweating, and water was puddling on the ceiling causing a few small damp patches in the bedrooms. I called through the loft hatch, "Condensation." Dick called back, "Rubbish, go and see how Dodd is getting on while I undertake a proper inspection of the loft." Dodd had pushed up a few tiles and found no evidence of a leak. I called up, "Look no further Terry, the felt is sweating on the underside." Just at that moment the householder invited us in for tea and biscuits and said to me, "Where is the funny little man?" I said, "I shouldn't worry about him."

Over the next hour Dick was in and out of the loft and up and down the outside of the roof. Eventually he said, "I can't find the water ingress, what are we to do?" "Mr Douglas," said Dodd in a commanding voice, "I have been roofing for over thirty years and I am telling you that both John and I know the problem is caused by condensation, and will easily be resolved by placing an air brick either end of the gable to give a much-needed through draught; end of story." Dick pondered for a while and then said, "I am going to ring the technical department for advice." A minute or two later the lady asked me to close the loft and remove the ladder, which had been blocking the bathroom door, and I duly obliged.

I then said to Dodd that I was fed up with 'this hassle' and in any case was late for another appointment. I left assuming that Dick would instruct Dodd to insert a couple of airbricks.

When I finally returned to my office late that afternoon once again I had a message to phone the boss. "Yes Dick, how can I help this time?" I asked. "You and that fool Dodd left me trapped in the loft with no access ladder!" he bellowed. After I had left, so did Dodd, and the lady of the house had to borrow a ladder from a neighbour to free the angry man. My promotion prospects diminished somewhat that day.

Our storeman, Jim Juden, ran a smallholding in his spare time to supplement his meagre wage. Jim asked permission to use the company's pickup truck in his lunch hour to collect manure for the market garden, which of course I was happy to grant. We were due our annual management inspection by Dick together with his boss John Witt, the divisional managing director. They would take all day, checking the recent results, looking at our projections and assessing our individual and joint performances. No problem; everything would be in apple-pie order to ensure a perfect day, or so I thought.

Charles, Dick, John and I were assembled in my office when, to my horror, Jim drove up with his company vehicle piled high with steaming manure. Jim spotted the boss's car and immediately swung the truck around and headed for the main gate. Charles and I spotted the truck, as did Dick, yet John Witt who was facing the other way, did not. "Did you see that? Did you see that? One of my trucks piled high with shit!" Dick squealed and then chased out of the door in hot pursuit. Unsuccessful in the chase he returned and said "Well, Madell, what's doing?" "I have no idea what you are talking about Dick, did you see anything Charles? John?" Well of course they both said no, which in John's case was true. Dick then turned to Charles, "You were right next to me; you had to see the truck." "No I did not; look Dick you are making no sense, please let's get on with the job in hand," Charles lied convincingly.

Half an hour later Jim once again drove up in the now empty and sparklingly clean vehicle. Dick rushed out and combed every inch of the truck for any sign of manure; he found none. John Witt turned to Charles and said, "I think old Dick has been working too hard and must be seeing things; we will be off soon, he could really do with an early night."

Some years later, top management finally found a way of moving Dick sideways: fluent in a number of languages, he was appointed as the chief executive officer of the French subsidiary. At his regional leaving do, Dick took me to one side and whispered, "Tell me, you did see the lorry-load of shit at Storrington that day?" "Sorry Dick, I really don't know what you are talking about," I replied, expressionless.

Stories about Dick were legendary and my old colleague Dan Davis was always happy to relate the best of the lot. Dan was ordered to follow Dick down the dual carriageway (pre-motorway days) to Bristol. Dan had an 1100 Escort, and Dick with his top-of-the-range Granada, was renowned for his fast manic driving. Struggling to keep up with the boss, Dan was pulled over by the police for speeding. 'You were clocked doing ninety miles per hour in a seventy limit; have you anything to say, sir?' the police constable stated. 'Yes', Dan said, 'I couldn't help it officer, my boss told me to keep up with him.' 'Where is your boss, sir?' the policeman asked. 'Waiting for me in the layby just up ahead.' Dan responded. 'Well that is very interesting sir, thank you; we need trouble you no further.' With that remark the policeman jumped into his patrol car and pulled up behind Dick's waiting Granada and promptly issued him with the speeding ticket instead.

I was working out of our Teddington office on Christmas Eve when Dick telephoned just as we were about to decamp to the pub in Waldegrave Road. All week he had been chasing me up hill and down dale to nag me about one disaster or another. I thought, I really can't put up with this hassle any more. I picked up the phone and before he had the opportunity to dish out yet another bollocking, I said, "Good evening Dick, I have had more than enough of you and your job, which you can poke up your arse where the sun doesn't shine." Complete silence; finally a very weak and rejected voice whimpered, "I only rang you up John to wish you a Happy Christmas." Well you can just imagine how happy my Christmas was after my untimely tirade!

Throughout my Marley career I worked alongside Charles Theodosius Brandon Ward-Boughton-Leigh. Sometimes brilliant; at other times a total, completely incompetent, buffoon. He bore a remarkable likeness to a cross between Boris Johnson and Billy Bunter; and he was always, as his name suggests, unique.

A twenty-stone rugby enthusiast who proclaimed to anyone remotely interested, to be teetotal; twenty stone that is, until the day he joined Weight Watchers and shed seven stones inside a year. Meeting Charles for lunch most working days was quite an experience; witnessing him shrink before my eyes in less than one year. It took him the next year to work his way back to twenty stone; the reverse was just as disconcerting.

Marley had a policy that two managers would always conduct a recruitment interview, and then in the event of a successful candidate proving to be a hopeless employee, at least the decision to appoint was a joint error. On many occasions Charles and I interviewed potential employees; one in particular will remain indelibly imprinted on my memory. We had placed an advertisement in the local paper for a storekeeper to supervise the ordering and issue of flooring products and Peter Gurney turned out to be the only applicant. Company pay scales were set centrally with little flexibility and on this occasion the wage package on offer was below local rates; hence we had only had one applicant, who appeared, on paper, to be quite unsuitable; nevertheless, we decided to interview him.

After I had run through the job specification, Charles asked the candidate to expand on his application form and explain the duties he undertook in his previous employment. Gurney described his job as a cowman on a farm near East Grinstead. The majority of the time he had spent tending to the cattle and, in addition to other general jobs, he was instructed to repair perimeter fences. He told us that after five happy years working with livestock an unfortunate incident caused him to resign. Charles asked Gurney to be more specific. Reluctantly, he told us that his employer had often sent him, usually on a Friday, to remote parts of the farm to work on the fences. One Friday, job done, Gurney returned home early to his tied cottage to find his wife in bed with the farmer, and of course he had no other choice than to leave the farm there and then.

Well, I just did not dare to look at Charles, although I was aware that he had produced his hanky and was blowing his nose long and violently. Desperately trying to keep a straight face, I quickly asked Gurney to describe his next job at Crawley Taxis. He said he was very fortunate to be offered accommodation above the taxi office and was happy to undertake any job his boss asked him to do. Most of the time he operated the switchboard and directed the taxi jockeys to the collection points. Sometimes his boss sent him on the long-distance runs. One day he was called on to make an airport run which, it turned out, had to be aborted. Returning early, he popped upstairs to his flat for a cup of tea only to find his boss in a compromising position with his wife. Once again Gurney was forced to leave his employment.

With this revelation Charles jumped out of his seat and rushed from the room promptly closing the door behind him. The office was directly adjacent to the tile store and the walls were paper-thin and therefore it was painfully apparent that the moment Charles shut the door he started howling with laughter. This left me and Gurney looking at one another in puzzled disbelief. After what seemed like an age Charles reappeared, red-eyed and blustering about an imaginary phone call. Charles, now composed and with a deadpan expression informed Gurney that it was necessary for him to expand on the job specification. Charles explained that it was very important for Peter to appreciate that although ninety per cent of the job would be based in Storrington, he would also be expected once a fortnight, normally on a Friday, to drive thirty miles to our un-manned store at Havant to distribute floor tiles.

Gurney leapt out of his seat and demonstratively informed us that he had now divorced his unfaithful wife! With that the three of us collapsed into uncontrollable laughter. After we had all finally calmed down, Gurney asked point-blank if we would give him the job. I looked at Charles and he turned to the bold applicant and said, "Can you start on Monday?" Peter Gurney proved to be an excellent storekeeper and stayed with us for at least five years. We attended the wedding of Peter to his second wife, which thankfully proved to be a far more successful union than his first marriage.

A few weeks later we were once again interviewing, this time for a general clerk; the same scenario, poor wages and only one applicant. Ernie was fifty-nine and barely over five feet tall. He had spent all his life as a bespoke tailor working in an upmarket West End clothing store and taken early retirement to live in Storrington. On a good pension, he was really looking for a job to fill his time and the salary was a secondary consideration. Charles and I were unimpressed with Ernie and after half an hour informed him that we would be in touch. Three minutes after Ernie left the office we heard an almighty crash, more like an explosion.

We rushed out to the main car park, which was located next to the display ground, with garages and greenhouses on show to the general public. There was Ernie prising himself from his black A35 car, which was completely encased by a glass and metal greenhouse. Obviously, he had backed his car into the newly displayed Marley greenhouse. Like Ernie, the almost vintage car was (or had been) immaculate. A bewildered Ernie covered in particles of glass and with a tear in his eye shuffled towards us and in a weak and emotional voice quivered, 'It wasn't there when I arrived.' Clearly the Buildings Division had erected the greenhouse while we were interviewing Ernie. Feeling partly responsible and sorry for the tiny man, we gave him the job; he turned out to be hopeless!

Marleyfold Doors (large room-dividers) were a product that fell into my lap from almost day one of my career with the Marley Tile Company. Cliff Ware, the general manager in charge of non-core products, called at Storrington and asked if there was anyone interested in undertaking responsibility for the supply and fix of the product for the South East. I volunteered and for the next eight years ran that section of the business as an addition to my normal roofing duties. I spent a couple of days at the factory in the West Country studying their manufacture and soon after secured regular orders for the doors. They were always made-to-measure and usually fixed at weekends to avoid disrupting the environment they were intended for, such as schools, hospitals and colleges. I estimated the cost of the door, transport, and labour and then added a high profit-margin. Great for the bonus, yet more importantly, I undertook the fixing myself. I could make more money on a Saturday than I could earn all week. Fixing was not a one-man operation and on most occasions Charles accompanied me; if the doors were very large, I recruited a couple of floor tilers to help.

I sold a giant door to the Post Office, to be fixed on the sixth floor of the GPO building in Brighton. It was so large that I had organised a mobile crane to lift it through the double-glazed windows, which had to be removed to facilitate the operation. I met Charles and a couple of 'Jack the Lad' floor tilers, Taylor and Redman, early one Saturday morning outside the building with the knowledge that it would require all four of us to lift the partition into place. The Marleyfold was packed in an enormous wooden crate that seemed to be as heavy as the double door. The four of us took five hours to complete the job and it became painfully apparent that as big a task would be the removal of the packing case. It would be necessary to saw it into manageable lengths, carry them into the lift, and out to the car park. Then we would have to collect the pickup truck from Storrington some twenty miles away and transport the wood and metal bracings back again. As Brighton and Hove Albion were playing at home that afternoon none of us were keen on this prospect.

Just as we were debating the problem a guy in a suit appeared. "I work on the fourth floor and couldn't help notice the packing case that was craned-up yesterday. It would make a great shed, would you be prepared to sell it to me?" Quick as a flash Johnny Redman replied, "More than our job is worth mate, the case must be returned to the factory on Monday." The suit said, "I'm prepared to pay £5 cash." Redman sighed, shook his head, and then commented, "Well, we might look the other way for £10." Pulling out his wallet the suit counted out £8 and gestured to us, waving the money aloft "£2 each lads?" With a wry smile Redman said, "Not really guvnor; make it £2 each for my workmates and £3 for me, OK?" The two men clasped hands and the deal was done. By this time we had packed our tools and were heading for the lift. The new owner of the packing case called out. "Hang on, how do I get the crate down and out of the building?" Tightly clutching nine £1 notes Redman called back just as the lift doors were closing, "Funny you should ask, we were wondering that before you turned up, cheerio mate and up the Albion!"

It took only two of us to fit an acoustic door in Rustington one evening. Fifty per cent of the doors I sold had acoustic properties and were popular in offices where privacy was called for. The problem with an acoustic door was that although the door itself was expertly manufactured to a high specification, the surroundings into which it was fitted could not be accounted for and might be unsuitable for the purpose. For example, sound, although muffled by the partition, might well carry over a plasterboard ceiling or under a wooden floor, or even through the internal walls. I was always very careful to point this factor out to potential customers.

By the time we had completed this job it was painfully obvious that sound was travelling via the ceiling. After shutting the door with Charles one side and me the other, we could speak clearly to each other even if we only slightly raised our voices. Job done and as we were about to leave, the clients walked in. "Oh, it looks lovely," the woman exclaimed. "How sound proof is it?" asked the man. Charles immediately responded, "Most impressive, sir; you stand that side with Mr Madell and I will shut the door." We then barely heard a muffled voice say, "Can you hear me?" I yelled, "Speak up Charles." His reply was even less audible. "Can we try the other side?" The two clients joined Charles and shut the door. I took out my handkerchief, held it over my mouth, and said in a low voice, "Can you hear me?" Charles bellowed back, "Not really." I repeated the farce, opened the door, to find the couple beaming. "Splendid," the man said, "this will very much suit our purpose." "What purpose is that?" Charles enquired. The lady said, "This side will accommodate a probation office and the other side is for a marriage guidance counsellor." Charles and I looked at each other with a knowing and resigned expression. Unbelievably, the invoice was settled on time and we never heard a dicky-bird, which is probably more than can be said for the future occupants of the now 'divided' room!

Shortly after I moved to head office in Sevenoaks to run Dick's old region I discovered that the company was planning to close the contracting division. Charles and I called a meeting with the directors and resigned. With our former employer's blessing we set up Cobsen-Davies Roofing Ltd, and started our own business.

I Heard It Through The Grapevine!
Performer: Marvin Gaye
Composers: Whitfield and Strong
Number 1:   February 1969

Chapter 12 – Fred

Proverbs 27:17
People learn from one another, just as iron sharpens iron.

It would be an exaggeration to say that Littlehampton has many famous sons and daughters, although one or two well-known personalities have spent brief spells wandering along the beach and the riverbanks. These include a few artists and writers, such as Percy Bysshe Shelley, Samuel Taylor Coleridge, Lord Byron and Ian Fleming.

More recently, John Inman, famous for his part as a camp counter assistant in the long-running comedy series *Are You Being Served*, also starred in a TV sitcom based in and around Littlehampton. The thankfully forgettable series, *Odd Man Out*, had Inman playing the part of Blackpool fish and chip shop owner Norman Sutcliffe who inherits a half share in the fictitious Littlehampton Rock Factory. Amazingly, the show lasted for seven episodes based on its one and only joke: 'Little Hampton', a slang reference to a small penis. Ronnie Barker lived for some years on South Terrace and often popped round the corner to his local convenience store.

One of the most popular long-running comedy shows on TV starring Ronnie and David Jason, *Open All Hours*, was partly based on the actor's experiences when being served by the eccentric proprietor of the shop in Norfolk Road.

Sometimes it is too windy to hoist the four flags on the promenade; in the past the strength of a howling gale has torn them beyond repair. Invariably, a high wind results in us having to treat people for sand in the eyes, and as I write today it will cause a great deal of hassle to the team of men attempting to erect a marquee on the greensward in preparation for the *Pebbles on the Beach* concert scheduled for tomorrow. Also known as 'LA Pebbles', the event takes place on the last Saturday in August and is sited halfway between the Windmill car park and Banjo Road. It is designed as a showcase for local musical talent and provides an eclectic mix to cater for all tastes.

The show is professionally organised and marshalled within a purpose-built arena surrounded by security fencing, with the artistes and bands performing alternately on the back of two static flatbeds. The entrance fee is reasonably priced and designed to cover only the costs of the facilities provided as the performers generally perform free of charge. It is a great idea, giving a stage for young bands and soloists, and a golden opportunity to show what they can do in front of a large audience; some, no doubt, facing a crowd for the first time will be discovering the excruciating joy of stage fright. If the wind and rain that we are experiencing today continues, then sadly, tomorrow, the event may well be cancelled – fingers crossed.

In 1979 I received a bonus of £360 from my employer The Marley Tile Company. Still dreaming of riches and fame to be found in the music business, on the spur of the moment I spent all the money on a new drum kit. I timidly erected the gleaming set in the lounge of our home in Downlands Avenue and, to my astonishment, found Jean to be as excited as I was by our new pieces of 'furniture'. The year before I had purchased practice pads and spent hours, more or less recovering my speed. I guess Jean may have felt very slightly responsible when I sold my previous kit to fund a much-needed three-piece suite back in 1973; to justify the rash acquisition, now I had to find a band to join. I did sit in with a Christian band playing at church functions and the experience clicked me back into holding fellow musicians to a fixed rhythm; yet not being commercial, it was no real test. I think most musos would concur that a fee for performing endorses an individual's credentials. Anyone can play free concerts, open mike or busk, but the real test is whether a pub, club or the public is prepared to pay; if so, then the musicians are more than likely on the right track.

One Friday night, shortly before Christmas, my wife Jean and I went for a drink at The Downview pub opposite West Worthing Station, where we found a duo called Three's a Crowd playing. In the interval I engaged the lead singer John Horan in conversation and asked, somewhat tongue in cheek, "I am about to form my own band; would you both like to join?" To my utter amazement after a short conflab with his musical partner Jeff, they invited me to rehearse with them. Within a couple of months Three's a Crowd became three and I found myself performing once a week in the local pubs and clubs.

My comeback gig was in the Locomotive pub, located next door to Hove Station, where 'we' had a regular spot; it was, however, something of an ordeal. Having not played professionally for about seven years I was understandably nervous. After setting up my kit I ordered a beer at the bar and chatted casually to the barman. Clearly he had not connected me to the band and said, "I wouldn't hang around if I were you as we have a real crap band playing here tonight!" Whatever self-confidence I had managed to muster deserted me at that moment; it was all I could do to hold on to my drumsticks when, a few minutes later, I took my seat for the first set. As it turned out we went down well with the crowd, although the landlord was enraged by Jeff's farewell comment: 'Goodnight, thank you and remember, keep doing it until it hurts'! Never mind, at least I was back.

John on lead guitar and vocals harmonised very well with Jeff who sang backing and played rhythm guitar, but the three-piece line-up was a little thin without a bass. It was soon to become even more lightweight when Jeff decided to leave and form a duo with his girlfriend. John and I soldiered on for a couple of months as guitar and drums, which (although we got away with it) did not really work. To make up a third member John persuaded an old acquaintance to sit in.

I met Steve Davis one Friday night in June when he turned up to play with us at The Southdown pub in Broadwater. Steve, a tall, slim, handsome man walked into the room with his beautiful wife Gilly; he looked every inch a rock star with his long fair hair and stylish leather jacket. "Hi John, it is a great pleasure to meet you," said Steve, his cut-glass accent greeting me together with a firm handshake. Without rehearsal, or any discussion on repertoire, we kicked in and within twenty minutes the place was really rocking. Clearly, Steve was a talented guitarist, a competent singer and one of life's good guys. From that day on until he died in 2003, we were firm friends. Back in 1980 Steve was committed to his band Kite, and consequently John and I were unable to retain his services.

I placed an advert in Broadway Music for a rhythm guitarist/singer and bass guitar. By the end of August, Steve Smith and John Hunt had joined. Steve, then aged twenty-nine, had played guitar and sung backing vocals for a couple of years with a popular local disco band called Carousel. Previously, Steve had performed on the folk club circuit. John, twenty-three, had just graduated from Swansea University where he had played in a punk band.

On Friday 5 September, Fred and the Ferrets were born and appeared in The Southdown pub. We started with The Eagles' *Peaceful Easy Feeling* and finished the evening with The Moody Blues' *Nights in White Satin*. Strangely enough, both numbers we still perform from time to time. For the next seventeen Friday nights we repeated the exercise, which proved to us that we must have been doing something right.

Fred and the Ferrets on European tour, 1990.   *Gordon Fraser*
(Left to right) John Hunt, John Madell, Steve Davis, Steve Smith

Why name the band 'Fred and the Ferrets'? Undoubtedly, the most frequently asked question. Somehow I don't think that any band name sounds appropriate; did the names The Beatles or The Rolling Stones feel right at the time of conception? Probably not; I guess we gradually became acclimatised and accepted them. I am sure we can blame Steve for the name. Who is Fred? Not one of us; sometimes all three of us; now and again just Steve. We used to joke to the audience about Fred's non-appearance: 'Fred is stuck in traffic', 'gone abroad', 'dealing with a family bereavement' or, 'undergoing a brain transplant' and always finished it with, 'don't worry, we promise he will be here next time'. We thought it was funny, until the secretary at Durrington Working Men's Club docked us 20% of our fee for his non-appearance! For at least ten years our agent Chris Lynn refused to book us out as the Ferrets and forced us to use 'Kestrel' or 'Daytripper'. However, we like the name, and it is without doubt memorable; having said that, a great number of people insist on calling us 'Freddie and the Ferrets'. What's more, the name suits our down-market image.

Daytripper, 1991. (*Left to right*) Steve Smith, John Hunt, Steve Davis, Elaine Bayford, John Madell

We have always delighted in playing scruffy joints: damp carpets, peeling paintwork, poor lighting, non-existent changing facilities and dirty loos feels rock 'n' roll to me. There is nothing better than the smell of warm amplifiers in a venue filled with weird characters to make us comfortably at home: the toothless women fist-fighting in The Whitehawk Inn, Brighton; the transvestite built like an Irish navvy who used to frequent Brighton Trades and Labour Club, or the two doormen at Chatsbar in Hastings: one a Jackie Pallo look-alike, the other a five-foot-tall wrestler/Kung Fu champion who could bring down the biggest and hardest yob, and eject him from the bar with his arm twisted behind his neck within thirty seconds flat.

The same venue had a sign behind the bar: 'No dope to be smoked here', which seemed to me to invite the illegal practice. We had to go to the loo in pairs and whilst one had a pee the other watched his back; absolutely one of our favourite haunts. When playing the same venue month in, month out, we became familiar with the audience and often had our pet names for some of them: Honey Monster, Rock-on-Tommy and Marty Feldman were always in attendance at The Whitehawk Inn that sadly closed in the Nineties when drugs, violence and one-too-many murders caused its demise.

Although the audience tends to stare at the band they are totally oblivious that we too are staring back at them. One night we were playing the Empire Club in Lancing when Steve Smith and I noticed two married couples at the far end of the hall. It was back in the days when we played strict tempo in the first set to pacify the 'silver-slipper brigade' and the couples waltzed around the whole room. (Perhaps Chris Lynn was right: Fred and the Ferrets was not appropriate for the ballroom environment.)

On this occasion it became clear that when the married couples swapped dancing partners then one of the pairs became, let us say, over-friendly by the time they were close to the stage and the furthest distance from their respective spouses. When the lights were down low I guess no one other than the band would notice the amour. The stage was about three feet above the auditorium's floor, which gave us a bird's-eye view. As they waltzed away from their table they gradually became closer and closer until they were immediately diagonal to their own husband and wife. At this point a passionate embrace and a snog would take place and gradually, as they approached the rear of the hall, they would very sedately dance past their respective partners. This happened maybe three times during one number, and again two or three times throughout the evening, causing the whole band to become mesmerised by this phenomenon. In those days we played the Empire every three months and this happened consistently over the course of a year, after which, we saw neither couple again.

Our agent Chris was quite a character; I first met him back in 1967 when I was with The Inventive Mr Jeff. Our paths crossed many times until he died in 2007 shortly after he and his wife Jean attended John Hunt's and my joint fiftieth and sixtieth birthday party. Chris was the master of the malapropism and mixed metaphor to such an extent that in the end I completely lost track of which were grammatically correct and which, hopelessly wrong. Some of his phrases only served to confuse: 'He is the rotten egg in the woodpile'; 'He is barking up a blind alley'; 'Leave the legalecalities to me'.

Chris's claim to fame was very nearly bringing The Beatles to play in Worthing; perhaps it would be crass to rephrase this sentence as failing to bring The Beatles to Worthing! He also claimed to have discovered Leo Sayer. To be fair, Chris gave me hundreds of bookings over forty years and I spent many fun evenings watching Bognor Town play as his guest.

Playing in a band is first and foremost a huge commitment. These days we play no more than a dozen times a year, and nine times out of ten these engagements take place on a Saturday night. Bookings are usually made three to nine months in advance and once the contract is agreed there is little chance of backing out. This can cause problems and major inconvenience, especially to family events. John, due to his family situation, can only play every other weekend. Steve is flexible and conducts his solo work when John is unavailable. As I deal with the bookings it can be quite a hassle teeing up the engagements.

What of my two long-term band members? John Hunt is most certainly a contradiction: a graduate with an exceptional brain who delights in portraying himself as an uncouth proletarian, which he does with casual ease. He has had to cope with two broken marriages, which amazingly, caused him to give away the same house twice in divorce settlements. The first was short-lived as Julie, like John at the time, was exceptionally immature, which led to a degree of flightiness on her part. The second, to Clare, failed mainly as a result of their twin daughter Alice developing a mystery brain disease; now in her teens, Alice has a mental age of eighteen months and is doubly incontinent. John has never sought help or sympathy, having the inner strength to rise above the wilderness moments that mental handicap can inflict.

He was nicknamed 'Le Gros' after being addressed by a French taxi driver as he attempted to sit in the back seat of his cab: 'The fat man must sit in the front seat.' It is true to say that John has a fluctuating weight problem and has been known to consume a cheese roll while playing his bass on stage. Yet, John, physically big as he is, has a much bigger personality and is great company.

I can only sum up Steve Smith as an exceptional talent, but somewhat flawed with a tendency to self-destruct; a man striving, and succeeding, to improve his guitar technique. When I first met Steve he had little or no singing ability, but was forced into taking on our lead vocals by default when John Horan left the band in 1981. Not wishing to be embarrassed on stage he has, through hard work, good equipment, a subtle vocal technique and a clever selection of the right tunes become, over time, a highly accomplished singer. Steve is the most complex of characters: often moody and abrasive, which may account for four broken marriages, yet on occasions, wonderful company.

His good looks and eye for the ladies sentenced him to his band label: perched on a bar stool in the cocktail lounge of the Grand Hotel in Eastbourne; dressed in a white tuxedo and smoking a long cigarette; accompanied by Elaine our then female vocalist (dolled up and at her glamorous best), Steve was hailed from the entrance by a dishevelled John Hunt: 'It's Julio', he yelled, to the delight of Steve Davis and me (a reference to Julio Iglesias the Eighties singer and heartthrob). John captured a moment in time and summed up Steve to a tee: the consummate lounge lizard. A talented man who for nearly twenty-five years ran a very successful business selling and servicing photocopiers and should have made a financial killing in either his business career or the music industry. Somewhere along the way he missed out – maybe he gave away four houses? I am very grateful to both Steve and John for their support and friendship over many years; it must be extremely frustrating having an out-of-time drummer sitting behind: being too fast in the early years and too slow in latter years. Incidentally, I am 'The Silver Fox'.

The Ferrets have professionally recorded twenty-six numbers over the years. Our first visit to the studio was in 1986 when we laid down twelve tracks in one day. John and I recorded each of the twelve in one take. In the studio next door was a band that had enjoyed many hit records, including a number one, *Don't You Want Me*; The Human League took time out from the album they were making to take in our hurried efforts. I was sitting in the control room when they came in to watch Steve Davis overdub lead guitar on *Peaceful Easy Feeling* and were blown away by his understated country picking, giving him a well-deserved round of applause. Their bass player said that our bass man was so good that he must be a session musician. (Don't tell John as this is the first time that I have revealed that little gem.) Our first album *In Search of Fred* only includes eleven tracks – the twelfth we dropped.

These days most of our gigs are within half an hour of home and we normally play between eight and eleven o'clock. This is a typical Saturday night:

6.30pm	Load up
7.00pm	Arrive at venue, unload and set up kit
7.45pm	Relax with a drink and discuss format
8.15pm	First Half
9.00pm	Break
9.15pm	Second Half
10.00pm	Break
10.15pm	Third Half
11.00pm	Encore
11.15pm	Finish
11.30pm	Pack up kit and load up
12 midnight	Leave venue
12.30am	Arrive home and unload kit
12.45am	Shower and relax
1.30am	Bed.

Steve has to rest on the day; John and I are generally wiped out the next day. Gigs are something of an unknown quantity. Factors that can affect our performance include the venue (though most we have played many, many times), the audience, the weather and our individual temperaments. All things being equal, nine times out of ten there are no problems. The weather can affect the size of the audience; speaking of which, the more the merrier please, as there is nothing worse than trying to entertain a handful of people for three hours. The band members must set aside external problems and ill health. Who knows if we are going to come down with a heavy cold or a bad back six months ahead? Do we suffer with pre-performance nerves? Steve, John and I have nerves of steel; though if we add new numbers there can be a little apprehension when we reach them on the list. As a rule, I introduce them towards the end of the first or early in the second set, to enable us to warm up and take the unfamiliar in our stride. Do we make mistakes? Yes, all the time. Although it is unlikely that the audience will notice, the culprit will most certainly receive a knowing look from his colleagues on stage.

Steve Davis, who played with the Ferrets for sixteen years, most definitely had stage fright, so the three of us do recognise and understand the condition. Dear old Steve was always a bundle of nerves and considering his musicianship and longevity this was a great mystery to me. Steve would turn up last and late, and faff around with his equipment allowing no time to relax before the first set. Ironically, we nicknamed him 'the late Steve Davis' which, very sadly, he became when he failed to wake up after a brain seizure. Although he drove us mad over the years the three of us loved him dearly and still miss his considerable stage presence. Spookily, I am sure I can hear him playing in the background from time to time.

I always anticipate that the next performance will be better than the last, or last year, or 2000, or 1990, or even 1980. Yet without a keyboard or a lead female vocal, the expectation could now be over-optimistic. Three-piece is tighter and there is certainly no place to hide.

The key to a successful evening is picking the right numbers to play at the appropriate time: nothing too heavy in the first fifteen minutes; more or less wallpaper music to settle in. It is unlikely the punters will dance until they have greeted friends and had a drink or two; they are generally happy to relax and listen to the first set. The second half always needs a lively start and if there is no dancing then, we are in trouble and the night will probably drag. We have always called the final set 'the third half' which makes no sense at all and neither does playing *Sweet Little Sixteen* at my great age. As we reach the end of the evening everyone wants to dance and for the band to carry on past the allotted time, therefore it is necessary to start the encore with at least ten minutes to go. If forced by the audience or management to carry on we will play a number that we know they will not care for and consequently bring the evening to an abrupt halt.

I guess we can call on a pool of about one hundred numbers; the average evening will consume approximately thirty-five. We have three distinct lists: an 'unplugged' sing-along set, a middle-of-the-road set for the Working Men's Clubs, and a set for the pub circuit, which tends to demand music played with an edge. By the way, we no longer do weddings!

I think the strangest element of being a member of a band is what I call the 'timeless factor'. I am still playing three numbers that I played in the mid-Sixties: The Beatles' *Can't Buy Me Love* and *Roll Over Beethoven*; Dylan's *All Along the Watchtower*, and half a dozen tunes from the Ferrets' first gig in 1980. The camaraderie is just the same; nothing can touch that sinking feeling at the end of the first number when greeted by total silence. We are in this together, we have been here before and it will happen again; the unspoken bond. Plus the constant joshing and one-upmanship is guaranteed to knit the team together.

The evening itself is timeless. Each number is perhaps four minutes in duration; each set contains a dozen tunes. For me, there is no concept of time whatsoever; one minute could be ten, and twenty could easily be one. Yet, curiously, during a rehearsal the time span is normal. Whether it is subconscious adrenalin, or the stage lighting, this state of experiencing the apparently suspended-animation of time can cause a problem or two; in particular, it is easy to lose the construction of the tune. For example, are we in verse two, or chorus three, have we done the lead break, are we close to the last four bars? John Horan often found this a challenge; after four pints John could quite easily finish the lead break and, totally unaware, continue with a different song. To make matters worse, neither I nor another band member might notice the error!

I really can't guess how many performances I have played alongside Steve and John; maybe somewhere between six and seven hundred. The largest venue: the Pier Pavilion, Worthing to an audience of six hundred; the smallest: a private party in someone's front room to about ten people. The farthest away: Rouen in France; the nearest: The Cabin pub fifty yards from my home. The longest playing time: the Wingspan Club, Gatwick, for five hours with one ten-minute break; the shortest: forty minutes at the Empire Club in Lancing when the loos blocked and the club closed due to health and safety considerations. The best reception: Wimbledon College, where we received a prolonged standing ovation for our rendition of *Sultans of Swing*; the worst reception: Haywards Heath United Services Club where we were paid up and asked to leave for our inability to play requested Jason Donovan and Kylie Minogue numbers.

I guess the best Ferret line-up was yours truly on drums, John Hunt on bass, Steve Smith on lead guitar and vocals, and the late Steve Davis on keyboards and vocals. Other notable Ferrets have included Elaine and Fleur on vocals, John Horan and Alan Hackett on guitar and vocals. At least half a dozen others have come and gone over the last thirty-plus years and I would like to mention the great support we have received from Jamie my son, Adrian, Steve, and especially Tony Haley, who has on many occasions commuted from his home in Champaign, Illinois to see us play. Steve Smith once said to me that of all the things he had done and regretted throughout his life he never would have missed the Ferret experience. I know John Hunt and I would say the same. From time to time as a band we have had the odd sabbatical. When this happened Steve Davis and I played with Six Five Special and The Elderly Brothers. How long will the three of us carry on? Hard to say; maybe best summed up by Jeff: 'We will keep doing it until it (literally) hurts'!

Above: The Elderly Brothers, 1995. (*Left to right*) Steve Davis, John Madell, Doug Eaton.

Left: Six Five Special, 1997. (*Left to right*) Paul Murdan, John Madell, Steve Davis.

One of the largest crowds I have performed for was at Hove Cricket Ground in the late Nineties with Six Five Special.

The very next day I was dining in The Green Room in the West End with my wife Jean, waiting for my favourite band The Zombies to perform a cabaret set. The Zombies, formed in the early Sixties, scored a massive hit in the summer of 1964 with *She's Not There* and continued playing together for another five years, recording along the way the cult album *Odessey and Oracle*, which included the haunting *Time of the Season* released as a single in the

States, where it reached number one. A Tom Petty throwaway comment that if he could join any band in the world it would be The Zombies, without a doubt applies to me too. In their revived format with original members Rod Argent and Colin Blunstone combining brilliantly to lead proceedings, the sound that evening was better than ever. However, on that wet night in London they were unable to fill the house, with maybe only sixty or seventy paying customers witnessing the event.

When we arrived I had a chat with their road manager and casually mentioned that I had played an open-air gig to a full house the previous night. After the meal I visited the bar to buy a couple of drinks and before returning to the table noticed the manager and Colin Blunstone having a drink in the corner. They beckoned me to join them and the manager said to Colin, "This is the guy I was telling you about." Then, turning to me, he said, "Tell us John, how large was your audience in Brighton last night?" I casually replied, "Four or five," Colin said, "Four or five hundred?" "No Colin, the audience was not in their hundreds, rather four or five thousand," I whispered with a smile. "Four or five thousand; an open air concert in November that is truly amazing. Your band must have a fanatical local following!" he exclaimed. Before I had time to respond Colin was called away by the house manager for his imminent appearance on stage, therefore I never had time to explain that the main event at the cricket ground on the Fifth of November was the annual Firework Party. My band was merely there to warm up and down the sell-out crowd. No doubt my favourite vocalist eventually worked out that the audience had not actually come to see me and my band; yet secretly, I must confess that I enjoyed giving a somewhat misleading impression to my hero Colin.

As something of a postscript to this chapter I will tell of my experience playing at Windlesham House School. Melody Pryce, a very talented violinist and vocalist, who performed with the Ferrets a number of times in the late Eighties, asked me to play drums for a concert held at a private school where she taught music. The format was for the school choir and orchestra to perform a selection of contemporary pieces including a Beatles selection. The orchestra was to be augmented by Nigel the musical director on keyboard, with Melody on violin and me on percussion.

We met in the late afternoon for a run-through before the evening performance in front of the school, parents and invited guests. The final piece was a medley including *Maxwell's Silver Hammer*, *Eleanor Rigby* and *When I'm Sixty-Four*. All well and good with three rhythms, umpteen stops and a couple of drum breaks, had I been provided with sheet music. Sadly this was not the case, so I wrote my own against a song sheet and hoped I could decipher it a few hours later.

Come the evening the hall was packed, with standing room only. I was positioned next to the choir with a poor view of Nigel conducting. Not to worry, as the concert progressed I managed to follow my notes to the letter and being very familiar with Lennon and McCartney was able to produce a faultless performance; however, when we came to the finale, to my horror, the most important 'Maxwell' song sheet was missing. I looked up as Nigel was counting 2/3/4, and away we went. Autopilot kicked in, after just one run-through, and now performing blind, I completed the medley without even one mistake. The audience rose and cheered.

Totally drained and feeling at least 'Sixty-Four', I thought, thank heavens that's over. The Headmaster thanked everyone for a splendid evening. Then what did he say? "Please Nigel, could you play the medley one more time as an encore?" "We are more than happy to oblige," Nigel eagerly replied. By the time we finished it I felt like a gibbering wreck hung out on a line to dry. More tumultuous applause, the auditorium lights were switched on and my ordeal was finally over.

As I packed away my kit one of the younger boys in the choir approached me and handed me a piece of paper. "Please sir, I hoped you didn't mind, but I lost my copy of 'Maxwell' so borrowed yours." Melody called over, "We are having a drink in the staffroom, would you care to join us?" Would I!

Needless to say I never found fame with the Ferrets, yet the experience has given me as much pleasure and amusement as the late, dear Ronnie Barker has given to his army of fans happily viewing *Open All Hours*.

When I'm Sixty-Four
Performers:　　　　The Beatles
Composers:　　　　Lennon and McCartney

Chapter 13 – Derek

Proverbs 26:17
Getting involved in an argument that is none of your business, is like going down the street and grabbing a dog by the ears.

'Attention, this is the Foreshore Inspector speaking. The public is reminded that at this time of year dogs are not permitted on the beach. Please remove your dog from the beach to the promenade, where your dog must be kept on a lead at all times. I thank you.' Dave announced formally over the tannoy. Between 1 May and 30 September dogs are banned from the blue section of West Beach and Dave is obsessively efficient at policing this bylaw.

At the time of the announcement I was sitting outside our office surveying the busy beach on a lovely sunny afternoon in late June. I could see a middle-aged woman with a Golden Labrador on a lead, about a hundred yards away walking between first and second beaches. "John, John, the bloody woman has taken absolutely no notice of my announcement, go and tell her to Foxtrot Oscar, there's a good chap," Dave said tersely. I duly picked up my walkie-talkie, donned my cap and wandered toward the lady and her offending dog. When I was within about ten yards I called out to attract her attention, as by now she was walking away from me towards the water's edge. She took no notice of my cry, although the dog seemed to look round and tugged the lead, which prompted her to turn her head in my direction. I smiled and started to explain the dog bylaw. She returned my smile and said, "Although I am profoundly deaf I can lip-read, please speak slowly to me." I repeated my 'no dogs on the beach' speech, this time somewhat timidly. "I understand what you are saying," and gesturing to the dog, she continued, "This is Ruby, who is by my side at all times and acts as my ears." Attached to Ruby's collar was a large tag: 'RUBY Hearing Dog for the Deaf'. Backtracking, I said, "Please don't worry madam, both you and your dog are very welcome on Littlehampton beach, have a lovely afternoon." Obviously, 'blind dogs' are permitted on the beach, but I had never heard of a 'deaf dog'.

When I returned to the office Dave gave me an old-fashioned look and said, "John, have you lost the plot, do I have to attend to everything myself?" I said, "Hang on Dave, the lady has a deaf dog." Before I had a chance to explain, Dave retorted, "Deaf dog! I don't care if it has three legs and two arses; it is not staying on my beach." With that my colleague beetled off towards the waterline in hot pursuit of the poor lady. Ten minutes later he was back in a rather flustered state and whilst hurriedly filling the dog bowl with water, told me to put the kettle on. "Do come in madam; John, I think you have met Joy and her lovely dog Ruby. Please take a seat Joy." Dave grinned, and speaking very slowly to the deaf lady said, "John has just made tea, would you like a bourbon?" Clearly, Dave had made a right prat of himself and was now in full flow with the sort of charm offensive that only he could achieve.

In high season there is no question that dogs are a problem. Every day we find at least half a dozen dogs on the beach and regardless of the heavy presence of signage, the owners continue to flaunt the bylaw. Sometimes we encounter a stray, which we attempt to catch, chain in the office, and then call for the Dog Warden. Julia usually arrives promptly and impounds the dog in kennels at Ford; the owner will have the opportunity to collect their pet, for a fee. Although I am a dog lover, they can prove to be a big nuisance, especially if they are poorly supervised. Offences I have witnessed include: biting people and other dogs, pissing and crapping everywhere, excessive barking, and frightening members of the public. Arun Council are fully justified in excluding dogs from the blue-beach zone.

Joy was a lovely lady and, although deaf, was exceptionally adept at communicating in an expressive and vivacious way. We learnt that she was booked into The Arun View Inn for a couple of nights to take in the Armed Forces Day. I offered to escort her to the hotel which is situated on the east side of the river, adjacent to the sliding bridge. We stopped off at the tourist office in the Look & Sea Centre and I found her a programme of events scheduled for the next day.

The Armed Forces Day is always a very popular attraction, provided the weather is kind, which it was on this occasion: sunny with a slight westerly breeze. The day commences with a Drumhead Service at 10.30am, followed by a multitude of activities taking place on the greensward, promenade, Harbour

Park and the river walk. The events, which vary from year to year, might include: marching bands, an aerobatic display, a Spitfire flypast, a mock air-sea rescue and sport parachute jumps. There are various military vehicles and memorabilia on show from contributors such as the UK Tank Club, and a display by The Light Cavalry Honourable Artillery Company demonstrating their lance and sword skills. There is always plenty for the kids to do, such as go-karting, together with the normal seaside playgrounds and funfair. All the profit made on the day goes to the Royal British Legion, with a large proportion being passed on to the Help for Heroes charity. It is certainly a colourful day, with Littlehampton at its very best. The parachute jump display is my favourite, and takes me back to January 1976.

I'm not entirely sure why I added my name, address and telephone number to the list on the notice board at Worthing Sports Centre. It read as follows:

Parachute Jump

All those interested in joining me for a long weekend at Dunkeswell Aerodrome near Honiton, Devon, on the last weekend in January, please sign up below.

We will leave the centre by minibus at 5pm on Thursday 29th, arriving Dunkeswell at 9pm.

Train with the Royal Marines on Friday and Saturday.

Jump from a height of 2,500 feet from a Cessna light aircraft on Sunday afternoon, weather permitting.

Leave Dunkeswell 5pm, returning to Worthing by approx. 9pm.

Total cost £8. Advance payment only.

Bring a sleeping bag and a strong pair of boots.

Derek Sheriff
Centre Manager

I had been a member of the sports centre for a couple of years, participating in fitness training, squash and badminton; occasionally passing the time with Derek who was a good organiser and an ex-Royal Marines officer. When Jean dropped me off at the centre the following week I boarded the minibus along with Derek and seven other men, none of whom I knew.

When we finally arrived at Dunkeswell it was pitch-black, deserted, and freezing. We dumped our kit in a first floor bunk-room illuminated by one 60-watt bulb dangling, shadeless, from a damp ceiling rose; I could just about see that the odd window pane was missing. "Well I didn't promise you the Ritz," commented Derek, who had spotted that we were less than impressed by our accommodation, "not to worry lads, there is a pub half a mile the other side of the camp and we have a least one hour of drinking time left."

The next morning we rose early, washed and shaved and had breakfast with the Royal Marines who arrived the evening before, while we were down the pub. We could see in the cold light of day that Dunkeswell would have been better named 'Dumperswell'. I guess built in a hurry during the early days of World War II, and no doubt little used since, almost certainly the buildings allocated to the Marines had not seen a lick of paint for thirty years. The camp is vaguely remembered for being where Joseph Kennedy Jr. was billeted in 1944. The elder brother of JFK, who would become President of USA in 1961, Joe was considered to be far more talented than any other member of the Kennedy clan; such speculation would never be tested as sadly he was killed whilst taking part in a secret mission towards the end of the war.

Breakfast was provided by the Marines' cook, and after egg and bacon rolls we were introduced to the one officer present, and the three NCOs. Derek clearly knew the senior officer and had agreed that his party would accept military training and discipline alongside the twenty-odd Royal Marine recruits. The physical training consisted of jumping off the back of a moving lorry, and from a platform the height of a first-floor window, to replicate the impact of hitting the ground after descending from 2,500 feet. It was all a little daunting, yet one paid full attention with an eye on what was to come on Sunday. That aside, the training was first rate and included, exiting the plane, chute failure, ground rush and parachute packing.

As I write, four decades later, I can recall every detail of the course and I must say that Sergeant Bob Leifman, a veteran of over 300 jumps, was a natural teacher. During his ten years in the service, Bob had faced just about every problem one might encounter; he relayed horror stories with great humour and provided 'triggers' that he knew we would instantly recall under pressure.

The other two instructors treated the eighteen-year-old recruits harshly, but us less so, presumably as we were roughly their age, and had not 'taken the Queen's shilling'. I can't say I minded the discipline; I could clearly see the necessity to follow all commands to the letter, yet one or two of my newfound friends from Worthing Sports Centre kicked against the heavy-handed style employed on both us and the young marines.

On one occasion, the oldest member of our group, Geoff, became incensed when one NCO continuously bullied a young recruit. Geoff was in his late thirties, six feet two inches tall and two hundred pounds, an ex-national serviceman and probably a Teddy Boy in the Fifties; and certainly confident that he could handle himself. On the second evening in the local pub, our trainers were invited by Derek to join us for a drink. Geoff took the 'offending' sergeant to task over his actions earlier that day. A heated row ensued leading to Geoff pinning the NCO against the wall. Fortunately, Derek intervened before blows were exchanged. I considered that Geoff was pushing his luck and told him that how the military train their recruits was really none of our business and it was most certainly unwise to alienate our temporary masters.

The majority of our group were upset by the ruckus and considered us privileged to be trained by top professionals, the most experienced of whom, Major Davis, had completed over 500 jumps. (Bob confided that when jumping 'out of hours', on the odd occasion he would not bother to pack the chute, but merely stuff it in the bag and in the event of a problem, unravel it on the way down!)

Our course was completed by Sunday lunchtime and it was arranged that our turn to jump would precede the recruits that afternoon. At 2pm we set about packing our chutes in one of the hangars, which somewhat took our minds off the fast-approaching ordeal. Happy that all the kit was correct, I donned my jumpsuit, parachute and reserve – very, very carefully ensuring that the groin straps were not going to inhibit my nether regions when the static line triggered the chute to open. By the time we lined up on the tarmac to wait for the Cessna single engine plane to return from dropping the last group of recruits, the weather had taken a turn for the worse. The senior officer approached and advised us that as the wind had considerably freshened and light rain was now falling, in his opinion it would be wise to abandon the drop. "It is your call lads, it will be dark in half an hour, so it is now or never.

Remember, once you climb on board the only way down is by chute from 2,500 feet. Put up or shut up!"

The four-berth aircraft had all seats (with the exception of the pilot's) removed, making room for six occupants. We didn't need a second invitation. First on board was the sergeant jumpmaster who crouched next to the pilot, facing the rear. I loaded third, which made me second out; third out was to be Geoff. The jumpmaster was none other than 'the bully', who was by now seriously eyeballing Geoff as the plane taxied across the airfield. We were jumping with the aid of a static line. As the jumpmaster systematically hooked us up he pressed his face against Geoff's and snarled, "Boy am I glad that it is me who is looking after you, hard man." As we took off I could not have cared less about how Geoff was feeling – which probably was not too good – because the reality of the situation suddenly hit me. With no door on the jump side, the engine roaring, and the freezing conditions, my head was pounding and I prayed to God 'please get me out of here'. A couple of minutes later He graciously answered my prayer, shortly after candidate number one had disappeared.

A tap on the shoulder was my order to move to the door; a second tap and I had to hold on to the wing bar as the pilot simultaneously switched off the engine, (with less than five seconds for me to position my feet) and a third tap to let go. The third command was irrelevant as it was near impossible to hold on for more than a second or two. The next job was to look up and count 'one thousand, two thousand,' and up to five, by which time the chute should be open and the line detached.

Although my chute had detached from the static line it had not fully opened. I was experiencing a 'candle'; the silk had not billowed out, as one would expect. Bob had taught us that on very rare occasions this could happen, and that I had two choices: either unclip and throw the main chute and immediately deploy the reserve sitting on my chest; alternatively, grab the support ropes and violently jerk the chute. I plumped for the latter and grabbed the opposite ropes and tugged. Instantly, I spun like a top and the chute fully deployed.

Someone jumping from 2,500 feet, without the aid of a chute, will take twenty-five or so seconds to hit the ground. With a parachute, somewhere in the region of two minutes, forty seconds. The striking feature of descending was for me the utter silence; until Geoff's untimely interruption. He was above and behind me singing 'Goodbyee, goodbyee'. Clearly he was a very relieved man to leave the jumpmaster behind without incident.

My next task was to look for the target: 'X marks the spot'. Steering the chute round in a circle there was no sign of it, in fact the wind was blowing me all over the place and I guessed by now I must have been airborne for at least ninety seconds. It was very nearly dark and I was way off course and drifting towards the edge of the airfield, with a hedge and trees fast approaching. What's more, the foliage was adjacent to a disused hangar and if I landed on it I would undoubtedly crash through the Big Six asbestos roof sheets.

I tugged hard on my guide rope to narrowly avoid disaster, but I forgot to look under my arm to gauge the ground rush, and neither did I remember to bend my knees. CRASH! Everything went blank. When I came to, I was being dragged across the grass. This time my chute was well and truly billowing. Once again I tugged on the ropes, this time towards me, and collapsed over the silk, trapping it beneath me. There was blood everywhere; it was pouring out of my mouth. As I detached the clips releasing the chute I fell backwards, both mentally and physically exhausted.

"You still in one piece John?" It was Derek driving the recovery truck. "I don't know, my mouth is bleeding profusely," I weakly responded. Taking a closer look at my wide open mouth, Derek said, "Don't worry, you have only bitten your tongue, we have all done that; I reckon that you forgot to bend your knees. Anyhow, it is still working, jump in." When we returned to base I found out our second group had not jumped; the pilot had called a halt, hampered by the high winds and fading light. Of the four of us who did fly, only one was unscathed. Apart from my sore tongue, one guy had an ankle the size of a football, and Geoff a cut head, presumably incurred on landing and not a present from the jumpmaster. Conversation during the journey home was somewhat stilted, with three in pain and four pissed off at missing out on the experience.

That summer I returned to Dunkeswell with the non-jumpers to complete my second descent. With near-perfect conditions I made a textbook landing, on target. To be honest, I had to return as the first jump scared me witless. To my amazement I was twice as frightened the second time and decided that I had had quite enough of this exciting hobby, and quit whilst I was still in one piece.

The following year I very sadly learnt from Derek that Royal Marine Master Sergeant Robert Leifman had suffered a serious accident while leading a display team. Bob had almost completed the perfect descent into a crowded football stadium on a hot summer's afternoon when, a mere fifty feet from the ground, his sport parachute collapsed. Apparently the rising heat from the spectators caused this freak occurrence. The fall broke his spine and the dear man never walked again.

Silence is Golden

Performers:	The Tremeloes
Composers:	Crewe and Gaudio
Number 1:	April 1967

Chapter 14 – Spider

Luke 12:6-7
"Aren't five sparrows sold for two pennies? Yet not one sparrow is forgotten by God. Even the hairs of your head have all been counted. So do not be afraid; you are worth much more than many sparrows!"

Attached to the Foreshore Office at the east end of the promenade is a small terrace of shops and takeaways selling fish and chips, doughnuts, ice creams and numerous beach-friendly items: crab lines, inflatable boats, buckets, spades and the like. Five hundred yards east along the promenade is the designer East Beach Café that tends to attract an upmarket crowd, young professional types and wealthy baby boomers, happy to pay a higher price for the fashionable dining experience. The proprietors of most of these establishments are licensed to trade by the council and pay an annual fee for the privilege. From time to time I am notified of the presence of an itinerant trader illegally plying their trade on the promenade; when I receive such a call I jump on the Beach Mule, find the offender, read the rulebook and advise them that the best course of action is to leave immediately. Generally, they are selling their wares out of a van, and as soon as they see my uniform they leave without any need for verbal encouragement.

On one occasion, however, I received a complaint from a local concession that an individual had set up a mobile coffee shop on the east section of the promenade. I drove to the far end of the promenade just past the Swimming Centre to find a man in his thirties trading hot drinks and confectionery from the rear of a vehicle, the registration number of which read, near as damn it, COFFEE. Being aware from the duty diary that he had been warned before and previously claimed that he had council permission to operate; and knowing that my colleague Charlie had contacted The Kremlin (Council Office) and been advised that no such licence had been granted, I politely requested that he close up and leave the promenade immediately. 'Coffee' stated that he had a licence, which, of course, he was unable to produce, and refused to move.

Coffee was no oil painting: blond hair, and stockily built with a Quasimodo-type gait. I pointed out that he was likely to incur fines for both illegal trading and illegal parking and therefore it was very much in his best interests to shut up shop and move on. To my utter amazement he verbally abused me, then moved forward swinging clenched fists at me. I quickly stepped three paces back holding my hands out flat and told him to calm down. Although he dropped his fighting stance he continued 'effing and blinding', so without further ado I informed him that I would call the police. I returned to my Mule and radioed base requesting police intervention. (Incident number: 748/29/03/08). Knowing full well that the police may or may not respond, depending on other priorities, I returned to the Foreshore Office and revisited the scene one hour later to find no sign of the unpleasant man.

Five months later my colleague Dave Strong was presented with the identical problem. Coffee was once more plying his trade exactly as before. In a similar manner to me, Dave confronted Coffee and politely asked him to move. On this occasion Coffee was accompanied by a photographer who was attempting to take pictures of the business operation for sales and marketing promotion. Coffee once again became highly abusive and began to swing at Dave. Unlike me, Dave stood his ground and when Coffee pushed him aggressively in the chest with his fists clenched, instinctively, Dave punched him on the chin. Then, once again, he told the now somewhat shocked and bruised man to leave. Dave climbed on to the Mule and returned to the Foreshore Office.

Approximately a week later Dave received a call from Sussex Police inviting him to attend Worthing Durrington Police Station regarding the incident. When Dave arrived he was promptly arrested, fingerprinted, charged with assault and bailed, all within one hour. After Dave had thrown the punch, Coffee complained to the police who took his statement and arranged for his, now black and blue, chin to be photographed. The matter was then referred to the Crown Prosecution Service. The alleged assault happened in August yet the court date was set for December; this was adjourned on the day as the court agenda was overbooked, and it was rescheduled for the end of January, only to be adjourned once again, this time on a legal technicality. Finally, the case was heard in March.

I regard my foreshore partner Dave Strong as an absolute gem of a man. Of rugged stature, standing five feet ten inches in height and weighing in at two hundred and ten pounds, at the time of the incident he was sixty-five years of age with ten years' unblemished service in the job. He joined the Royal Mail on leaving school at fifteen and worked his way through the ranks to a middle-management position running the local Postal Depot at Littlehampton, retiring at fifty-five, after forty years' service. Dave has been happily married to Sally for forty years, with four grown-up children and four grandchildren. Over the years Sally and Dave have also fostered ninety children of all ages, colours and creeds. Dave is very much considered a pillar of the community, liked and respected by one and all. Had he not had such a successful career in the Post Office then he could easily made his name as a stand-up comedian. Dave can, and does, crease me up all day with his witty remarks and cameos. The man is a natural mimic and will impersonate all and sundry at the drop of the hat; his Danny La Rue impression has to be heard to be believed.

The trial took all day and the three magistrates took over an hour to determine the outcome: Not Guilty. The bench chairman in his summary maintained that although Dave had been over-enthusiastic in defending himself, the one punch was justified under the circumstances. It had taken eight months for justice to be done. Costs were awarded against the Crown Prosecution Service.

The outcome of the hearing was always touch and go; had Dave been found guilty then he would have lost the Foreshore job, had to pay his defence costs of £10,000, and fined and/or otherwise sentenced. A criminal record would have prevented any future trips to America. To say that Dave and his family were relieved when we had a drink in the pub afterwards would be an understatement. Hopefully, my appearance as a key witness helped to sway the court in Dave's favour.

The only other time I had to attend the Magistrates Court was to support my son Andrew, twenty-two years earlier, ironically in the very same room.

Mark Robin Smith and Andrew John Smith were six and four years respectively when I met them for the first time at their grandparents' home in Durrington. It was the Fifth of November 1970 and a firework party had been organised in the back garden, followed by a late high-tea. Little did I know at the time that in less than three years they would change their name from Smith to Madell after I became their step-dad. Mark was fit, bright and full of life. Andrew on the other hand was a sickly, troublesome child. For the previous two years they had taken their grandfather Ron as their father figure. Ron was a fair, but strong disciplinarian and, as was often the case with someone of his generation, he did not 'spare the rod'. More often than not Andrew was the one on the receiving end of the corporal punishment, summarily administered.

Taking on responsibility for two growing boys as I did, aged just twenty-six, could have been very challenging yet both boys made the transformation easy and immediately accepted me as their dad. Perhaps they were subconsciously happy to escape granddad's heavy hand. I like to think that we still have as good a relationship today as we did during their childhood years.

Being a very young dad I enjoyed playing most sports with the boys and was able to encourage them to share my passion for soccer. Soon we were regularly attending matches together at Brighton and Hove Albion some ten miles from our home in Worthing.

It was at the Goldstone Ground that Andrew acquired his nickname 'Spider'. In 1974 the Albion purchased a tall, skinny centre-forward from Norwich City: Ian Mellor, soon to form what was to become a formidable strike-partnership with the precocious Peter Ward. The Albion manager, Alan Mullery, from time to time, left Ian on the bench and brought him on in the second half, if he deemed it appropriate. Andrew, then aged about ten, took Ian Mellor – nickname 'Spider' – as his favourite player. Never happy to see Ian as substitute, Andrew often chanted 'Bring on the Spider'. As we stood very near the dugout both the manager and player could easily hear the request. The surrounding fans usually picked up on Andrew's chant and soon the whole twenty-thousand-strong crowd joined in. Alan Mullery sensibly gave in to the majority and 'Spider' Mellor was ordered to warm up. Jogging up and down the touchline, and having become accustomed to the ritual, the sub waved and smiled to Andrew balanced on his wooden box. Andrew always beamed back, and from that season on became known to one and all as 'Spider'.

Spider struggled to keep up at school and slipped into the bottom set. We got up at the crack of dawn to study simple English and Maths with the aim of him catching up with his classmates. Although academically challenged he was good at sport, especially middle-distance running. He joined the local Harriers running club and won a number of prestigious races. Like his granddad Ron, he had the ability to engage all and sundry in conversation and consequently made many friends and acquaintances – hopefully all was not lost. Years later, Jean and I discovered that rather than attend St Andrew's High School, Spider, by now in his mid-teens, had found himself a morning job serving tables and washing-up in Cafe 29. In the afternoon he would walk down to the seafront and spend his wage on the fruit machines and games in the Pier Arcade.

Leaving school at the earliest opportunity Spider secured a job at a local fish and chip shop, moved into the flat above the shop and soon became self-sufficient. Despite his lack of formal education and acute dyslexia he was not frightened of hard work and continued in gainful employment throughout his teenage years, more often than not living back at home. Regrettably, he fell in with bad company and trouble was soon on the horizon.

One evening the doorbell rang and when I answered it, two burly and rather unsavoury characters that we shall call Pinky and Perky, confronted me and said, "Mr Madell?" "Yes," I replied. "We are from BJ's Casino and have come to collect the £500 you owe," Perky said. "You have the wrong house; I've never been to your Casino," I abruptly replied and attempted to shut the door, which proved difficult with Perky's size eleven boot in the way. "Mr Andrew Madell?" He continued. "No, that's my son." "Well your son owes us £500, and we are here to collect," Pinky said with menace. "Two problems old chap, my son is underage and gambling debts are not enforceable, goodnight," I snarled with my voice raised. Perky pushed me up against the inner door and said through gritted teeth, "If you don't have £500 in cash by this time tomorrow then we will smash down the door and inflict £500 worth of damage on you and your property." I pushed Perky off my doorstep and told him in no uncertain manner, "You've picked on the wrong man sunshine; I am a well-known roofing contractor and if anything happens to me or my property I guarantee that I will send at least thirty of my men to your Casino and when they leave there will be no Casino left, now fuck off!" Thankfully, they did just that. To this day I have heard no more.

Curiously, while working for the Marley Tile Company I had a similar episode and run-in, this time with a notorious slum landlord. I had been contacted by a property company located in Hove to price for strip and retiling one of their houses a couple of streets from their office. I did just that and after submitting the quote, in due course received an order to undertake the work. When credit-check results turned out to be a little patchy I requested a 50% payment upfront, and to my surprise, received a cheque by return. (Back in the Seventies, in the days before the World Wide Web, there was little financial sophistication; Marley policy was, if in doubt, ask for a deposit to cover the prime costs on the job.) With the work satisfactorily completed I submitted my invoice and waited for payment for the outstanding balance. After three months and a number of reminders I decided that my best way forward was to make an appointment with the owner of the company, now in my debt.

A few days later I walked into the office located in an old house and told the receptionist that I had an appointment with a Mr Nicholas Van Hoogstraten. "Please take a seat in the waiting room Mr Madell, he won't keep you long," she informed me, gesturing to a side door. I walked in and took a seat. To my amazement, also sitting in the room were half a dozen beautiful girls aged in their late teens and early twenties; they were all were dressed to kill and not surprisingly I soon found myself chatting to them. They turned out to be auditioning for positions as exotic dancers and waitresses in a string of nightclubs in Istanbul. Before I could learn more of this somewhat dubious-sounding venture, I was summoned by the receptionist to see the boss.

Sitting behind a rather imposing desk was a good-looking, dapper man, roughly the same age as me. Without any of the usual business niceties he addressed me curtly: "How much are you owed, man from Marley?" Rather taken aback (and mentally, still in the presence of the bevy of beauties) I dug out a copy of the invoice from my pocket and handed it to him. He opened and scribbled in his cheque book, tore out the cheque and said, "Paid in full, now piss off." This I swiftly did and paid the money 'special clearance' into the nearest bank without further ado.

For the remainder of my career I often remarked to those who owed me money that I had once successfully persuaded Mr Van Hoogstraten to settle his outstanding debt in full, though it was not strictly true, having not spoken even one word to him. I guess in his eyes my very presence was all that was needed to resolve our problem.

Gambling was not Spider's only vice. One beautiful Bank Holiday Monday, Jean, the younger boys and I were just about to set off to the Rackham Country Fair armed with a picnic hamper when the phone rang. "Mr Madell this is the Accident and Emergency Department at Worthing Hospital. We have your son Andrew here in a state of collapse." As Spider had only been discharged from the same hospital a couple of days earlier after an operation for appendicitis, I feared the worst. Leaving the family behind, I drove the three miles to the hospital. When I arrived I booked in at reception and was told to take a seat. Unusually, the place was empty with the exception of a rather unpleasant-looking yob aged about twenty sitting in the corner, who gave me the evil eye – which I ignored.

After waiting fifteen minutes a rather stern-looking nursing sister approached me. "Mr Madell, come this way," she beckoned. With a formidable look in her eye, a five o'clock shadow and burly appearance, I decided she was certainly not an individual to be messed with. "Is this your son?" she barked, drawing back the cubical curtain to reveal Spider, half hanging out of a raised-wheel bed. "Yes sister," I meekly replied. "Well you can take him home; we don't want him, he is drunk as a skunk." And he was – paralytic. "Come on Spider, we are going home," I shouted in his left ear. "No dad, I'm staying here," he slurred.

At this point, with the disapproving sister still very much in attendance, I pulled him off the bed and half-carried, half-dragged him toward the rubber swing-door exit. All the time my son was shouting and swearing. As we stumbled through the doors I felt an acute pain in the small of my back, which caused the two of us to fall over, and out into the hospital car park. Looking up I could see the yob from the waiting room standing over me and protesting: "You leave my mate alone, you prick." At the very same moment I spotted just a dozen yards away, the Worthing Carnival procession slowly wending its way to nearby Homefield Park with hundreds of people lining the route. Dazed and bewildered I picked myself up off the pavement to find not only the yob squaring up to me, but also my drunken son in a threatening pose.

The Carnival crowd appeared to find our altercation far more interesting than the float transporting Miss Worthing. "Come on Andrew, come home right now," I pleaded. "Just leave me alone and go away," he insisted. With that the yob took a swing at me. I immediately inflicted a left and a right punch to his head and he went down like a sack of potatoes. I thought, Pat Coleman would be proud – or would he? Andrew then grabbed me by the arm and cried, "You hit my friend; you hit my fucking friend!" By this time I had had more than enough of the pantomime, so placed a well-aimed punch to the side of Spider's chin and knocked him clean out. I picked him up, carried him back to my car and drove home. After I had dumped him on his bed, Jean, Jamie, Paul, picnic and I proceeded to the Country Fair.

Auntie Peggy, my adoptive mother's sister-in-law, came to stay and spend time with mum who, for ten years after Albert died, lived in the annexe of our large five-bedroomed house in High Salvington. Peggy was born in 1912, just one month after the Titanic sank, and lived until 2009. I had a great affection and admiration for my aunt who would have been pleased to be described as stoic. As a child I stayed on many occasions with her, Uncle Jack, and my two cousins Anne and Peter, at their home in Gidea Park, Romford. I found her to be strict, yet very kind to me; and believe me, no one could scramble eggs like Peggy. Well into her eighties she provided hospital transport in her ancient Morris 1000 and even today I can hear my aunt say, "Just running an old dear to the hospital, I will be back soon." The 'old dear' was more than likely ten years her junior!

Peggy, now widowed, retired to Barton-on-Sea and it was there that I would visit her from time to time. From her seafront ground-floor flat she was fond of walking the cliffs to enjoy the amazing views towards The Needles and the Isle of White.

One day after a hearty lunch Peggy, Nora, Jean, Paul and I climbed down to the beach to spin stones on the sea. Eventually we were faced with the climb back up the steep steps. Mum and Jean led the way followed by Peggy, who was a large curvy lady, with Paul and me bringing up the rear. Peggy hung onto the rail and every time she lifted her leg she passed wind, loudly. The first two or three farts could be ignored, but forty could not. Paul was beside himself, as any six-year-old boy would be. Not only could those of us at the back hear, but also those up front. Halfway up my mum could not resist saying, "Oh Peggy, really." This comment once again set Paul off laughing. Peggy, unperturbed, strode onwards and upwards. When we finally reached the top she turned to me with a wry smile and said, "Well ducky, that walk blew away lunch, I'm now ready for my tea!"

Back home, one night Jean and I went out leaving Peggy and Nora to babysit Paul and Jamie. Sometime during the evening the phone rang and Peggy answered. A young man's voice slowly and menacingly said, 'I'm going to cut off your toes.' He continued to repeat the statement over and over again, until a shocked Peggy retorted 'Well you just try!', and slammed the phone down in disgust. When Jean and I returned home, mum and Peggy relayed the tale of continuous calls before they thought of leaving the phone off the hook.

Shortly after Spider came home I confronted him. "What do you know about perverted phone calls?" By his body language I knew he had some knowledge. "Out with it, what's the score?" Sheepishly, he mumbled something about money he owed, which he was under pressure to pay. I shouted at him, "Sort this nonsense out right now, I will not have Nana and Peggy upset in this way!" Without further ado Spider sprinted out the door, jumped into his car and drove off. The time was now gone eleven o'clock. Two hours later I was asleep in bed when the phone rang. My immediate reaction was that I was about to receive an abusive call. I was wrong, it was the police; Spider had been arrested for using threatening behaviour.

His case came up at the Magistrates Court the next morning. Apparently, after he rushed out he went straight to the culprit's house, banged on the door and called for the individual to come out. When there was no reply Spider attempted to break down the door with a baseball bat. The police were called and promptly arrested him. Spider pleaded guilty and was fined £60 and bound over to keep the peace.

I thought that was that, but it wasn't, far from it. When the local paper came out on the following Thursday the headline ran as follows: 'LOCAL MAN GOES BERSERK WITH

BASEBALL BAT'. The article continued: 'John Madell of Mill Lane, High Salvington, was found guilty of threatening behaviour, etc., etc.' Spider had given his full name to the police: Andrew John Madell, but the press had omitted Andrew. I have always been one to attempt to turn a disaster into a triumph, and as luck would have it, on this occasion it worked. I made a dozen copies of the front page of the Worthing Herald and wrote across them in red ink, 'PAY UP OR ELSE'. Then I posted them to business customers who, for some considerable time, had owed me money. Within a week all outstanding debts had been settled!

By the late 1980s Spider was working for my company Cobsen-Davies Ltd. When a vacancy occurred at the Guildford branch he moved from Worthing to work alongside his old school friend, Shane Wiffen. Spider found a flat near the office and, finally, at the age of twenty-three, moved out of the family home. Jokingly, I said to him, "Your only real hope Spider is to frequent all the yuppie bars in the Weybridge area, find a rich girl and marry her." For once in his life he took his dad's advice and did exactly that. In 1993 he married Julia Penn and took a job with her father David's company. Spider did really well and David soon made him factory manager with a good wage, bonus and company car. Julia, a lovely girl, was a midwife and when their daughter Charlotte was born in 1996 they moved to a picture-postcard cottage in the heart of Claygate village. Life appeared rosy, but sadly, it was short-lived.

By 2001, David Penn had died, the marriage had broken up and Spider was living alone in a two-bedroomed flat in Ewell. Andrew once again fell in with a bad lot, lost his job in the factory (under new ownership) and quickly ran up debts in excess of £70,000. Heavy drinking soon found him in dodgy late-night clubs. On one drunken Friday-night-spree Spider was badly beaten by the club bouncers, to such an extent that his airway was cut off and he suffered a massive stroke, from which he has yet to fully recover.

Depression followed and the downward spiral continued after a failed suicide attempt caused him to be sectioned under the Mental Health Act. A cocktail of heavy prescription-drugs only seemed to worsen his mental state and he became paranoid. On one visit to the hospital the doctor took me to one side and said, "Would you like the good news or the bad news Mr Madell? The good news is that Andrew no longer believes that you are trying to kill him; the bad news: he now believes that you are trying to steal his money." The next few years saw Spider in and out of various mental institutions, and to top everything else, he developed the debilitating fibromyalgia.

To Spider's great credit he has never given up his faith in God and lives in hope of making a full recovery, maintaining a great sense of humour and a very generous spirit. Today he exists on Disability Living Allowance in a lovely one-bedroomed bungalow in Bookham, Surrey. He sees his daughter Charlotte on a regular basis.

Summer Wind
Performer: Frank Sinatra
Composer: Mayer and Mercer
Number 36:   September 1966

Chapter 15 – David

Ecclesiastes 7:14
When things are going well for you, be glad, and when trouble comes, just remember: God sends both happiness and trouble; you never know what is going to happen next.

The coveted Blue Flag is awarded to beaches that reach a very high standard of excellence. The Foundation for Environmental Education makes the award annually to beaches complying with the required standards in five categories: water quality, safety, environmental management, education and information. The basic requirement is to ensure that no industrial waste or sewage is discharged into the water near to the beach.

The foreshore team is responsible for providing first aid, lifeguards, disabled access, ensuring the toilet facilities are of a high standard, environmental management, education and banning both dogs and barbecues from the beach. The only towns in West Sussex that regularly qualify for the flag are Hove, Littlehampton, Bognor and West Wittering. The relevant stretch of beach at Littlehampton is approximately two-thirds of a mile in length, between the pier to the west and Norfolk Road at the east end. The foreshore policed by colleagues and me is probably the best-managed beach in the UK. We take our duties extremely seriously to make our town's promenade area safe and sound for both local people and visitors by enforcing the Council bylaws, including no cycling and the curtailment of excessive alcohol consumption.

When it comes to discouraging the riding of bikes on the promenade, my work partner, Dave Strong, is zealous in the extreme. There is no doubt that at busy times cycling can prove a hazard, and does need strict control. Dave has become incensed when repeatedly ignored by the same individuals, and one in particular: Eric, a beach hut owner who, on numerous occasions, has taken great pride in riding his unicycle up and down a crowded prom. The tall, well-built Frenchman in his early forties, relished entertaining the day-trippers with his ability to balance, spin and weave in and out of the various obstacles on the tarmacked area.

From time to time, I reminded him of the bylaw and he always complied with my request by dismounting and moving onto the greensward, where cycling is permitted, to continue his show.

Over the years Eric had become very skilled in riding the one-wheeled bike and, by and large, he didn't really bother me. Dave however, was a tad less tolerant and at every opportunity confronted Eric, often adding to the day's entertainment by chasing him back down the promenade to the haven of his beach hut.

One day the regular circus turned ugly when Eric banged on the office door and confronted Dave over his perceived persecution. A heated row ensued and Eric, who is, incidentally, black, accused Dave of being a racist. "Don't you play the race card with me, old son!" Dave exclaimed. Sensing that the situation was about to worsen, I stepped in and told the two of them that they were acting in a silly and childish manner. With that, the Frenchman jumped back on his bike and rode off. "Bloody bloke, fancy Chalky calling me, of all things, a racist," said my friend, the-now-incensed Dave.

In late October 1972 another 'Dave' entered my life when he walked into the saloon bar of my local the Red Lion in Pulborough. Around 9pm on Friday nights a crowd of perhaps eight to ten met in the bar, and being a village, usually I knew everyone who might venture into our domain; however, not the guy who had just ordered a pint of Brickwood's Best Bitter from the landlord Les Morrison. I had never seen him before. The stranger, in his late twenties was short, yet fairly stocky, with a presence. Pointing to the pint that Les had just poured, I said, "I'll get that, come and join us." David shuffled along the bar, thanked me for buying the drink, and introduced himself. In turn, I introduced him to the three or four people I had been talking to. It turned out that David had just moved to Pulborough having bought one of the newly constructed houses located north of the recreation ground. From then on David joined us most Fridays, and soon became one of the crowd.

Over the 1973 Easter holiday I left Pulborough for good and took a cheap room in a house in Harrow Road, West Worthing. I wouldn't describe the accommodation as a slum, although it is true to say that two of my mates sent me a 'Red Cross parcel', complete with a cake with a file buried inside! Over the next eighteen months most of the pub crowd got married and we inevitably drifted apart. Yet David and I made a point of meeting up at least once a month for an early evening drink, and this became a tradition that was to continue for the next thirty years.

David married Jane in 1975 and our families met up for barbecues and meals celebrating birthdays and other special occasions. We also enjoyed a couple of winter-sunshine holidays together in Lanzarote. Unbeknown to me at the time, one of these breaks was the beginning of David's rather unusual story.

One night in the holiday apartment the four of us played 'Consequences': a silly game where one has to tell the truth, or not; prompted by a carded question. To our astonishment, Jane hinted that if he didn't sharpen up his act she might leave David when the children were of an age when they would be able to fend for themselves. David merely laughed off the threat, and I put it down to the wine talking. Jean later confided to me that in her opinion Jane was deadly serious.

Seven years later when their youngest son was just sixteen, Jane packed her bags and left her husband. David was totally shocked, devastated and utterly inconsolable. The year was 1997 and I had decided to celebrate my fiftieth birthday by driving Route 66. David asked if he could join me on the trip. I was a little reticent, as I had rather looked forward to the challenge of travelling alone on the sixteen-day journey. Yet it had become clear that my friend was in desperate need of moral support, and anyway, I knew that we would get on OK.

We arrived in Chicago, appropriately, on the Fourth of July. The six-hour time difference caused jet lag, which meant that we retired to bed at 10pm, only to be woken up at midnight by the sound of a massive firework-display, sited just a block away at Navy Pier. For a moment I thought the city was under nuclear attack and, in fact, when we arose early the next morning we found the centre of Chicago utterly deserted. The good citizens were no doubt sleeping off the excesses of the night before.

After two days sightseeing and the inevitable body-clock adjustment we collected our hire car and headed west, whenever possible following the old Route 66, which straddles Interstate 40 for most of the journey. This took us through eight states: Illinois, Missouri, Kansas, Oklahoma, Texas, New Mexico, Arizona and California, in total 2,278 miles.

David became far more enthusiastic in maintaining the integrity of our trip than me. He was not just satisfied with visiting all the famous landmarks surrounding the route, but insisted on returning to the very junction that we left to make the detour, thereby attempting to cover every inch of the road between Grant Park, Chicago and Santa Monica Pier, L.A. We enjoyed viewing the world's tallest Totem Pole, Boot Hill at Boys Ranch, Cadillac Ranch and a couple of wonderful ghost towns. We even followed the 1926 pre-alignment to take in Santa Fe. The only time we missed a stretch was between Kingman and Barstow to visit The Grand Canyon and Los Vegas. David was very keen to double back to Kingman to be able to claim that we had indeed travelled the entire length of Route 66. Thankfully, I managed to persuade him that this course of action was a little extreme.

During two weeks travelling together we covered many topics and had great fun, although there was one subject that however hard I tried, I could not avoid – Jane. I fully understood that David was suffering emotionally and gritted my teeth whenever the 'J' word was uttered, which seemed to be on the hour, every hour, or roughly every forty miles: perhaps sixty times along the route. By the time we reached L.A. I was not sure who hated her most, David or me. Funny that, as I had always liked Jane.

Early in 1998 on one mid-week afternoon, whilst working in my office, I received a distress call from David: "I can't go on like this John. I'm at the end of my tether, help!" I knew immediately that he was in a bad way. David had not driven to work that day, which was totally out of character, and clearly needed my company. I jumped in my car, and thirty minutes later I found my old friend in the depths of despair.

We sat opposite each other, together with two glasses, a bottle of gin, a bottle of tonic and a bucket of ice. Fortunately, I don't much like gin so it was easy for me to drink 95% tonic to obviate the problem of driving home. I had a sort of a brainwave: "David, you need to find a woman to replace Jane in your life." As I said it, I thought that he probably did not want to replace his now ex-wife in his emotions. "That sounds a plan John, but I don't know how to go about finding a woman," he said, surprising me. "Advertise David, you are a good salesman; instead of selling office furniture, sell yourself! Place a one-liner in the local lonely hearts column."

There and then we composed the advert: '54-year-old professional gentleman, equally at home in dinner jacket or jeans, seeks lady for friendship and maybe a little more.' David telephoned through the advert before I left that afternoon. As I drove away I thought at least my friend had something to look forward to, even if there were no takers. Anyway, two weeks would pass before the advert would appear and by then, maybe, 'the black dog' mood might lift.

No takers? Not many, a total of forty-eight! David, a meticulous man, set about the task with organised enthusiasm. Armed with a phone and a spreadsheet he called all the ladies. His tick list included the following questions: Age, height, weight (I have no idea how he broached this question), number and age of children, status (divorced/widow/etc.), location, number of GCEs, ethnic group and speaking voice. This effectively meant that the lady had to be five feet, four inches or less, white, with children over eighteen, a reasonable standard of education and live within twenty miles of Pulborough. This test eliminated twenty candidates. The remaining twenty-eight he arranged to interview on the hour, every hour, during weekday evenings at The White Swan in the nearby village of Steyning, over the course of a three-week period.

Twenty-four accepted the invitation to meet and twenty-two actually turned up. Ten ladies agreed to what David termed as a 'first date'; six made it through to stage two: a second date. David then narrowed the list down to three candidates (or, perhaps they narrowed him down) and continued to see all three for three months, and then only two, for a further three months. After a long deliberation Amanda was selected. I am quite sure that none other than David could have dealt with the emotions of the heart in such a clinical and efficient manner. I often have wondered what the landlord at The White Swan must have thought of the procession of middle-aged females through his snug bar.

The romance between David and Amanda bloomed, and twelve months later she moved in. Amanda eventually sold her house in Lancing and a couple of years later the couple bought a property in France. Their French home was furnished with the contents of Amanda's property. David hired a three-ton vehicle, and together with his son, the three of us set off fully loaded for the village of Duravel, in the department of Lot. The five-hundred-mile drive from the port of Ouistreham, near Caen, took us twelve hours.

They had purchased a fantastic house/villa two-and-a-half miles from the village, set in three acres, with a large outdoor swimming pool, *pigeonnier* (a converted, towered pigeon loft), double garage and wine cellar. With wonderful views south over the Lot valley, and a seemingly endless forest behind, it was very much rural France in the heart of the Cahors wine-growing region: wild mushrooms aplenty, truffles and even boar hunting on Sundays, when in season. The house was holiday let by a local agent and the couple decamped to France whenever work permitted. David took early retirement in 2005, and placed his Pulborough house on the market with the firm intention of leaving the shores of England for good. "Sun on my back John; that has always been my long-term ambition," David smiled. "Not before we get married, David," Amanda firmly stated. Married they were, one week prior to the move south.

Everything in the garden appeared rosy, but life is never that simple. David's father died the following year and when David and Amanda returned for the funeral, things did not appear entirely right; there was talk of acquiring a one-bedroomed flat in Worthing as a *pied-à-terre*. A short time later, back in France, Amanda threw a complete tantrum and caught the first available flight back to England. Within a month she filed for divorce, returning to Duravel just one time to collect her belongings. David was alone again, this time in a foreign country with no friends or family for support, and what's more, facing a considerable divorce settlement. Adding to David's despair, his long-term employer went into receivership, leaving his pension fund in limbo.

I visited as often as I could, as did both his son and daughter. David's consumption of the local wine had increased alarmingly, and I suggested that he should return to England for Christmas and the New Year to stay with me in my converted railway carriage in Pagham. In fact he stayed for six weeks, and then decided to return home to remain alone in Duravel for as long as it would take to get over his second 'lost' wife. I never figured out whether Amanda had planned the wedding and a short stay in France to maximise the divorce payout, or she had genuinely had enough of her life in a foreign land with her husband.

David stuck out his exile with true British grit, gradually forcing himself to socialise with both the ex-pat community and the locals. Two years after Amanda's sudden departure he met Dominique, a lady born and bred locally; yet living a hundred miles away in Toulouse. Her younger sister Valerie was married to Tony, an English builder, who had settled in Duravel fifteen years earlier. Tony introduced David to Dominique at a village gathering, and as they say: the rest is history. Dominique placed her flat on the market, gave up her job and returned home to Duravel intending to refurbish and move into her late father's house. In fact she moved to David's house, and after extensively renovating it, rented her property out to holidaymakers.

Curiously, whilst staying with me in 2011, David and Dominique went out to lunch, only to bump into both Jane and Amanda in the car park of The Black Horse in Findon Village. Small world.

I am pleased to say that David's stoicism and British stiff upper lip saw him through a very torrid period in his life. David and Dominique tied the knot, which thankfully brings this quaint tale to a happy ending.

Route 66
Performer: Nat King Cole
Composer: Troup
(Released in 1946 before official charts existed)

Chapter 16 – Wayne

Proverbs 20:1
Drinking too much makes you loud and foolish.
It's stupid to get drunk.

The promenade train runs between the coastguard tower and the East Beach Café, a return distance of just over half a mile that takes ten to fifteen minutes, depending on the degree of congestion on the promenade. Accommodating up to thirty passengers, the train is very popular with visitors and locals of all ages. Kim, a slim blonde in her forties holds the concession from Arun District Council and runs the attraction between eleven and six on fine days. The Foreshore Office is located just a few yards from the train's starting point and rarely a day goes by without the occurrence of some minor incident involving the train. Nothing too serious: skateboarders might be hanging on to the last carriage; kids jumping on or off when Kim has to slow the train because of the crowds, and once I had to reprimand a couple of teenage boys for 'mooning' whilst riding the train. To be fair, Kim is a dab hand at frightening offenders without my intervention; until David Baker was employed as a Foreshore Inspector in 2009.

Geoff Taylor, my boss, invited me to sit in on the interviews at the start of the year. Being a seasonal job, the council dismisses all part-time beach staff when the schools return for the autumn term in early September. Consequently, there are always vacancies to fill the following Easter when the beach starts to come alive after the long winter. The lugubrious David Baker, a retired Metropolitan Police sergeant, appeared to be tailor-made for the position. Geoff did have some doubts; not me though, having interviewed and employed dozens of people over many years I was convinced that David was the ideal candidate, and along with two others, he became a Foreshore Inspector.

Within a few days Dave Strong and I were beginning to have serious concerns about Mr Baker. The first hint of a problem was his inability to hoist the flags. Our first job in the morning is to raise four flags: the Littlehampton Town flag, Arun District Council flag, the Quality Coast flag and the Blue Flag, signifying a clean beach. Likewise, at the close of play we drop the flags and store them for the night. They perform the function of making it clear to the public that the beach is manned. Actually, the flags can be a bit of a fiddle and on the odd occasion all of us have lost control of the rope, resulting in the jamming of the pulley roller at the top. When this happens it becomes necessary to drop the pole, re-engage the mechanism and then raise the pole again. Just what one wants to do, especially at the end of the day! In reality, the job normally takes one person five minutes, morning and evening. David Baker was totally incapable of undertaking any part of the process; simply, his shaky fingers did not work. Because of this Dave and I were particularly concerned about his likely inability to undertake first aid, which in high season becomes a major part of our job.

Patrolling the riverside and the promenade is continuous. With two Foreshore Inspectors on duty every day, one stays in the office/first aid station and the other shows a public presence outside. David Baker, however, was unwilling, or maybe unable, to walk. Whenever it was his turn to patrol, he chose to take the Kawasaki Beach Mule instead and very often disappeared for hours on end; a walk around the patch should normally take between forty minutes and one hour. At the end of the day David usually made a beeline for the 0-2-Club watering hole, a brisk walk from our office; no problem for him walking there! Stinking of cigarettes, unable to communicate first thing in the morning, shaky hands and alcohol on the breath added up to a big problem, if not to the public, then certainly for his duty opposite number.

Before long it was clear to Geoff, Dave and I that we had to confront the problem head-on. Fortunately for us though, David Baker engineered his own departure: he confiscated a few bottles of beer from a couple of teenagers hanging out in the Banjo Road beach shelter. Then he cadged a lift from Kim and climbed on the back of the train, gleefully swigging down the beer in front of all and sundry, including Helen, another new Foreshore recruit. Helen reported the incident to Geoff who instantly requested, and accepted, the ex-policeman's resignation.

We later discovered that rather than patrol the designated area, our erstwhile colleague had pub-crawled, taking in: The Arun View Inn, the Littlehampton and District Angling Club, the Nelson

Hotel, the O-2-Club and the Bowling Club bar on his way round. Regrettably, none of the locals had let on to us and I guess we felt let down by the beach community. Clearly, the man was an alcoholic and a potential hazard to the public, in or out of uniform. For many years David had trained guide dogs for the blind, which was very laudable; although one of the lifeguards, rather cynically, suggested that his dogs would always find their way back from the pub after a skinful. Shortly after his downfall, David developed throat cancer, presumably caused by his considerable appetite for fags and booze. I am pleased to say that remarkably, he made a full recovery.

If I were able to rewind my life, I would not smoke my first cigarette, nor take my first drink of alcohol.

It was a racing certainty that I would become a smoker. Dad was a heavy smoker; therefore I became a passive smoker from the age of six weeks. What's more, my parents shop, The Chocolate Box, was crammed full of tobacco, cigars, snuff and cigarettes. I smoked my first cigarette at Lee-on-the-Solent in 1958 whilst holidaying with my two cousins, at an old aunt's house in Hampshire, for a week during the summer break. Most days Peter, Anne and I visited the amusement arcade on the seafront.

The grab machine fascinated us. For a threepenny bit there was a chance to grab and win one of the prizes, which included such items as key rings, golliwogs, chocolate bars and, the ultimate triumph, a ten-shilling note wrapped around a ball. To operate the machine one had to insert the coin, press the trigger and guide a miniature crane over the object of desire, drop the handle and simultaneously close the claw and, if lucky, capture the prize. Next, very gently guide the arm towards a central trapdoor, release, and hey presto! the prize dropped through into an outside receptacle. Easy it was not, ninety-nine times out of one hundred the claw would miss and not capture the item, or frustratingly, grab but drop it, before reaching the trapdoor.

The hundred-to-one chance happened for me at my second attempt when I most skilfully secured a packet of five Weights cigarettes. Without further ado, Peter and I, despite protests from Anne, purchased a box of matches from the cafeteria and made for a secluded area of the beach. We lit up, Peter smoked two, and being one year older and worldly-wise, I smoked three. Disgusted, Anne returned home threatening to split on us. Very soon Peter's colour changed from grey to green and before I had finished my last fag he was honking over the side of a nearby groyne. Five minutes later I followed suit.

I became a regular smoker in 1962 and soon progressed from ('You're never alone with a...') Strand to (The flip-top that was sure to win the girl) Peter Stuyvesant. Eventually, I moved from cigarettes to cigars and finally gave up the habit in 1984, much influenced by my father's death from lung cancer. Without question, smoking had a detrimental effect on my sporting stamina, not least when playing football and squash.

My mother was teetotal and my father was not a big drinker. He liked a glass of cider with Sunday lunch and a scotch or a sherry before bed. Yet he could, and did, go for weeks without a drink. My first experience of alcohol at the age of ten was cider consumed under my parents' watchful eyes. At sixteen, my mates and I, from time to time, popped into the Red Lion where the landlord would serve us alcohol: Brickwood's Best Bitter, better known as 'boy's beer'. It was strictly against the law to serve anyone under the age of eighteen, yet more often than not the local 'bobby', Terry Fox, was in the bar and happily acknowledged our presence.

The same also applied to the Oddfellows Arms, run by two spinster sisters. Curiously, it was one of the last beer-only pubs in Sussex, and did not sell wine or spirits. Even to be served at the Oddfellows was something of a challenge. Firstly, one had to enter the sparsely furnished room and run the gauntlet of elderly men, playing cribbage on a scrubbed table, who were clearly highly disapproving of our presence. Then knock on a hatch (behind which was the old girls' living room) that may, or may not, be answered depending on their mood or the volume of their radio.

The older sister was willing to serve us boys, the younger was not. I don't think the older sister was mid-twentieth-century enlightened, but merely suffering from poor eyesight. Not surprisingly, we tended to patronise the Red Lion.

Shortly before my eighteenth birthday Skeyne House Youth Club closed and when the old house was finally demolished and the land redeveloped for flats, the only entertainment to be found in the village was in one of the nine local pubs. By the time I reached my nineteenth I had been barred from six of them. I was now desperate to escape the confines of village life. I managed to persuade dad to buy me an old Morris 1000 for my birthday and six months later, having passed the driving test first time, I was free. Have car and drums; drummer will travel.

A word of advice for dads: never, ever, attempt to teach your son to drive. My first and last driving lesson from my father lasted all of four hundred yards on a deserted country lane. After only five minutes starting and stalling, he yelled in panic and rage, "Stop the car and move over, you will never, ever, learn to drive; you have no aptitude whatsoever!" Thereafter I relied on my friends Terry Roberts and Pete Haynes to instruct me, which they did willingly. Thankfully, both were natural teachers. However, Terry lived about a mile from my house and after a late-night driving lesson, quite reasonably, he expected me to drop him off first, before slowly and gingerly driving myself home, unaccompanied.

On passing the test I arranged to meet my instructors to buy them a drink in the Red Lion to celebrate my success. Sitting by the fire enjoying a pint with his wife was PC Fox. He said hello as I was ordering at the bar, and then exclaimed, "Congratulations John, your success is partly down to me, you can buy us both a drink too." Puzzled, I responded, "Certainly Terry, but how did you help?" "Simple, on at least three occasions I turned a blind eye to you driving home alone after dropping him (pointing to Terry Roberts) in Stane Street Close." As our local bobby, Terry Fox was a star.

The test itself was a very strange experience. The examiner arrived fifteen minutes late at the Broadwater test centre and in torrential rain we drove towards Worthing Pier. Within a minute a ten-year-old girl stepped from the pavement, right in front of my car. I was probably only travelling at twenty miles an hour when I slammed on the brakes, narrowly avoiding what could well have been a very serious accident. The examiner, in an era before seatbelts, smashed his head against the windscreen and a large egg-shaped bump quickly grew on his forehead. Shaken, he ordered me to drive on and mumbled something about my emergency stop being of 'textbook standard'. As the heavy rain turned into hail we drove to the pier roundabout and then headed back towards Broadwater.

After less than ten minutes we pulled up in the test centre car park. My examiner then turned to me and asked, "Can you do a three-point-turn, reverse round a corner and do you know the Highway Code?" Before I could reply he said, "Of course you can, can, and do. Many congratulations Mr Madell, you have passed without one single fault." He then signed his carbonated notebook, tore off the top copy and handed it to me, shook my hand and wandered back to his office rubbing his forehead. I sat in the car park in a daze and can only liken my helpful examiner to the Australian who always answered his own questions:

'What colour do you like, Blue?'
'What's your name, Sheila?'
'Have you a favourite hobby, Sport?'
'What job do you do, Digger?'

As one of just a few car owners in my age group, my mates often called on me to drive them to parties, night clubs and favourite bars in the nearby towns. They paid for the petrol and my soft drinks. Free nights out; alcohol free! Consequently, for three or four years I drank very little. For me, drinking started in earnest when I joined Gripperrods International.

The company had a drinking culture from the chairman down. As office manager I was very much linchpin between manufacturing, distribution and sales, and invited to all company functions, both casual and official. It did not help that following an after-work session with sales representatives and the female office staff, I could always jump on a train home from the nearby Horsham station. Yet I had two golden rules: no drinking before 6pm; and however bad the hangover I might inflict on myself, I would always be at my desk fifteen minutes before the official start time the next morning.

From the age of twenty-four I was already a disciplined drinker, which, sadly, I still am. The days at Gripperrods were fast and furious. The managing director was a real shit of a man who delighted in finding fault where there was no fault and viciously reprimanding me in front of my staff. By 6pm I had 'earned' a drink and always found time for a couple of pints; but to award sterling work with a drink is a big mistake. Without doubt there were very few occasions when John Madell did not deserve a drink. Has drink had a detrimental impact on my life? Yes and no; at work: no, socially: no. In my relationships: yes! In my health: I guess only time will tell.

I had two great drinking buddies, both of whom are now dead. Over-imbibing cost Wayne his life. Indirectly, the demon drink killed Brian. Both were fabulous company and I miss them terribly.

Brian, a quick-witted raconteur, was always a joy to be with. I was vaguely aware of him at The Weald School, yet as two years my junior I only really made friends with him when he turned up at the Red Lion one evening. Brian soon became one of the crowd who met twice a week from nine o'clock onwards. Like me he was a keen squash player and very soon there were four of us who played on a regular basis.

Brian was an only child and lived with his old eccentric parents in the next-door village of Fittleworth. The three of them lived in a tied bungalow on a large private estate where his mum was the housekeeper and his dad the general factotum. The owners were retired and only too happy to grant Brian exclusive use of the concrete squash court sited in the woods to the rear of the main house. Here we whiled away many hours, often playing doubles. The one disadvantage to a concrete floor was shoe wear. Within a few months I had purchased four pairs of trainers before switching to the old-fashioned inch-thick bumpers sometimes referred to as 'brothel creepers'; they lasted for well over a year.

Practice, they say, makes perfect and in time we all became very good at the game. Back in the early Seventies, squash was a rich man's sport, due mainly to the lack of public courts; as a result we played matches against those privileged to have access to a private court. Venues included Chantry Lane in Storrington and Knepp Castle, West Grinstead.

A London stockbroker, Douglas Binden-Howe, nicknamed 'wind and bowel', also drank in the Red Lion from time to time; he eventually recognised our enthusiasm for the game and challenged me to a match. "Think you are good at squash John, then play me for a wager; shall we say best of five games for a crate of Scotch?" he said, loudly enough for the whole bar to hear. Doug claimed he was the undefeated Sussex squash champion and laid claim to many achievements, which we all took with a pinch of salt. I was twenty-four years old and at my peak fitness, whereas Doug was ten years older and a couple of stone too heavy; I accepted the challenge.

There was no question he was a very accomplished player and took the first two games. However, I had guessed correctly, Doug was not fit and over the next three games I ran him into the ground. "Play fair and pay up," I said. "Don't worry, I will see you in the Lion during the week," he replied. As I had expected, I never received the dozen bottles of whisky. After a month or so he left one bottle for me behind the bar. We never saw Doug again; although we did hear through the grapevine that he was struck off the Stock Exchange Register for insider trading.

One night at the pub Ron Swann came up with the idea of a trip away for all those who wished to go. Ten of us were up for a four-day-break abroad. We plumped for Majorca and Ron made the arrangements: just £20 each, half-board in a four-star hotel in Magaluf. Amazingly, not one of us had experienced plane travel before we set off for the sunny Spanish island. Well, it would have been sunny had it not been the month of January. Package holidays were in their infancy back in 1973 and when the plane landed at Palma Airport spontaneous applause broke out, accompanied by the odd cry of 'Nice one Cyril'.

I was allocated to share with Brian and when we arrived in our room we found a complimentary bottle of wine. Brian took one swig and decided the wine was only fit to be used as a shampoo, and promptly washed his hair with it. Even though the unheated pool was on the chilly side, we took a dip. Standing on the poolside Brian turned to me and said, "Do you think ice and lemon has been added?" I replied, "Without doubt." With great style Brian dived in.

The 'in crowd' had a great time, with visits to nightclubs, beach football and coach excursions being a few of the entertainments we managed to cram into the short holiday. Street traders attempting to sell watches, dolls and other unwanted items constantly hustled us. Leaning up against a beach bar one afternoon we were approached by an itinerant cobbler who offered to sole and heel shoes, Brian agreed a price and to our amazement the Spaniard proceeded to undertake the task while Brian was still wearing them. Incredibly, the man did a good job.

Our last night on the island was set aside for paella and flamenco dancing somewhere in the capital city of Palma. Brian and I picked up a couple of Welsh ladies. Attractive, yet not in the first flush of youth; to be kind, let us say they were in their forties. We moved from the event to a nearby nightclub. I guess we had been in the club for about an hour when a photographer approached the four of us and invited us to have our picture taken. I waved him away for obvious reasons; but not to be discouraged, he took the photo regardless of our protestations. Sometime later he returned with the developed picture and asked for payment. I told him politely that we had not ordered the photo; we did not want the photo, and please go away. He then became agitated and loudly demanded money. Standing on no ceremony Brian told him to fuck off. Instantly, the Spanish photographer produced a flick-knife and menacingly held it under Brian's nose. Clearly, the man had a very good understanding of the English language. Had I not been trapped in the middle of a half-round bench seat I may well have made a run for it. As cool as a cucumber, Brian said to his potential assailant: "I do not want the photograph, nor do I wish to buy your knife, so as I previously requested, fuck off." The Spaniard did just that.

Needless to say we decided that it was time to leave, Brian disappeared with Gwen and I returned to the hotel alone. Our party arrived at the airport at nine for the ten o'clock flight. No sign of Brian though. After the last call I figured he had decided to stay behind with Gwen. Having taken my seat next to the empty one, we awaited take-off. Suddenly, Brian appeared from nowhere. "You certainly cut that fine mate; I think we need a drink," I said as he sat down. With that comment in mind Brian reached into his inside jacket pocket and produced a full glass of gin and tonic, complete with ice and lemon, and handed it to me. "Be my guest," he said, smiling.

As a postscript to the break away, we subsequently discovered that having booked ten places Ron received one free. Brian, Tony Haley and I hit upon a practical joke to get even with Ron. We decided to place the following advertisement in a local newspaper: 'Good home wanted for two-tone Welsh-speaking parrot, breaks ice at parties. Apply (Ron's phone number)'. Two days later the advert appeared in the paper. A feature article in a subsequent edition explained that Ron's mother had received calls from many people who said they had seen the advertisement and were interested in the Welsh-speaking parrot. She didn't understand what was going on until she realised that it was a practical joke. Aware that Ron had been on holiday in January with friends, she also knew that he had caused a bit of a stir one day at the hotel when he imitated a parrot, and had everyone searching for it. Altogether, there were twenty calls about the non-existent bilingual bird; she said she could have made a fortune had such a polly existed! I think Ron got the message.

Shortly after we returned from our trip abroad Brian's father was arrested and charged with the theft of wine and spirits from the local grocery shop and was sentenced to six months, which he served at Ford Open Prison. Brian was mortified and his heavy drinking was fast becoming out of control. Very soon he was running up massive debts and using one credit card to pay off another. Then along came Jane.

Jane was loud, fat and common; the total opposite of Brian who was well-spoken, slim, with a highly subtle turn of phrase. The two were the ultimate mismatch. As a close friend I was just about able to ask, why? "John, I'm barely hanging on to my sanity, I desperately need somebody to love." Six months later they were married and Brian dropped off the radar, although I did hear a few years later that they had had two children. Well before his thirty-fifth birthday he connected a hosepipe to the exhaust of his car and committed suicide.

Twice a week, after work, I would pop into Findon Village for a couple of pints either in The Gun or the Village House. I think it was about 1990 that I first met Wayne and Penny. I noticed them standing at the bus stop in the pouring rain and stopped to offer them a lift. Having previously seen the pair of them in the Village House, I suspected that like me they were headed for the pub.

From that day on I became firm friends with Wayne and Penny. Wayne was about my age and Penny ten years his junior. Wayne, bald with a ruddy complexion, a little less than six feet tall and carrying well over twenty stone, would certainly have been a handsome man in his younger days, but the drink had taken its toll. Thankfully, we never bought one another drinks as Wayne could, as a conservative estimate, down five pints to my two in the hour I spent at the pub.

Like so many of my generation, he had left school on his fifteenth birthday and signed indentures for a five-year plumbing apprenticeship. At twenty-one he started his own business, first working as a site sub-contractor and later moving into domestic plumbing and heating. By the time I met Wayne he was property-developing. As we both worked in the building industry we had a great deal in common and were able to offer one another mutual advice and moral support. Wayne was a brash, and sometimes, abrasive fellow who, if he did not like someone did not hesitate to tell them so. Consequently he had both friends and enemies in the local community. To all appearances Wayne seemed brim full of confidence, yet I was sure there was a deep insecurity about the man.

One day, Penny told me that a teacher at his secondary school had told him that he was 'useless' and would most likely prove to be good for nothing in the world of work; these words, though possibly just a throwaway comment, haunted Wayne all his life. It just goes to prove how important it is to feed positive vibes to young minds. Wayne may have sunk to the C-stream at school, yet in 'the real world' he was a highly successful and astute operator. The standard of work he achieved when taking on a derelict property and almost magically producing a state-of-the-art refurbishment, was sublime. He would invite me to view the newly acquired wreck and delight, a few short months later, in my inspection of the finished article. Wayne usually undertook two projects a year; generally sell the property just before completion, and acquire another to move seamlessly on. Such a feat is not easily achieved.

Wayne's great passion was Findon Cricket Club or, perhaps more accurately, Findon Cricket Club bar. For years he ran the bar, which was open on match days and for various social events. Much like his business ventures, tight controls and astute management returned a handsome profit for the club when the takings were totted up at the end of the season. Somehow he talked me into making my company club sponsor, and me into being Vice Chairman of the club.

The cricket ground is situated a mile west of the village. Nestling a stone's throw away from the South Downs Way and within what is now the South Downs National Park, it is in one of the most picturesque settings in Sussex. With good facilities, three teams, and a thriving junior section I was delighted to play my part in a small administrative role for a few short years. The first team attracted the best local players and invariably won the league and, more often than not, produced an exciting cup run. In 2006 Findon was very narrowly beaten in the Village Cup Final at Lords.

In 2002, Anne, the wife of the local butcher, Steve Duffield, died of cancer. The following year Wayne, Penny, Steve, Ian Hart and I arranged a charity cricket match in memory of Anne and in aid of the local St Barnabas Hospice. Ian, the local undertaker and radio personality, agreed to raise a team of sports stars to play a Findon Cricket Club team. Six months prior to the day we earnestly set about organising the event. We decided that we would not charge admission but merely rely on the sale of programmes to be the main source of income. Each programme was numbered and there was to be a grand prize for the lucky number, to be drawn on the day. We felt the best way to promote the event was to visit the pubs and clubs in the Worthing area and sell programmes.

The very first attempt to make a sale was early one Friday night in Broadwater Conservative Club. After permission to approach the membership was granted by a committee member, I entered the main bar area and offered a programme to the nearest man; he violently pushed me to one side and told me to 'piss off'. Not the best start to our endeavours perhaps, although the other club members appeared shocked and embarrassed by the incident and not only did they all buy programmes, but also gave us a drink by way of apology. The culprit by then had been shamed into leaving the premises.

From then on, wherever we went we were well received, in fact many people wanted to talk about their deceased loved ones who had received palliative care at the hospice. The match was a great success with at least half a dozen of the local Brighton and Hove Albion footballers taking part. Steve and his son Matthew opened the batting and the event was finalised, after Findon had gained a narrow victory, by Ian conducting a charity auction on the pitch. Well over £10,000 was raised for St Barnabas.

How much drink could Wayne consume? If our visit to the Oval cricket ground was anything to go by, then it was something of a miracle that he actually celebrated his sixtieth birthday. I drove to Wimbledon and we caught an underground train to the Oval, where we arrived around midday. First stop, the bar; a Coke for me and a pint of bitter for Wayne. We had super seats; sitting next to us were a couple of lads in their early twenties and Wayne very soon befriended them. Wayne never moved, amazingly, not even to find the loo, while his two new buddies fetched and carried at least six more pints for his consumption. He had a charisma whereby people just happily did his bidding.

On the return journey we stopped off for a 'wet' and Wayne consumed another three pints. By the time we reached our local curry house, Anaz in Findon Valley, it was around 8pm. We enjoyed our meal – washed down with two bottles of wine and five or six large Cobra beers. By this time I no longer had to worry about driving, so my liquid intake now matched Wayne's. For a nightcap we visited the Caledonian Bar where Wayne moved on to spirits and consumed three double gin and tonics. I really can't say whether he had a drink after he walked home from the Valley Parade. Not for a moment during the twelve hours of drinking did my friend appear under the influence of alcohol, yet if his consumption was converted into units of alcohol, then they must have reached fifty. At that time the Government's recommended maximum safe limit for a man was twenty-four units per week.

In a mad moment, I agreed to a night out with Wayne and the landlord of a local pub. We met at the pub and the landlord elected to drive downtown. In Worthing we had a Thai meal and then moved across the road to the Hare and Hounds for their Tuesday jazz night. I do not recall how many pints we consumed; but by closing time I felt pretty much pissed. The fact that the publican was driving did not appear to limit his intake. When, a few minutes later, we climbed into the car, Wayne and I did not realise that we were about to experience a nightmare journey.

For the driver, one-way streets became two-ways, red lights were green, and either direction around roundabouts was good enough. We were travelling at sixty miles an hour at all times in a thirty limit, and I am certain we became completely airborne, 'Starsky and Hutch style', crossing over Broadwater Bridge. When the car pulled up outside Wayne's bungalow I quickly exited the car and told the landlord that I lived 'just around the corner'. The fact that I had a two-mile walk home was of no consequence. Thankfully, I was still in one piece and wished to remain that way.

I had many nights out with Wayne and Penny, sometimes accompanied by my wife Jean; laughter and fun were always on the menu, from start to finish.

One night in November 2005 Wayne complained of stomach pains. By January his complexion had turned grey and he was clearly in considerable pain. Hospital tests followed; by the summer, weight just fell off him and I was present when he suffered a massive stroke and was rushed into hospital. Three weeks later Wayne was dead. Officially, he died of stomach cancer; in reality, I am sure that it was alcohol that brought his life to a premature conclusion.

When my wife Jean and I attended an Alan Ayckbourn farce at the Connaught Theatre in Worthing in the early Noughties we decided to have a quick pre-performance drink in the theatre bar. Whilst queuing up I noticed a late-middle-aged man sitting close to the bar in a state of inebriation. He was being propped up and simultaneously chastened by his wife to whom he was making loud incoherent responses. Standing behind me in line was James Bolam a well-known TV actor, probably best remembered for his starring roles in *The Likely Lads* and *New Tricks*. I casually enquired if he was performing; he commented that he wasn't actually appearing that night but merely attending the performance to support a fellow-actor friend. When finally it was my turn to be served, and the barman asked me what I wanted, I pointed to the drunk and said, "I will have what he is drinking please." James Bolam tapped me on the shoulder and said, "Oh, I have always really wanted to say that!"

Though it may not be for me to moralise, or advise, I invite the reader to take his or her own view on the emotive subject of alcohol consumption.

Wide-eyed And Legless

Performer:	Andy Fairweather-Low
Composer:	Fairweather-Low
Number 6:	December 1975

Chapter 17 – Paul

Psalm 23:4
Even if I go through the deepest darkness,
I will not be afraid, LORD,
For you are with me.
Your shepherd's rod and staff protect me.

I guess that all those working on the beach who have responsibility for the safety of the general public, hope for the chance to save a life at least once during their career, whether it be by raising the alarm, actually fishing someone out of the water, or even performing resuscitation.

Curiously, my opportunity occurred at home in Elmer whilst looking out of the window, and not when I was on foreshore duty. It was very early one Sunday morning when I pulled the bedroom blinds and spotted a small open rowing boat drifting about fifty yards to the south of the coastal rock defences. At first it appeared to be empty, although there seemed to be some object on the floor of the vessel. I woke my wife Jan, and sleepily she rolled out of bed, found her glasses, and took a long look at the boat. "What can you see Jan, is that a body in the bottom of the boat?" I asked quizzically. "I can see something John, but I can't really tell; I will find the binoculars," Jan replied. We both looked long and hard through the high-powered glasses, yet still could not see clearly.

With the sea becoming increasingly choppy, I thought, if in doubt it is best to err on the side of caution. I looked at the clock on the wall and saw that it was just 6.30, and decided that as time was of the essence, I must call 999. "Which service do you require?" the operator asked. "Coastguard please," I replied, and was soon able to give the Solent Coastguard a description of what we could see, together with other pertinent details: location, the sea condition, and my name, address and phone number. "Thank you sir, I will call out the Littlehampton Lifeboat."

I know some of the lifeboat crew and regardless of the time, the day or weather conditions I am aware that they really do relish a call, especially if someone may be in a life-threatening situation.

I stayed on the line to the Coastguard to give an eyewitness account of proceedings and redirect the lifeboat should they miss their target. Within fifteen minutes they had sighted the tiny boat and the Coastguard reported to me that a body was clearly visible. Sure enough, I could see that a couple of the crew were transferring what appeared to be a man into the lifeboat. The duty coastguard then said, "They have recovered a middle-aged man who is alive but hypothermic; I'm going off the line now to call the paramedics and will phone you back when he is transferred to the ambulance, many thanks, goodbye."

Twenty minutes later he did call back and said that the man, although in a bad way, was expected to make a full recovery and my call had undoubtedly saved his life. The coastguard then asked me to keep an eye on the empty boat until the lifeboat returned to recover it, which in due course it did. The moral of this tale is that if you happen to be in a similar position, always make the emergency call; the authorities will not mind in the least if it turns out to be a false alarm. Far better safe than sorry!

One Friday in the spring of 1996 my son Paul was struck, accidentally, by a medicine ball in the gymnasium at Durrington High School, and knocked out. He was taken to Shoreham Hospital where he fell into a deep coma and for four days it was touch and go whether he would actually pull through. I vividly remember that on the following Sunday morning in church, the guest minister never found the pulpit, as our pastor Graham Jefferson, invited me to share my concerns for Paul's plight, and subsequently the congregation became fixed on prayer and intercession on behalf of my son.

When Paul awoke his personality had completely changed: putting it bluntly, he had turned into a raving lunatic. From Southlands Hospital, Shoreham, Paul was transferred to a hospital in south London where he underwent extensive tests for brain damage. The diagnosis was not good: the medical notes stated that he was suffering from paranoid schizophrenia. I cannot describe the pain and soul-searching that Jean and I suffered over this dark period in our lives.

Paul was once again transferred, this time to the adolescent secure unit in the Chalkhill part of the Princess Royal Hospital in Haywards Heath, where he was to remain for the next nine weeks, under the care of Dr Venables. During this time, a suitable drug was found to stabilise Paul's disturbed condition; the voices in his head disappeared and gradually we were once again able to communicate with our son in a reasoned manner. When he finally returned home Paul's memory, and indeed his vocabulary, had dramatically diminished. Our fifteen-year-old was like an eight- or nine-year-old child. A couple of months passed by and Paul relapsed and once again returned to Chalkhill for further treatment; coincidentally, spending another nine weeks in the hospital. The doctor tried various medications and eventually found Clozaril to be the most effective. Once again Paul returned home, and to school this time, dropping down a year. During the early part of his illness our son had missed vital school exams and two football cup finals, one for the school team and the other for Rustington Otters.

Slowly but surely, Paul's mental health improved although when, eventually, he did take his GCSEs, the results bore no resemblance to his original expectations. Paul left school with no qualifications and enrolled on a two-year catering course at Worthing College of Further Education. With a great deal of love, prayer and help from both my family and church, Paul very gradually shook off the demons that tormented him. His mum spent many a long hour teaching him the meaning of everyday words that the illness had inexplicably removed from his memory.

He secured a job in the kitchen at Goring Hall Hospital where he remained for five years. During this period in his life Paul learnt to drive, passed his test and slowly, slowly recovered. Frustrated by his lack of progress and opportunity at the hospital, Paul applied for and secured a part-time job at the Post Office and after a six-month trial period, became a full-time postman in 2003.

At the same time that he started at the Post Office, Paul met Soumely, a midwife, whom he married in 2005 and his recovery continued to improve, partly thanks to Soumely's patience, calming influence and medical insight. The couple bought a semi-detached house in West Worthing and soon Holly, Shannon and Josiah arrived on the scene to fill the family home.

Paul's recovery has been quite remarkable, confounding the medical profession's preconceptions about schizophrenia. When the terrible diagnosis was made we were told that our son was very unlikely to ever work or form a meaningful relationship, let alone marry. Paul's great determination to overcome an illness with such an awful stigma, and God's influence through the power of prayer, added up to an amazing story of recovery against all odds.

My son has asked me tell his story to encourage all those suffering from such a debilitating mental illness to stay positive, be patient and anticipate a full recovery. His brothers and I fully expect that now Paul is nearly back to normal, he will continue to progress and surprise us with bigger and better achievements over the coming years – watch this space.

Despite all the doom and gloom surrounding the early days of Paul's illness there were two or three amusing incidents that momentarily lightened the darkness. I was invited to attend Littlehampton Football Club's ground to watch the cup final that Paul would have appeared in for the Rustington Otters' under-sixteens eleven. The Otters lost 2-1 with both goals conceded by poor right-side defending; the team manager and I agreed that had Paul been playing in defence that evening, the likely outcome might well have been very different.

At the end of the game after the cup had been presented to the winners, both teams lined up for each member to receive a commemorative medal. To my surprise, Neil, the manager of our team, told me to join the end of the line to receive Paul's medal. The cup organisers, on hearing of Paul's serious illness, had decided to award him a medal even though he did not take part in the final; it seemed to me to be a very kind and touching gesture. When my son's name was called out I proudly walked forward and shook hands with the chairman of the junior section of the Sussex Football Association who, as he handed me the gong, smiled and said, "I have heard of over-age players Mr Madell, but I think you are stretching the rule a little too far."

At the secure unit in Haywards Heath hospital Paul was surrounded by teenage girls with various issues, one of which included anorexia. These girls, who apart from the obvious symptoms of their illness, seemed quite normal, were keen to help Paul (a good-looking lad) through his dark moments. He, in turn, was only too happy to help them make their food disappear! Joking aside, I do believe that understanding one another's mental disorder can prove to be extremely therapeutic.

Over the two periods that Paul spent under close surveillance he was physically restrained on a number of occasions. The male nurses had a remit to prevent self-harm and if a patient 'kicked off' they had no alternative other than to calm down, hold down, and even, tie Paul down. A staff member told me that they knew my son was in a bad way as Paul continued to insist that Brighton and Hove Albion Football Club were the current Premier League Champions. Deluded indeed!

Paul is a fanatical Albion supporter; likewise, to a greater or lesser extent, all my other sons; and I must take some of the blame for the longevity of their support for our local football league team. I dragged them all along to the Goldstone ground when they reached an age when ninety minutes of football would hold their attention. When it comes to the Albion I could easily write a book on the 1,000 or so games I have witnessed both at home, away, and on neutral grounds, including three visits to the old Wembley Stadium. The reader will be very pleased to know that I am inclined to avoid that trap, although I am going to relate a couple of strange occurrences with regard to Brighton and Hove Albion.

In the mid-Eighties my colleague Charles and I occasionally received a call from the Albion Commercial Manager, Ron Pavey, to advise us that there were spare tickets available on the plane that he had privately chartered for away games up north. If we were free, we joined the directors, manager, players and John Vinicombe, the Evening Argus sports writer, on the journey which was generally to a mid-week fixture. As my company had for some years paid for an advertising board behind both goals, I had a good rapport with Ron, and that was the reason for the invitation.

Flying out of Gatwick to a provincial airport we normally arrived two or three hours before the game, and enjoyed an early dinner at a local hotel together with John and the club's board of directors, before catching a coach to the away ground with the players. Upon arrival, the team headed off to find the away dressing room whilst we made for the bar before taking our seats in the Directors' Box. A glamourous trip if we went to Anfield or Old Trafford, a little less so Oakwell, the home of Barnsley, on a cold wet Tuesday evening. Charles and I became familiar travelling companions to the Albion contingent.

One morning in 1986 I was sitting at my desk when I received a call from Bryan Bedson the club chairman. "Hello John, would you and Charles join me for lunch in the boardroom next Saturday when we are playing Blackburn Rovers. If you could arrive early I have a proposition to run past you both, let us say 11.30am, OK?" the main man requested. "Sounds all right by me; I will check Charles's availability and confirm later today Bryan," I responded. When I finally caught up with Charles, he said excitedly, "We are on the way up John; maybe they are going to invite us to join the board!"

When we arrived at The Goldstone Ground that Saturday morning we were greeted with great deference by Bert Smith: "Honoured guests, the chairman has asked me to take you up to the boardroom without delay, follow me gentlemen." As we were walking up the stairs I said, "We have met before Bert, you are looking very well." Bert replied, "When was that sir?" "Many years ago Bert; it is lovely to see you again after all this time." (Twenty-five years previously, Bert had thrown Denis and me out of the ground on a number of occasions after finding us illicitly walking the corridors under the West Stand in search of the players' autographs.)

Fortunately, before he could delve deeper into our past, Charles and I were greeted by Bryan Bedson, who immediately introduced us to the senior partner of a local architectural practice. "Gentleman, we are planning on erecting a new stand and I understand that you may be willing to fund the project?" Bryan said enthusiastically. Before we could comment the Blackburn Rovers contingent turned up and Bryan went outside to greet their directors alighting from the team coach. "What on earth have you told them Charles?" I exclaimed, prodding my business partner in the ribs. Charles replied sheepishly, "Nothing, absolutely nothing; I know nothing."

On his day, Charles could 'spruce' for England so I suspected he was not being entirely honest. "Well you have certainly done it this time, how on earth are we going to wriggle out of this?" I whispered tersely in his ear. "John, Charles, come and meet the boys from Blackburn," Bryan called over from the bar, and we did the rounds of the opposition's board of directors before sitting down to enjoy a three-course lunch. I sat next to Jack Warner who was later to fund Blackburn's rise to win the Premiership in 1995. "Very well done John; Bryan tells me you are going to provide a new stand for the Albion which is the same thing I'm about to do at Ewood Park, I think we have a duty to help our local club as best we can," he said sincerely. I responded sheepishly, "I am sure you are right Jack." Lunch completed, we sat and watched a boring 1-1 draw from the Directors' Box and then returned to the boardroom for after-match tea and biscuits.

Amazingly, nothing more was said about the 'stand', although on our departure Bryan indicated he would ring me later in the week, which he duly did. "Sorry we were unable to complete our little bit of business last Saturday; briefly, we plan to build a stand for the disabled to provide cover for those in wheelchairs and I know that both you and Charles have handicapped sons. The supporters club has raised half the money; could your company, by way of sponsorship, please provide the other half which will be in the region of £2,000?" I quickly responded, "Bryan, delighted, I will send you a cheque, just let me have a receipt." Bryan replied, "No problem, many thanks. We will invite you to an opening ceremony when the work has been completed, bye-bye." Charles and I had envisaged a multi-tier state-of-the-art stand, but this would only be a lean-to to house a dozen wheelchairs and their owners, what a relief; £2,000 was cheap and what's more, within our limited budget for advertising.

Having established ourselves and our company as a 'main' sponsor of the Albion, I arranged a golf day between the company and the club to be played at West Chiltington Golf Club on an annual basis. The 1990 event was in aid of Steve Gatting's testimonial fund and, as usual, we defeated the footballers. Steve played for Arsenal, Brighton and Charlton Athletic, and made over 300 appearances in the Albion defence. Charles and I played Steve and his brother, the then England and Middlesex cricket captain, Mike Gatting. I think our match was a draw. We had a fun-filled day, with Mike striking the ball a country mile, yet rarely in the right direction, and regaling us with stories of England's Test tours which had fortunately escaped the attention of the press.

Curiously, Charles resembled the Gatting brothers in height, weight and facial appearance and when the wife of the golf club's owner asked for their autographs, Steve and Mike were only too pleased to sign the menu and pose for a photograph. "Come on Charles, join in; your mother must be very proud of the three of you," the lady said, smiling. Charles obligingly added his signature alongside those of Mike and Steve, autographing the menu: 'Best Wishes, Charlie Gatting'!

I have enjoyed what is, effectively, an all-of-life-relationship with the Albion. Imagine my feelings when, a couple of years later, I was approached by a board member who had been sent to sound me out to ascertain whether I would be interested in becoming a director. After due consideration, I gracefully declined that most tempting opportunity.

Rescue Me
Performer: Fontella Bass
Composer: Milner, Smith and Bass
Number 11:   Released December 1965

Chapter 18 – Charles

Proverbs 23:4
Be wise enough not to wear yourself out trying to get rich. Your money can be gone in a flash, as if it had grown wings and flown away like an eagle.

Littlehampton Golf Club's eighteen-hole course is situated next to the west bank of the Arun and is offered some protection from the wind and sea by the sand dunes on West Beach. It is a quality links course and a true test of golf, even to a scratch player on a wild and windy winter's day. To a hopeless hacker like me, this game is best reserved for a calm summer's evening.

I once played a round on the course with Brian Barnes, the Ryder Cup player best remembered for beating Jack Nicholas twice in one day. When Brian and I tackled the long par five, he demonstrated how to cut a ball through the wind by taking a one-iron off both the tee and then the fairway to reach the green in two. I think it most unlikely there is a present-day top-ten golfer who could achieve that result with such an old-fashioned club; indeed a joy to behold. Not so, the three putts that followed!

To reach West Beach the public can either walk over the slide-bridge situated adjacent to The Arun View Inn, or take a three-mile road trip. Dave Strong and I normally drive to this part of our patch once a week as our beach buggy can just squeeze through the slide-bridge chicane.

At the end of Rope Walk a large public car park and West Beach Café can be found on the site of the former Redoubt fort, built in 1854 to protect the mouth of the port from potential French invasion. The five-gun defence never saw action and the fort was decommissioned some twenty years later; now dilapidated and overgrown, it can be viewed from a wooden walkway winding through the sand dunes. Once we have unlocked the gate allowing vehicle access to the beach and crossed the pebbled area (created twenty-five years ago to prevent erosion of the beautiful dunes) we can, at low tide, drop down onto the vast sands. It is a truly wonderful sandy beach stretching from the West Works on the

Arun estuary to the rocks at Middleton-on-Sea, a distance of just under three miles.

Part of the sand dunes behind the café is protected as a Site of Special Scientific Interest, and is fenced off to preserve the rare plants and wildlife. The unrestricted dune area covers an area of just under a mile and, in places, up to forty yards wide, providing a natural windbreak and suntrap. The area has for many years been popular with naturists, who are not a problem in themselves provided the participants use discretion. Sadly, more recently, the dunes have been unofficially advertised on the internet as a gay beach, which has caused the authorities some concern.

With families keen to spend time at this beauty spot, we have been asked by the police to regularly patrol and discourage overt nudity and any inappropriate behaviour; consequently, Dave and I are less than comfortable riding West Beach solo. The sound of our beach buggy driving over the pebbles will disturb any activity that may be taking place, and usually, the all-male inhabitants pop up like meerkats from behind the long grass at the sound of our engine.

On one notable occasion, a rather 'over-excited' naked man exposed all. Startled by this bizarre sight, Dave stood on the passenger seat and waving the broomstick he generally carries on this patrol, bellowed at the individual, "Pull up your trousers, you dirty bastard!" This intrusion caused the naked man to instantly drop to the ground behind a dune. I turned to my colleague and said, "Don't hold back Dave; tell him exactly how you feel." The reason why my colleague carries a broom handle only when visiting West Beach has always been something of a mystery to me, and I guess is best not pondered for too long.

A few weeks later Dave and I were in the self-same spot clearing rubbish into black sacks when a couple in their early sixties slowly walked up to us. "My husband is diabetic and I think he's drifting, can you help please?" the worried lady requested. Being familiar with the condition, having witnessed my best friend Dave Brown slump over on more than one occasion in desperate need of a sugar hit, I quickly helped him into the passenger seat. Fixing the belt I said, "Hang on tight, I will get you to West Beach Café in less than ten minutes." His wife insisted on coming, and Dave and I helped her into the back of the pick-up buggy.

Our activity had attracted the attention of the 'meerkat population' with at least a dozen heads popping up above the sand dunes, and just as I was about to pull away Dave said, "Don't leave me here John." Well, with the mountain of rubbish we had collected, there was insufficient room for two in the back. I called back as I drove away, "Don't worry Dave, I will return as soon as possible." Dave was alone and surrounded by not only what he perceived to be his worst childhood nightmares, but also a beach community he had previously persecuted.

Helping the diabetic into the café, I told his wife he would be fine as soon as he had taken some sugar, and left him with a Mars bar and sweet tea. I had visions of Dave bravely fending off hordes of meerkats with his trusty broomstick. Twenty minutes later I found him just where I had left him. "Are you all right mate?" "Yes John, but no thanks to you," he snorted pointing to the sand dunes, "they crowded round me, and then offered me a cup of tea!" "That was kind Dave," I replied, trying desperately not to laugh.

Another 'exposure moment' happened within fifty yards of my office. Disturbing my tea break, a rather prissy schoolmistress arrived at the office in a particular state of fluster. "I need you to do something quickly," she exclaimed. "How can I help madam?" I responded. "I… I have in my charge a large class of eight- and nine-year-old boys and sitting on the beach right next to us is a topless female sunbathing; I will show you, follow me." Always one to help, especially under these circumstances, I duly followed the troubled lady. Sure enough, next to the third groyne I found a cluster of boys pointing, whispering and sniggering. Their reason for amusement: a rather plump lady just a few yards away, semi-naked and seemingly oblivious to the commotion she was causing. Tits up, so to speak!

As it happens I had noticed, by chance, the same individual about an hour earlier, and long before the school party arrived. I turned to the teacher and said, "It is not an offence to sunbathe topless on the beach and in fact she was here first, so perhaps you chose the wrong spot to park your class." The teacher, who bore a close resemblance to Peggy Mount (who often played formidable mother-in-law types in Fifties B-movies), was singularly unimpressed by my observations and I therefore decided to back-pedal. "However, I will, under the circumstances, politely ask the lady to cover up." By this time the topless lady had spotted my uniform and promptly attached her bikini top. I thanked her for her discretion and returned to Peggy and commented, "All's well that ends well madam." No thanks were expected, or received.

I have always wanted to be my own boss and never, ever felt at ease 'working for the man'. The sixty-four-thousand-dollar question is, when to start? The right time for me was when I felt comfortable enough with myself to kick off a business in an industry, of which I had in-depth knowledge, and was aware that there was a gap in the market a new company might squeeze into.

Sir Stanley Matthews, with John Madell and Charles Boughton-Leigh, both of whom are clearly overawed by the presence of the great man.

When Charles Boughton-Leigh and I jointly made the decision to jump in the deep end, we both had a wife and four children to support. So with twelve mouths to feed, the economy on the rocks and neither of us with a spare penny to invest, we might have appeared quite mad to tender our resignations. Yet we both wanted to have a go, and there was indeed a market that we could harness our experience to.

The senior management of the Marley Tile Company, where we both worked, were disillusioned with the cumbersome contracting business and keen to concentrate resources in production, wholesale and retail. I had recently transferred to running the supply-only business in the south out of the head office at Sevenoaks, and was conveniently situated next door to Charles who covered the same territory for the contracting division.

When my director informed me that contracting in our region would be closed within a year, and moreover, the existing business would be transferred to preferred contractors to maintain production volumes, the scene was set. "Charles, *we* shall be the preferred contractor for Sussex; what do you think?" I said excitedly in his office one late afternoon in June 1982. As we had both toyed with the idea over the previous eighteen months Charles knew this was an opportunity not to be missed: "OK John, let's do it." However, one hurdle needed to be overcome. The process of purchasing product was effectively cartel-led by the two main manufacturers: Marley and Redland. There was no way that we could become a preferred contractor without a trading history and, of course, we had no trading history: catch-22!

Not quite catch-22 though. John Elms, an old acquaintance in the industry who ran a very small roofing contracting business called Cobsen-Davies Contractors Ltd from his dining room, had long-standing accounts with both suppliers. What is more, John had approached me to join him with a view to me taking over his business when he was due to retire, within the next twelve months. Consequently, Charles and I met John in his office/dining room and agreed to set up a parallel business, provided Marley were happy to support the arrangement.

Charles and I made an appointment to see our immediate bosses to tender our resignations. Waiting in the hallowed hall outside the boardroom the very next day we felt like two naughty schoolboys waiting to see the headmaster. In this instance the head was the grandson of the founder, Company Chairman Trevor Aisher, together with Managing Director John Witt (Charles's boss), and Sales Director Russell Day (my boss). When we unveiled our plan they shook our hands, wished us well, and promised us their full support. They were true to their word; we kept our company cars for a couple of months and were quoted, in writing, very favourable terms including sixty days unlimited credit. We were, understandably, immediately relieved of our duties and as we walked down the corridor and into the unknown Charles turned to me and complained in a forlorn voice, "Oh dear, I thought they would offer me another £1000 a year to stay on." I thought, typical, and replied, "Somehow Charles, I think you have missed the point. Come on, let's get started."

As I had been planning a move for at least a year and was by this time hyped-up and raring to go, I had already built an office in the garden and cleared the double garage to store felt, batten and ancillary items. John Elms lent us a spare pickup truck. We immediately incorporated Cobsen-Davies Roofing Ltd as the sister company to Cobsen-Davies Contractors Ltd, set up a bank account and quickly made contact with our potential customer base. Curiously, the manager of Littlehampton's NatWest Bank was most accommodating, extending us a £25,000 facility merely requesting joint guarantees from the three of us. As we walked back to the car park, John winked and said, "He turned down Anita Roddick's request for a £4,000 loan to set up The Body Shop and was not about to make the same mistake again."

We started on 1 July 1982 and by the end of August had secured and completed a couple of jobs. We hit breakeven by October month end. In our first financial year we turned over £680,000 with a gross profit return of 21% showing a small net profit and a positive cash flow. My wife Jean placed an advert in the local paper to sell a pair of curtains, just as we started our first week in business. As we were also using our house phone number for the company, all we received in our first week of trading were numerous enquiries for curtains, which I am sure we could have sold twenty times over. Sod the curtains; all we really wanted was roofing work.

By Christmas it was very clear that we needed separate premises for the business, so we rented a small unit in Dominion Road, Broadwater; within a year we had outgrown this corner plot. Early in 1984 we purchased a shop, with a flat above, in Goring, which served us very well for the next five years.

One of the first jobs we undertook was for a Mr Bull at Fontwell on a plot situated the other side of the A27 immediately opposite the racecourse. The job was new build, a substantial four-bedroomed house with a plain tile roof, for which we quoted in the region of £10,000 to supply and fix. George Bull's appearance and persona exactly fitted his name: in his early forties and slightly overweight, he was a powerfully built man though rather squat. With just a hint of aggression he whispered in a gruff voice, "Pop over next Monday and I will pay you the £5,000 deposit." Obviously a didicoy; as I knew they only dealt in cash and George had almost too readily agreed the quoted price, the alarm bells should have started to ring.

When Charles and I arrived the following week George invited us into the caravan that he, his wife and children were living in while the new house was being constructed. The caravan was perhaps fifteen years old yet beautifully decked out with tasteful *objets d'art*; all four walls had high fitted shelves to show off a magnificent set of hand-painted china plates depicting Romany scenes. When I commented on the *décor,* Mrs Bull proudly proclaimed that they had commissioned the plates to be painted to their specification. Over tea George counted out 500 ten-pound notes and handed them to Charles. "When the job is complete I will pay you the other half of the money, again in cash."

Well, the job went according to programme and I phoned George to arrange to collect the money. "We are very happy with the roof, come over at 6pm on Friday to collect your money. Upon arrival a distraught Mrs Bull greeted us. She was standing next to the burnt-out frame of the caravan. "Oh Mr John, Mr Charles, all my worldly possessions have gone." As she sighed, George appeared from inside the partly completed house. "What's more, I am very sad to say that I had just drawn out your £5,000 from the bank and that too went up in smoke," said George, and added, "I just don't know what to say." "I'm sure you don't," retorted Charles sarcastically, "you will just have to find another £5,000 to pay us with; we shall be back the same time next week to collect our money."

Both Charles and I had dealt with didicoys for long enough to know that it was very, very unlikely that we would ever see the money, but legally, as the tiles were fully fitted they were now his property. Week in, week out, we called Mr Bull to no avail, and through investigation discovered that he was the subject of umpteen County Court Judgements. Three months passed by and we knew, along with dozens of other creditors, that George Bull had indeed bumped us. A very hard pill to swallow in such an early stage of our business venture.

Just when we had given up all hope, Bull phoned: "Mr Charles, I have your money, please come over at 5pm tomorrow to collect it." Somewhat in disbelief we arrived, and at once Mrs Bull invited us into the now completed house and showed us into the lounge where George Bull was seated. "Gentlemen it is such a pleasure to see you both," he said gripping our hands tightly, "here is all the money I owe you," Bull said, and promptly presented a brown envelope to Charles. "No need to count it, and I will tell you for why," he said, and then continued, "my wife and I saw you in Montague Street last Saturday together with your twin Down's syndrome boys. Well us type don't do people with handicapped children. Sorry you had to wait for your money; we had no ideas of your family circumstances." Tongue in cheek, Charles responded, "Well George, how about an extra £1,000 for our lost interest? What you don't know is that John also has a handicapped son." "Sorry, can't do Mr Charles, we only received £5,000 from the insurance." As we left Charles pointed to the main wall in the lounge and winked at George, "Your unique plates look grand, set in your new home, good evening." I wonder how George Bull's long list of creditors would have viewed his ability to 'keep the plates up'!

By the end of the first couple of years in business we had made a good profit and continued to rapidly expand throughout the Eighties: more contracts, more staff and more vehicles. Charles ran the administration and I looked after the contracts. We shared the selling, both having good contacts, and between us secured enough work to cover our overheads and continued to turn in a healthy profit. By the end of the decade we had opened six branches in the South East of England and set up separate premises to facilitate the administration and computerised systems. Our £10,000,000 turnover, with a high nett margin, made us the largest independent roofing contractor in the country. In addition, we had set up a Roofing Supplies Depot in Horsham Station's old rolling-stock yard.

One of the keys to our success was the ongoing support of our main suppliers who crucially provided substantial discounts, annual rebates and extended credit terms, without which we would have been unable to finance the rapid expansion. Steetley who owned vast clay pits in the West Midlands were not one of our biggest suppliers of roof tiles, but were without question our best supporter. With premium products to offer, Charles and I often met with Steetley's two senior directors, David Hennessey and David Scott, for lunch or dinner to discuss existing and future projects.

In any long-term business relationship it is imperative to maintain integrity and complete trust between the two separate entities. It must also be remembered that the other party has to make a reasonable profit return just as one's own organisation must. Fortunately, Cobsen-Davies and Steetley enjoyed a long and fruitful partnership.

One evening, Charles and I collected the two Davids from their hotel in Worthing and drove to the Village House Hotel in Findon. We enjoyed a good meal without any mention of business (generally, this was conducted in the office beforehand) and left the restaurant just after 11pm. Charles, who as usual had drunk only Diet Coke, elected to drive. He turned right out of the car park and drove erratically in a southerly direction down London Road and back towards Worthing. Having been driven thousands of miles by Charles over many years I had become accustomed, and even oblivious, to his appalling driving techniques.

After travelling half a mile we were pulled over by a police patrol car that had been following us since we exited the hotel. The young police officer tapped on Charles's window and indicated that he wished to speak. Charles obliged by winding down the window, poked his head out and said, "Yes, officer how can I help you?" The policeman curtly retorted, "The inconsistent control of your vehicle, together with you leaving the Village House Hotel at closing time, leads me to believe that you may have been partaking of alcoholic beverage. Sir, when did you last have a drink?"

Well, this statement slayed the two Davids and me; we had indeed, had more than enough beer and wine. Our laughter further aggravated the young man. "Well sir, when did you last drink alcohol?" he barked impatiently. By this time Charles had worked out the answer to the question and responded angrily, "Twenty years ago on 2 August, 1968. That was the day before I got married; I over-indulged and was taken to Worthing Hospital where they took me into Accident and Emergency, and the duty doctor, rather unpleasantly, administered a stomach pump. I was so ill that night that I have never taken another alcoholic drink."

Clearly, the answer threw the policeman and he said, "So you mean that you have not had a drink tonight?" Charles had had quite enough of the conversation and asked for the constable's name and number adding, "I know your Chief Constable." It was time for me to step in; I said to the policeman, "Charles is teetotal, and that is why he is driving, to enable our companions and me to safely enjoy a drink. Looking Charles straight in the eye, the officer said, "OK, I am happy to let you go on your way, but sir, please be sure that you take extra care and drive home safely, goodnight."

Once a year, we the directors of Cobsen-Davies, had a four-day-break abroad to play golf and chill out. We visited Estepona, La Manga and Moraira in Spain, Penina in Portugal, and Dublin in Ireland. The format rarely changed: a late breakfast, a round of golf, then a swim followed by a drink in the hotel bar and a trip to a local restaurant. No great extravagance, or misbehaviour, just time to unwind and maybe discuss the company's forward plan. Generally, Charles and I shared a twin-bedded room.

After a long night out in Marbella we all returned to our hotel in Estepona. Charles and I retired to our room on the fifth floor overlooking the hotel courtyard. Charles promptly fell asleep and within ten minutes was snoring like a 'good'un'. Within an hour he had turned up the volume fivefold. For me, having failed to wake him, there was only one answer: drag my mattress into the room's corridor and close the inner door. The plan worked and almost instantly I fell into a deep sleep.

Unbeknown to me, sometime later Charles woke up in urgent need of the loo. He was unable to open the inner corridor door, now blocked by me and my mattress, and apparently shouted to me, to no avail. Desperate for a pee he decided, at such a late hour, the only option open to him was to pee over the balcony, hopeful of not being detected. As we men know only too well, with a full bladder, once the flow has started, it is nearly impossible to stop until the fluid is no more. Well, Charles by all accounts had a very full bladder indeed. I guess it is fair to surmise that pouring a liquid from the fifth floor onto a stone-slabbed courtyard in the still of the night, was going to make some noise; however, I am sure nobody could have predicted the decibel count that dear old

Charles actually achieved on this beautiful late spring evening in southern Spain. It was described to me by those who heard it as sounding like machine-gun fire; a possible terrorist assault in the offing! The full effect was accentuated, no doubt, by Charles's utter inability to stop the flow.

Within half a minute lights were being switched on from all adjacent rooms, floodlighting the courtyard, and soon sleepy heads were peering over the balconies of the six-storey complex to investigate the hullabaloo. Voices in the night called to one another in a variety of European languages: 'What is that terrible noise?' 'Are we under attack?' 'Call the manager'. Eventually, Charles was at last able to retreat to the sanctuary of our darkened bedroom.

From my alcohol-induced sleep I was rudely awakened by a plaintive cry, "John, John, help, help, we are in desperate trouble; please, please open the door!" Now wide awake, I jumped up and propped my temporary bed upright against the corridor wall and opened the bedroom door. Simultaneously, I could hear the cry of distant voices from the main corridor. Charles blurted out the immediacy of the problem, "Words fail me John, it is your entire fault; when the management find out that 'we' have piddled over the balcony they will throw us out, or even worse call the police! Quick, you must think of something," Charles squeaked as panic drove his voice higher and higher.

Well, I did instantly think of a partial solution to the dilemma: "Pass me the bottle of unopened Cava. If we open the bottle, pour the contents down the sink and leave the empty bottle under the balcony rail, the manager will assume that the contents accidentally dribbled over the side onto the courtyard and in the process woke his guests. Problem solved, provided that you were not in fact seen flashing." "I was not flashing!" retorted Charles indignantly, "but, I must admit it is a good wheeze."

Charles grabbed the fizzy wine and instantly popped the cork. Bang! The cork flew off and took out the mirror hanging above the dressing table. The sound of breaking glass led the hotel manager, who had just knocked loudly, to open the room door with his pass key. Entering the room with two other members of staff, he encountered a somewhat bizarre sight: Charles bending over in his boxer shorts, frantically attempting to remove the broken glass from the carpet with one hand, and the other clutching a by now half-empty bottle of wine. For my part, I had wedged myself and the mattress half in and half out of the bathroom doorway in a vague attempt to swing the bedding back into the bedroom. "You drunken English are far more trouble than you are worth, such perverted sexual games are unacceptable in my hotel, kindly dress quickly and follow me and my colleagues to my office on the ground floor," he proclaimed in very good English.

We felt like two very naughty boys when the manager had finished dressing us down. Charles was just about to argue when I quickly intervened and apologised profusely. As no reference was made to the peeing incident I offered to pay for the mirror. Charles, sensing the mood, said, "We would very much like to leave you and your staff a substantial gratuity. I only have sterling; I hope £100 is acceptable." The manager beamed. I guess all's well that ends well, although it did seem to me to be a very expensive way to spend a penny.

After the heady days of rapid expansion of our business in the Eighties, the 'yuppie' years came to a grinding halt. Between 1990 and early 1992 the company's turnover shrank by 50%, profit margins all but disappeared, and the value of the seven properties we had acquired plummeted by 30%. Maggie Thatcher had been driven out of Number 10 and interest rates rose to 15%. The housing bubble had well and truly burst. The consequences for Cobsen-Davies were severe: a write-down of assets triggered the bank to call in our overdraft facility. Our suppliers became reluctant to continue with our favourable credit facilities, and the customers who didn't go bust were hard-pressed to pay on time. The classic cash-flow nightmare; very soon Charles and I were staring into a black hole.

Maurice Van Tritt was a sixty-five year old Dutchman from Amsterdam who I decided to engage as a business consultant for the outrageous fee of £50,000. Maurice had all the answers to our dilemmas: experience in company turnarounds, connections in high places and best of all, access to funds. Within six months he had cut our overheads by half, sweet-talked the bank manager into extending our overdraft facility indefinitely, and on more favourable terms, and somehow persuaded our main suppliers to increase their credit to us. Maurice was a six feet two inches tall, straight-backed, distinguished gentleman who bore a strong resemblance to Victor Borge the Danish comedian and musician. Yet without a hint of humour, he convinced all who came into contact with him, that the unlimited funds at his disposal would be available to Cobsen-Davies as soon as his well-planned blueprint had revitalised the balance sheet. This, he confidently revealed to all interested parties, would take him between six months and a year to achieve. Unbelievably, not one person, even for a minute, doubted his word, and for Charles and me sanity was restored.

At our first meeting in Holland, Maurice took me in his car on a trip to the tulip fields. As we surveyed the beautiful surroundings in the serenity of the spring sunshine, he told me of his teenage years under the jackboot of the invading German army. "They were dark days in my country during World War Two, John; for years we had little hope, precious little nourishing food and certainly no candy," he explained, "then all of a sudden the enemy had fled, and just like magic, the liberating American GIs were handing out numerous bars of chocolate! Today, my newfound friend, you can see no future for your business; please believe me, very soon you will be eating chocolate again." In just a few words not only had the man given prospective to my dilemma, but also shown me the light at the end of a long dark tunnel.

Not surprisingly, no funding was forthcoming. Charles and I suspected from the outset of our arrangement with Mr Van Tritt that there were never any funds, and yet, perhaps there just might have been. That was the man's talent: plausibility. Everyone who came into contact with Maurice either believed him, or wanted to believe him. Without a shadow of doubt Maurice singlehandedly saved the company from insolvency.

Unlike many of our competitors, Cobsen-Davies weathered the storm; however, it was a long and painful recession and in 1994 Charles and I decided to sell the business to Asphaltic, a large roofing merchant. Firstly, we sold the Roofing Centre in Horsham and soon after the core contracting side. Asphaltic retained the name Cobsen-Davies and I continued as managing director with a brief to expand by setting up new branches throughout the country. Charles immediately stepped into the holding company with a brief to streamline their hotchpotch of tatty roofing yards. I know that we both did a very good job for our new masters. Regrettably, we no longer worked together and after twenty-two years our formal and informal partnership ceased. Two years later Asphaltic sold out their roofing merchant business to the Sheffield Insulation Group for £25,000,000; Charles became a regional director for SIG and I stayed with Cobsen-Davies, reporting to the two owners of the company. This arrangement suited neither me nor my bosses and within a year I had bought back the company.

Life was never the same without working alongside Charles (basically it was no fun anymore) and in 2005 I sold my shares in Cobsen-Davies to two junior directors and left the company.

Charles resigned from SIG in 1999 to become the Sussex Director of the charity Age Concern. This job provided him the opportunity to enhance the lives of many elderly people until he retired in 2011. He was so successful that he was awarded the MBE.

Sadly, his liver failed in 2012 and he died after a brief illness, at the age of sixty-eight. His lovely wife Ann collected Charles's gong from Buckingham Palace a couple of months after his well-attended funeral. RIP my dear old friend.

Sussex by the Sea
Composer: Ward-Higgs in 1907

Chapter 19 – Anita

Although I never met Anita our paths have crossed on a number of occasions. Back in the early Sixties I used to spend the odd half hour in her mum's coffee shop, the Roma Café in Littlehampton. Rather than sit and wait for a connecting train between Pulborough and Brighton I often nipped out of the old station entrance and crossed the road into the tiny brightly lit café for a cup of tea. There I could easily spend twenty minutes or so playing on one of the old-fashioned 'push' pin-tables located in the corner of the room.

Just as my parents, who owned The Chocolate Box in Lower Street Pulborough, press-ganged me into working in their shop whenever one of them wanted a couple of hours break, I cannot believe that it was not the same for Anita; the chances are she served me at least once.

Back then, Littlehampton itself was quite small, yet for me the nearest town; and the only hope of some form of high life for a lad from Pulborough was to visit the coast at weekends, often to end up in the Top Hat Club. I am sure that Anita must have frequented the same clubs, bars and cinemas as I did and it is not beyond the bounds of reason to suppose that she might have seen me playing with my band, The Inventive Mr Jeff, in one local venue or another.

I am certain that I would not have been granted such a generous bank facility by NatWest in 1982 had it not been for Anita's indirect and unwitting help (See page 198).

Who was this woman? Anita Roddick is the most famous daughter of Littlehampton; it was she who set up the first Body Shop in Brighton in 1976, and over the next thirty years grew the business into a world-wide brand with 2,200 stores operating in fifty-five countries. The business was based upon green principles, using sustainable products and upholding ethical beliefs; all of which were previously alien to the cosmetic market and consequently became the key to maintaining the support of her loyal customer base.

In 2006, she and her husband and business partner, Gordon, sold out to L'Oréal for a reported £652,000,000. By the time she died, the following year, she had donated her entire personal wealth of around £51,000,000 to charitable causes. The magnificent building that she had constructed in the late Eighties as the company's head office is located alongside the A259, diagonally opposite the Littlehampton Cemetery roundabout. Standing at the entrance to the town it is, almost accidentally, a shrine to her memory and lifetime achievements.

Not long after Anita died, a sizable donation by her husband made the construction of The Longest Bench possible. Located on the west end of the promenade between the ice-cream parlour and the East Beach Café, the 354-yards-long innovation, commissioned by the Council, was to make the job of Foreshore Inspectors a great deal easier.

Prior to the bench there were two old-fashioned shelters on the promenade, probably erected just after the Second World War. The shelters were often frequented by tramps, dossers, winos and druggies who were a real pain in the arse to us: loud, abusive and prone to urinating in the adjacent bushes, Dave and I frequently received complaints about their antics from both the local traders and general public. Upon receiving a shout, we had to lock up the office and jointly clear them off the promenade and the greensward, as a lone inspector, without support, would be very vulnerable if confronted in a violent manner by these bewildered people.

As soon as the old shelters were removed, the nine or ten regulars thankfully retreated to the town centre, well out of our way. We both thought that The Longest Bench might become a target for vandals, but this proved not to be the case; the two metal canopies, with their clever wavy design, and housing part of the structure, were more or less graffiti-proof. A year or two later, when the outdoor theatre was built nearby, the two features perfectly complemented one another. The East Beach Café, though, with its iconic copper roof and metal cladding, is the jewel in Littlehampton's crown, and the worthy recipient of the many design awards bestowed upon it.

I was born into a Catholic family; brought up by my adoptive parents in The Church of England; went missing for ten years, and from the age of twenty-seven for the next forty years, worshipped in two Free Baptist churches: firstly, for thirty years, at New Life Church in Durrington and thereafter, until December 2014, at Opengate Baptist Church in Bognor Regis. Worry not; I do not propose to ram my beliefs down the reader's throat as I think that we are all entitled to make own decisions when it comes to spirituality. For that reason, I only share my convictions when asked to do so, or occasionally from the pulpit when invited to speak in public.

I do believe in the power of prayer, and in early 2011 I asked God to give me a job to do, specifically for the advancement of his Kingdom and for the good of the local community.

A word of advice: do be careful what you pray for; within a few days I seemed to be bombarded with information about The Trussell Trust. Everywhere I looked I saw news items in the papers, on television and the internet, and when a work colleague casually mentioned that he was providing a van, free of charge, to help the Worthing Foodbank, I knew what I had to do. I immediately made contact with Jeremy Rvan the CEO of The Trussell Trust to ascertain whether there was a foodbank in Bognor, or even a need for one. One week later I was at their head office in Salisbury to find out how the charity operated, and to quickly discover how keen Jeremy was for me to set up the Bognor Regis Foodbank.

Unless someone has started a business previously, from scratch, it is impossible to know how difficult it is to successfully accomplish. Think of hitting a golf ball off the first tee; nothing will happen until the golfer strikes the ball! Likewise, with every aspect of a new business, absolutely nothing at all will happen until it is *made* to happen. Over the years, I have set up a number of businesses, some through the franchise route which, believe me, is a great deal easier than going it alone. Trussell operates a simple, though sophisticated, franchise template to start off each member of the foodbank network. Provided the new recruit follows, to the letter, the instructions in the operating manual, then the new start-up business will happen. Great, I knew this venture would work with such good systems in place and, more especially, with God on my side.

Next stop, Opengate Baptist Church and an appointment with my pastor, Graham Banks, to gauge his reaction to my proposition. "Well John, if God has told you to start a foodbank, then we had better do it!" said Graham boldly, and confirmed that he would meet at the earliest possible time to seek the support of the church leadership. Within a week, he not only confirmed that the church was wholeheartedly behind the idea, but had also made contact with Vineyard Church who had contemplated such a venture the previous year and were more than happy to lend their support. Along with Mike Sartin from Vineyard, I once again visited Salisbury to discuss detail and to sign the agreement. We were now Bognor Regis Foodbank, member number 146. Once we had paid our joining fee we were issued with an Operating Manual, and were very soon enjoying a training session.

The basic principle of the foodbank is to provide a three-day food supply to people in crisis. To facilitate this service we needed to find the following: premises, food, and hungry people. Before these, we needed funds and charitable status. The two churches agreed to provide limited start-up funding and a charity to 'plug into', temporarily. Vineyard made part of their church office in the centre of Bognor available to the foodbank to work from, and included a large cupboard to store the food. Within a couple of months we had Mike as a part-time paid manager, and four Trustees, one of whom, with the specific role of directing the operation, was me. Julie, the Opengate Church administrator, undertook the onerous job of applying for start-up grants, and Mike and I recruited volunteers from both churches. Mike very quickly made contact with the relevant local agencies: Citizens Advice, and others, who in due course would be sending their clients to us for food.

The next step for me was to get in touch with the local supermarket managers to request a meeting to explain where we were at and what we needed them to do to help us source the food. That was easier said than done; nevertheless Morrisons' local manager came onside as soon as I sought permission from his Head Office via our Trussell Trust contact. We printed a list of basic, nutritious, non-perishable food; set up a foodbank sign and for eight hours asked Morrisons' customers to select one item of food from their weekly shop and then place it in our collection basket. By the end of that cold March Friday in Morrisons' shop foyer we had collected just over half a ton of food.

In April, we officially launched the Bognor Regis Foodbank with a service in Opengate Baptist Church. The invited congregation included the Mayor, the local clergy, our volunteers, heads of our forthcoming agency partners and the press. The guest speaker, the manager of Portsmouth Foodbank, spoke passionately about his two years running the operation. After I had shared my vision for the distribution of free food within our community, Graham prayed that God would bless our endeavours. Having sent foodbank vouchers to as many local agencies as could be found, we opened for business in early May and issued the first food parcel the same day. Six months after my first meeting with Jeremy Rvan in Salisbury, my golf ball rolled into the hole on the first green.

When Mike resigned in August 2012, one of our original volunteers, Sandie Bolton, took over the coordinator's role, a job she now shares with Jopie Reeves from Vineyard. In late 2013 we acquired our own premises in the centre of town and opened four days a week.

We are now in partnership with over one hundred agencies and able to spend quality time with those people who are desperate for help; thereby meeting needs beyond just food: accommodation, debt, employment, and other real-life problems.

Once we have discovered the client's needs we redirect them to the appropriate agency that can attempt to lead them back to normality. They are free to use our computer terminals to make job applications and we can assist them in filling in all sorts of confusing forms to seek help with benefits, free fuel, and the like. We also offer basic cookery and/or money-management courses. Most important of all is to make people who are in crisis feel comfortable, wanted, and at home in our premises; the majority of those who walk through our door are really embarrassed to ask for free food. We always offer tea, biscuits, someone to talk to, and prayer if they so wish; it never ceases to amaze me that four out of five of our clients are happy to be prayed for. We issue approximately 2,000 food parcels per year.

Over the years I have heard many a sorry story: single mums who have gone for days without eating to ensure their child/children are fed; clients with mental health problems that make it impossible for them just to manage living; old people who cannot make ends meet on their meagre pensions; a teenager not long out of a children's home struggling to make his lonely way in the world – the list is endless. I know there are some who disapprove of the foodbank concept and I do understand their concerns; I have encountered the odd ne'er-do-well, but they are generally given short shrift by me. In truth, they are few and far between and we do not let them spoil our service, which is very often a real lifeline for those in genuine crisis. Trussell Trust estimates that only 4% of all food parcels issued, go to those not entitled to receive free food.

I *almost* encountered two such undesirables whilst enjoying a giant sausage and egg bap, with chips on the side. I was sitting in the Westside Café diagonally opposite the foodbank; a greasy spoon; nevertheless, the food is *par excellence* so it is not at all unusual to find me in there. On this occasion, I was gazing out of the window and admiring my highly polished BMW parked on the foodbank forecourt, when out of the shop doorway stepped two men in their mid-twenties carrying a couple of parcels of food issued by one of my colleagues; both men were scruffy and covered in tattoos. They placed the food on the ground next to my car and lit cigarettes; one of them, wearing a hoodie, casually keyed the boot of my car. Then, picking up the food, they both strolled off down the road, laughing.

How about that for a dilemma, what on earth does one do? My first instinct was to chase outside and remonstrate with the culprit, but in my mind I saw the headline in the Bognor Observer: 'Bognor Foodbank director arrested after punch-up outside the Bognor Regis Foodbank', which I instantly interpreted as: 'How to undo the good name of the foodbank in thirty seconds'. This was indeed a 'grin and bear it moment', which I guess one only learns with age.

The compensating factor about doing nothing on this occasion was the thought that my old boxing trainer, Pat Coleman, would have been proud of me; notwithstanding the very real chance of ending up flat on my back in the gutter. Never has the expression 'Biting the hand that feeds you' felt so poignant to me, as on that day.

The Roddick Foundation, through its management team and trustees, chooses to support organisations that aspire to make the world a more caring and just place. I am very proud to say that in 2015 the Bognor Regis Foodbank was selected to receive a generous grant, and felt greatly honoured that the Foundation had recognised our efforts. Once again, the late Anita Roddick had crossed my path.

The Snake
Performer: Al Wilson
Composer: Oscar Brown, Jr
Released: 1968
(Although not a hit, this song was ranked No. 4 of 500 Northern Soul singles)

Chapter 20 – Uncle Jack

John 10:10
The thief comes only in order to steal, kill, and destroy.
I have come in order that you might have life—life in all its fullness.

With a mainline station and plenty of cheap parking, Littlehampton is a great venue for a day out by the seaside, although holidaymakers may be hard-pressed to find a wide range of accommodation within the town boundary. It is true to say that there is a campsite near the council tip, a variety of B&Bs, and a few apartments to let, but for hotels there is very little other than The Nelson in River Road, The Arun View Inn next to the slide bridge, and a Travelodge in Worthing Road. The upmarket Bailiffscourt Hotel and Spa is a couple of miles east in Climping and there are a couple of motels at Crossbush just south of Arundel. Having never had reason to stay at any of these venues I am not in a position to make recommendations, and from my foreshore experience I know that the vast majority of visitors are day-trippers with no intention of staying over. With Butlin's massive holiday centre only five miles away in Bognor Regis there is little or no demand for a flagship hotel in Littlehampton.

Elmer Sands, however, was once a different proposition; situated exactly halfway between Littlehampton and Bognor, it may well have been considered by the pre-war vacation-starved population as a summer-break Mecca. A very swish holiday centre, The New City, was established in 1922 catering for the wealthy with every possible comfort and entertainment for that time, including a swimming pool, tennis courts, restaurants, a dance hall and an indoor garage to house over one hundred cars. By the end of the decade another holiday camp had sprung up nearby; the Elmer Sands Holiday Resort targeted the lower-middle-class market. In addition, there were six hotels, a number of boarding houses and numerous bungalows to let, including quaintly converted railway carriages, which could also be found in Bognor Regis, Pagham and Selsey. With the vast expanse of golden sands at low tide and an attractive greensward, Elmer made a fabulous destination for a family holiday.

When mum and dad booked a two-week stay in a seaside bungalow, Elmer was still in its heyday. The year was 1955; long before package flights abroad were to decimate summer trade for the traditional British holiday destinations. I soon discovered the wonders spread out either side of the main road: the Sussex Club Holiday Resort, the putting green on Sea Way, the Elmer Hotel and numerous little shops; yet the main attraction for an eight-year-old boy was always going to be the beach.

Although my Pulborough home was only about fifteen miles north-east of Elmer Sands I really thought I had been transported to paradise. Joining us for the two weeks in August were Uncle Jack and Auntie Peggie, and my cousins Anne and Peter, who travelled down from their Gidea Park home in Essex. As my cousins and I were roughly the same age we had a fabulous time playing in the safe environment of the tiny seaside resort. The sweltering, sunny days were filled with swimming in the sea, building sand castles, picnics and ice creams on the beach, and in the evenings we were taught board and card games by the adults whilst swigging pop and scoffing numerous bags of sweeties.

Uncle Jack, then aged forty-five, and company secretary of the Hudson Bay Company, like my parents aspired to be middle-class. Jack had a Brownie box-camera and seemed to be taking photos constantly, which habit was to prove spookily fortuitous for me. Some of the snaps were taken on the beach; not looking out to sea as could be reasonably expected but, curiously, looking back towards the land.

The bungalow we were staying in was a few yards from the main Elmer road, in The Layne, and about a hundred yards from the beach. Leaving our holiday home we turned left out of the front door and walked to the main road junction. We crossed the road into a little alley leading to the wooden steps used to access the beach, and plonked ourselves down, along with the usual beach paraphernalia, on the nearest available patch of sand. Immediately behind us were the Manor Hotel and a line of detached beachside houses, all of which were to feature as background in the family group photos.

Many years later I met, and married, Jan who owned Manor Lodge, the house next door to the Manor Hotel divided by the very same alley leading to our favourite spot on the beach!

When I first visited Jan's house I casually mentioned to her that I had spent a childhood holiday nearby and might have a photo or two to prove it. I found an old case and within half a dozen of Jack's snaps, were three that clearly showed Manor Lodge in the background.

On the day after our wedding in June 2013 my cousins and I posed for a repeat of one of the photographs that my uncle had taken fifty-eight years before. Never could I have imagined, that in my retirement years, I would be living in the same house I passed by every day on the way to the beach on those long-ago August afternoons, nor that I should settle in the fabulous village of Elmer. The Manor Hotel is long gone, making way for retirement homes, yet the neighbouring houses to the east of Manor Lodge are all still intact and much the same as they were over half a century ago.

Above: John, Peter and Anne in 1955, and *below:* in 2013

I have mixed feelings about holidays: trying to cram into a week or two all the things there is no chance doing when working full time; expectation over realisation maybe, and just sometimes, wishing one was not here at all. My parents always aspired to two weeks away every year and I have followed suit, which leads me to a few strange experiences when on vacation.

Originally through necessity, yet in later years by choice, I have launched myself, and sometimes reluctant family members, into the joys of camping; be it caravan, motorhome, or simply under canvas – they have all come and gone, and come back again.

On one memorable occasion back in the 1970s I borrowed my out-laws' caravan and set off with Jean, Mark and Andrew to the New Forest. Upon arrival, Jean insisted that we find a secluded spot well away from the hoi polloi. After arguing over the pros and cons of various potential sites we both settled for a little glade at least one hundred yards from the next camper.

In my/our defence: it was the first time I had towed a caravan, and with two naughty boys squabbling in the back of the car during the journey down, by the time we finally settled on our chosen patch, our nerves were a little frayed. Very carefully and gingerly I started to unhitch and position the caravan on level ground, plug in the battery which had been charging in the car boot, and organise water and slops, before my wife said, "What about the awning then?"

If ever there was anything designed to frustrate and anger a virgin camper then it is, without doubt, the awning. My first advice to the novice camper is: never, ever be tempted to acquire an awning. Don't do it, take this as a warning: please, don't do it. A caravan awning is designed to be a second room and when erected will double the living space; made of canvas with plastic windows and a zipped doorway, it is, in short, a three-sided tent.

The trouble starts the moment the camper removes it from its sheath and attempts to position the thick plastic thread that attaches to the van. Take care to thread it from left to right and, vitally, before starting, ensure that it is not inside-out. An able assistant is required to waggle the cord up through the lip of the caravan. A steady hand is essential, as any minor deviation will result in the cord jamming; when this happens, as it surely will, the process will need to be reversed and the exercise repeated until both parties, now in sync, by pushing and pulling very gently, are able to coax the awning 'A' into place. Next, position the poles 'B' (beware of the white plastic joiners); the guy ropes 'C'; the groundsheet 'D'; and finally, the curtains 'E' (Why would anyone want curtains in a tent?) Trust me, none of these procedures will be any easier than the first.

Finding the Able Assistant is something of a conundrum, yet essential to the exercise; it is generally best not to ask a family member, and most certainly not the wife if one is keen for her to retain that title for any length of time. Of my five sons the only one not to run for cover at the sight of the awning has been Mark. He always proved the most capable of undertaking the job, so much so, that our roles have reversed into Dad becoming the able assistant.

Probably the best bet is to find the campsite know-all; he is very easy to identify as he has already spotted the awning novice scratching his head and wandering round in circles looking bewildered. He will call over, 'Having trouble sport? Want a hand? That make of awning you have is a real devil'. By now the novice will probably have noticed the immaculate array of equipment on his plot with a degree of jealousy, yet know, without doubt, he is the man for the job and in all haste wave him over. 'Hello my name is Dick, whatever possessed you to buy that load of rubbish?' As tempting as it may be, the appropriate reply is not 'Piss off, arsehole', quite the reverse in fact; smile, offer him a hand in friendship and say, 'Lovely to meet you Dick, my name is John. You couldn't possibly give me a hand for five minutes or so?'

With honed perfection Clever Dick will erect the awning in no time at all. 'There you are chief, all done. Anything else I can help you with?' Although the novice will be absolutely delighted that the awning is up, he will feel a little pissed off that despite CD's demonstration, he can never expect to achieve the same level of perfection in such a short space of time. Getting shot of Dick now that his expertise is no longer required is quite another matter, so best make pretence to leave: 'Many thanks for your kind help, now I must pop into town to get some supplies; do hope to catch up later for a drink, bye!'

Back in the New Forest, Mark and I successfully erected the awning in just less than two hours. With a sigh of relief I flipped open a can of cold beer and was slumping into my deckchair when I detected a faint roaring noise. My first thought was to check and see if the water pump was correctly connected; this being my inaugural caravan adventure I was ignorant of the fact that all campers are paranoid about their equipment. However, there was no problem with the pump; seconds later we were surrounded by motorbikes generating the offending sound, at least a dozen or so, and no ordinary bikes either: 750 Nortons, Bonnevilles, and Harleys; some three-wheelers and others with chairs (sidecars) attached.

The leader dismounted and announced to his compatriots 'We will camp here.' I soon noticed that they all sported the same insignia on the back of their leather jackets. A swastika and printed underneath: North London Chapter Hells Angels. "John," Jean called over, "go tell them to camp elsewhere as we were here first." I have done many a stupid thing in my life, but carrying out Jean's instruction on this occasion, was certainly not one of them. I beckoned to Mark and quietly said, "Please come over here and help me dismantle the awning as we are moving to another part of the site."

On another occasion I was in Bude, Cornwall, a spot that the family has tended to visit annually for a week or so in the summer; a tradition I have kept up since 1976. As I recall, this time we had the motorhome parked on the Budemeadows site four miles south of the main town. To fully enjoy a family holiday it is very important to attempt to maintain some level of sanity, therefore sometime during the course of the break I find a reason to escape alone for an hour or two, either to a pub and/or for a long walk in the country.

On one beautiful late June afternoon I discovered a lovely cliff walk just south of Widemouth Bay and strolling along a rather overgrown track I happened upon a courting couple in a passionate embrace, lying in the middle of the remote path. I consider myself unshockable; however, in this instance I was bordering on being a little unnerved as the pair were not only starkbollock-naked, but also 'fully connected', if you get my drift. What does one do in such an embarrassing moment? Thinking quickly, I stepped over them and said, "Good afternoon, a lovely day for it." Without waiting for any response, I rushed down the path, which just happened to lead to the beach. Fortunately, I didn't have to retrace my steps as the tide was well out. Now over a hundred yards clear of the amorous pair, I was able to walk casually back to Widemouth Bay over the rocks and along the beach.

My youngest son, Dan, and I have had many far-flung one-to-one holidays, including trips to Berlin, Paris, Dublin and Johannesburg, but the most memorable was a whistle-stop tour around England and Scotland.

In the early Sixties my dad, Albert, took me in his Standard Vanguard car to Blackpool, the Lakes, Gretna Green, Glasgow, Edinburgh, Inverness and St Andrews. The adventure with dad had given me a fantastic understanding of the geography of our wonderful island. I decided it might be fun to retrace the steps I had made some forty years earlier, and that a repeat of the journey could only enhance my twelve-year-old's education. I am sure it did; we climbed a mountain in the Lake District, fished in Lock Ness, stayed in the appropriately named Albert Hotel in Inverness, caught a ferry to the Isle of Skye, visited the Culloden Moor battlefield, and played golf at St Andrews – not on the Old Course at the home of golf, but on one of the six other public courses.

My enduring memory of our eight-day jaunt was without question experienced in Blackpool. The Imperial Hotel is *the* hotel at which to stay; positioned north of the piers on the seafront, the nineteenth-century building is certainly imperial. My dad loved its Victorian opulence and pointed out that my behaviour in the dining room required my best endeavours as the well-to-do guests would expect nothing less.

After the obligatory visit to the funfair, Dan and I decided that on our first night a fish-and-chip supper was a good bet, and found a fantastic restaurant just off the Golden Mile; our first visit to the hotel dining room would have to wait until breakfast the next morning. My well-chosen words as we walked down the stairs in search of the dining room were soon to ring in my ears: "Dan, if you watch and follow the other guests' behaviour you won't go far wrong this morning." The posh diners I was anticipating had, just like dad, become ghosts of long ago; now replaced by a couple of dozen dart players, accompanied by wives, girlfriends and supporters. I easily recognised Eric Bristow, John Lowe, Jocky Wilson and Bobby George who were obviously in town for the World Matchplay Darts Championship at the nearby Winter Gardens.

I can only liken their behaviour that morning to the Mad Hatter's Tea Party; yet far worse, as the language would not have gone amiss in a four-ale bar. Bread rolls were flying around the room, the genteel tea cups were replaced by pint mugs of lager, and the dress code appeared to be jeans and football shirts. "Dad, do you really want me to behave this badly?" Dan queried with a cheeky smile.

Undoubtedly some of my best holidays have been travelling around Europe in the motorhome. There is nothing better than catching the car ferry from Newhaven to Dieppe and parking up in Les Andelys, not far from Monet's garden, before pushing on south toward the Pyrenees in search of sunshine.

On one such occasion I called on David in Duravel before heading for Andorra to load up with duty-frees. After finding a stopover in the mountains I crossed the border into Aragon and drove south-east towards the Spanish Costas. The sun was shining and I found myself singing along to *High Ho Silver Lining* from a CD compilation, then bang, it happened: the fan-belt broke, quickly overheating the radiator, and 'Doris' (Jan's pet name for the vehicle) slowly ground to a halt. It was on a Sunday afternoon a few miles north of Valencia. Very fortunately, I was only a hundred yards short of a layby when Doris finally decided she could go on no longer and was just capable of free-wheeling to it.

It took three hours for the Spanish version of AA to turn up and they soon carried me and the motorhome on the back of a rescue transporter to a car park on an industrial estate in a suburb of Valencia. No one spoke English and I don't speak Spanish, yet the driver walked me across the road to a vehicle repair shop that was, of course, closed on a Sunday, and indicated a sign in the window with the opening hours displayed. Pointing at the Monday opening time, he pretended to knock on the door, which he intended I should do the following day.

At least being stranded in a motorhome is not like being marooned in a car; with a fridge full of food and beers, and plenty of DVDs to watch, it was no problem to lie back and wait for the morning. All would have been hunky-dory had it not been for a massive storm, followed by torrential rain beating on the roof all night long, and by first light I could see that the car park was flooded. As it turned out, at nine o'clock the garage proprietor knocked on *my* door, and pointing to his garage, made a steering action and then touched the wheel. I gingerly drove across the road at five miles per hour. After checking the damage he quickly ordered the part, which arrived that afternoon and was promptly fitted.

The boss handed me his invoice and made it clear that only euros were acceptable to him. I was €25 short of the €140 bill and evidently there was no cash machine nearby. A problem; no problem; the man was a smoker and I had in my locker over a hundred packets of cigarettes. I gave him all my euros and ten packs of Stuyvesant and instantly, a grin appeared from ear to ear, before the swarthy Spaniard hugged me: deal done. As I drove out of the garage the heavens once again opened and my new-found friend waved me down. From his gesturing I gathered that it would be unwise to proceed so I thanked him and found my way back to the car park, this time to a space on the high ground in the far corner. The weather that night was a repeat of the previous, once again the car park became a lake and I was therefore unable to risk completing my journey south until the Tuesday.

Yet on the Monday night I witnessed a crime. Sometime before midnight I turned off the TV and began to settle down for the night. Having just switched off all the lights I heard a lorry drive into the dimly lit and, what was by now, near-deserted car park. I half drew my curtain and through the torrential rain could see two men drop open the back of a high-sided transporter and, rather strangely, wait patiently outside their vehicle in the pouring rain. Two or three minutes later a very smart new Mercedes sped into view, drove up the ramp and into the lorry. The driver jumped off the back of the transporter and the three of them quickly closed the back door, hopped into the cab and within twenty seconds, were gone.

Luckily, as my vehicle, tucked away in the corner, was in pitch darkness, they did not spot me. I dread to think what my fate might have been had they done so. I am sure the top-of-the-range Mercedes must have been stolen to order. Thankfully, my guardian angel was on duty once again.

Although Jan and I still love the odd break away, living in tranquil Elmer we now see ourselves as permanently on holiday; hoorah!

Summer Holiday
Performer: Cliff Richard
Composer: Bennett and Welch
Number 1:   Released February 1963

(During one of my many visits to The All England Club at Wimbledon, I was 'availing myself of the facilities' when I noticed that standing next to me in the urinal was none other than Sir Cliff Richard. I am especially thankful it wasn't Shakin' Stevens!)

Chapter 21 – Dawn

Song of Songs 6:10
Who is this whose glance is like the dawn?
She is beautiful and bright,
as dazzling as the sun or the moon.

After reflecting on my five summers working on Littlehampton beach I realise how much I found the job a refreshing change from my lifetime working in the construction industry. It was also a sobering shock to be paid just above the minimum wage and to come to the realisation that had I needed to rely on this level of income, it would have been an impossibility for me to have managed. Yet that was exactly what some of my colleagues were faced with, and in some ways this wake-up call later led me to appreciate the plight of those forced by circumstance to visit foodbanks.

On further reviewing my foreshore experiences, I consider the most enjoyable time was probably during the first year or two. After completing my initial training with Dave Strong I found myself paired up for the Easter weekend with Charlie Thwaites. As Charlie and I had started on the same day just two weeks previously, it was a case of the blind leading the blind. Charlie, an attractive, single, blonde lady in her mid-thirties had three major assets: a great personality and an enormous chest!

We soon found out over the next four exceptionally hot and sunny days that there was a small community of elderly immobile men who, to overcome their various states of handicap, had all acquired disability scooters and very soon made a habit of calling at the Foreshore Office. It became very clear that they had no time for me, far from it, as to them I was invisible. Not so, Charlie. With her platinum-blonde hair tucked under her cap and her ponytail swinging seductively down her back, tight black trousers, stylish black boots and a pullover two sizes too small, she was without doubt a far better model for our uniform than I was. Add a walkie-talkie hanging low beneath her belt, strapped down her right leg like a six-gun, and our recently acquired disabled friends seemed to rapidly acquire a zest for life over the 2007 holiday weekend. Sitting in the office I knew precisely when Charlie was about to complete her patrol by the whirr of the electric motors arriving at my front door. Little gifts of chocolate, flowers and miscellaneous fluffy toys appeared like magic on the shelf behind me.

They were not the only uninvited guests to find any manner of irrelevant reasons to knock on the door.

John, the resident cleaner who looked after the public toilets located immediately behind our office, eagerly regaled us with tales from the deepest depths of his domain; when he was not endlessly scrounging food from the fish and chip takeaway next door. Whilst John, armed with a recently 'acquired' steak and kidney pie, explained how the Ladies was always far messier than the Gents – and the many obnoxious reasons why – we listened in false wonderment, carefully ducking the spray from his gravy-soaked pastry; I am not certain he had, by this performance, adopted a good ploy to seduce the delectable Charlie.

Another would-be Lothario ran a seafront concession. He continuously tried to capture my colleague with offers of exotic dinners in the local curry house, or romantic rides in his open-topped car to find a country pub in the wilds of Sussex. This abruptly stopped when his wife found out about his dastardly plans. It is true to say that there was never a dull moment for me when working alongside Charlie.

Our introduction to the job of Foreshore Inspector was undoubtedly a baptism of fire, yet in those few short days we were to experience nearly every aspect of the job and from then on confidently undertook the full responsibility of our new-found career. First aid, lost kids, drunks, careless cyclists, faulty equipment and numerous enquiries about every aspect of life on the beach came and went between 9am and 6pm. Without a break for lunch and absolutely no one to refer to for advice, we cheerfully soldiered on. By the end of each day we were both knackered. All I could do was to go home, collecting a take-away en route, eat it, and go straight to bed.

On Easter Monday afternoon I was patrolling on foot next to the colourfully painted beach huts at the eastern end of the promenade when I spotted four or five horses and riders on the beach. The beach was packed, mainly with families enjoying the balmy weather; with young kids paddling in the sea, the horses were very much a hazard to their safety. "Beach patrol to Foreshore office: come in please, over," I stated into the walkie-talkie and a few seconds later Charlie replied, "Foreshore office to beach patrol, I can hear you loud and clear. How can I help? Over." I explained the problem and suggested that it was important to make an announcement over the public address system. "Copy, over and out," Charlie said with confidence.

'Attention please, this is the Foreshore Inspector speaking. Horse riding is not permitted on the beach at this time of year; please dismount immediately and lead your horses off the beach. Thank you.'

I was nearly a mile away from the office and the message over the recently upgraded sound system was indeed, very loud and clear. The horse riders certainly heard it as I could see them dismounting and slowly making their way off the beach; I thought to myself: that's good. I was then distracted by the sight of a lit barbecue and had to remind a middle-aged couple that this activity was not permitted on the beach.

When I returned to the office half an hour later I was confronted with a tearful and flustered Charlie. "The horse riders shouted and swore at me and said they had every right to be on the beach; and I could find nothing in the bylaws manual to support my announcement," Charlie complained. I said, "I don't care what is, or is not, in the rule book, those horses were a major health and safety hazard on a crowded beach. Without question we made the right call, and after all, we are in charge of Littlehampton beach today, no one else." Charlie seemed happy with my reassurances and soon cheered up enough to treat a little girl's cut foot.

I never did quite clarify the rule, although Geoff Taylor, our boss, did confirm we made the right decision when the riding stable proprietor made a formal complaint the very next day. As the bylaw manual was printed in the Fifties all agreed that a revised edition was long overdue – it never arrived.

Charlie was great to work with and just a little younger than two of my daughters-in-law: Dawn, my eldest son Mark's wife, and Julia, Andrew's wife; and a little older than Soumely, Paul's wife. All three girls were great company and I count myself very lucky to have had them as part of our family.

I first met Dawn in late 1985 when Charles employed her as a bookkeeper working out of our Goring office; a vivacious young lady of twenty-three who was destined to become an invaluable addition to the then young company's administrative team. At that time Dawn was just getting over a difficult divorce and threw all her energies into her work. Mike Scott, Cobsen-Davies' external accountant and auditor, said that Dawn was the very best bookkeeper he had ever met. She soon settled in and became very popular with both management and site staff alike; not least with my son Mark who was by this time working as a qualified roof tiler on sites all over Sussex.

In February 1986 I was arranging a Valentine's Dance in Findon Village, with all proceeds going to the St Barnabas Hospice, and to boost numbers invited all my work colleagues to attend. One afternoon, Mark phoned me to say that although he would like to attend the event taking place on the following Friday night, he didn't have a partner. I said, "No worries; Dawn has the same problem, if you hold on the line for a few seconds I will put you through to her, bye." I gave Mark no chance to argue and said to Dawn when she picked up the phone, "I have a call for you." They attended the dance on 14 February, fell in love and were married in the summer of 1989. Just call me Cupid!

A year or two later Dawn was taking driving lessons and needed to practise for the forthcoming test. I cheerfully volunteered my help and once a week, for a month or so, we set off for a drive around the Sussex countryside. One late afternoon in Storrington I noticed that the fuel was running low so I told Dawn to indicate and turn left into the service station situated next to the shopping centre. She followed my instruction and made the turn in, then without slowing down, drove past the pumps, out again, and back seamlessly onto the road. I said, "Dawn that was a perfect manoeuvre, except for one small thing: you failed to stop to fill up the tank." Dawn laughed with embarrassment, "I am aware of that; I completely forgot how to stop!" Women drivers, don't you just love them? Regardless of that momentary aberration, Dawn passed her driving test first time.

In time, Mark and Dawn had two lovely children: Rebekah and Luke, and Dawn gave up her job with my company. Likewise, Mark progressed with Cobsen-Davies into a management position and finally left to set up his own small roofing company that proved to be very successful. Life was good for all the family: a spacious three-bedroomed house in Tarring, which Mark refurbished to a very high specification, a nice car, and regular holidays abroad; they seemed to want for nothing.

Out of the blue, one January evening in 2015, I received a call from Mark, who was clearly in an emotional state: "Dad, Dawn has been diagnosed with terminal cancer and has been given less than a year to live," Mark tearfully blurted out.

They had been in Mexico on two weeks' holiday back in October and when they returned Dawn had difficulty breathing. Her doctor thought that she had picked up a virus and treated her symptoms accordingly. When she failed to respond to the medication she was sent for a full evaluation; X-rays and scans soon identified advanced cancer in both lungs. It all seemed so unfair: Dawn had never smoked, and throughout their married life had attended weekly aerobic and dance sessions to keep fit.

Following the diagnosis everything possible was done to delay the advance of this terrible disease. The chemotherapy did, for a short time, slow the cancer's progress, and Dawn and the family managed to enjoy the odd normal day, even to the extent of Dawn being able to drive once more. Yet as the months marched on it became painfully clear that it was only a matter of time. At least Mark and Dawn had time to plan the family's future without her, and this they did, with the utmost care. Macabrely, and coincidentally, her father, Spence, was also diagnosed with terminal lung cancer shortly after Dawn had received her own devastating news. Although a strong and powerful ex-Para, Spence's life gave out at the age of seventy-eight in October 2015; Dawn bravely attended her dad's funeral with the help of breathing apparatus.

As we age, we all start to think about dying. When I die, unless suddenly, I hope I will possess at least some of the same dignity and grace that Dawn maintained right up to the second she stopped breathing in December. Not once did she complain; not once did she feel sorry for herself; her only thought was to make her demise as easy as possible for all around her. In fact whilst desperately poorly in (ironically) St Barnabas Hospice, she scolded Mark for going to football one Saturday in November: 'That's right, you leave your wife on her deathbed to watch your beloved Albion.' Dawn said to her husband, tongue in cheek.

Her funeral was a real celebration of her comparatively short life (Dawn was fifty-three when she died) and I doubt there was a dry eye in the packed Findon Crematorium on that cold winter's day.

In my first season on the beach there were only three Foreshore Officers employed at Littlehampton, so I was on duty either with Dave or Charlie, both of whom were great to work alongside. I think the reason we all clicked was our ability to share the same warped and politically incorrect sense of humour.

On a very hot summer's afternoon during the long school holiday we received a number of complaints in quick succession about inappropriate goings-on between a courting couple on first beach. I dug out the binoculars to check the problem and sure enough, I could see a male and a female, probably in their late twenties, indulging in passionate petting. I turned to Charlie and said, "Come on, we'll lock up the office and jointly deal with this: you talk to the woman and I will confront the man."

By the time we had walked down the sands we could see a half-drunk bottle of wine and few empty cans strewn around and about the pair. The girl had disappeared under a blanket that was covering the guy's nether regions and, judging by the expression on his face, it didn't take a great deal of imagination to guess what was going on.

Without hesitation, Charlie said to the girl, "Come out from under that blanket, young lady. We are Foreshore Inspectors investigating complaints from the public about your behaviour. What have you got to say for yourself?" Charlie's stern words had no effect at all, but by now she was certainly on a mission; before I could add my two penn'orth worth to the proceedings, she continued, "I am speaking to you!" With that, the man casually said, "Don't you know it is rude to speak with your mouth full?" I thought to myself, that's a good answer, and finally stepped in and shouted, "Right that's it! Pack up your belongings and clear off the beach, before I issue you a ticket for lewd behaviour in public, and another for consuming alcohol in breach of the Council bylaws." (Neither of which I could do without referring to the local police, but they weren't to know that.) Straight away they packed up their belongings and sheepishly slunk away.

The job was then, and is now, well and truly done and dusted!

You Didn't Have To Be So Nice
Performers: The Lovin' Spoonful
Composer: Sebastian and Boone
Released: 1966 on the *Daydream* LP

1951 – 1953	Old Place Manor (Private Infant School)	Pulborough
1954 – 1959	Arundale School (Private Junior School)	Pulborough
1959 – 1964	Weald School (Secondary Modern School)	Billingshurst
1964 – 1966	Worthing College of Further Education	Worthing
1966 – 1968 POSITION:	Sun Alliance & London Insurance Co. Ltd. Claims Clerk	Horsham
1968 – 1970	Crawley College of Technology	Crawley
1970 – 1972 POSITION:	Gripperrods International Ltd Office Manager	Horsham
1972 – 1982 POSITION:	Marley Tile Company Ltd Sales Representative, Contracts Manager, Area Manager and Regional Manager	Storrington
1982 – 2005 POSITION:	Cobsen-Davies Roofing Ltd Founder and Managing Director	Worthing
1987 – 1997 POSITION:	St Cuthman's School, Stedham, School Governor (Voluntary)	near Midhurst
2007 – 2011 POSITION:	Arun District Council Foreshore Inspector (Seasonal)	Littlehampton
2010 – 2015 POSITION:	Kingsley Roofing Ltd Business Consultant (Part-time)	Ferring
2011 – POSITION:	Bognor Regis Foodbank Founder, Director and Trustee (Voluntary)	Bognor Regis

QUALIFICATIONS: General Certificate of Education (Five passes) O-Level.

Ordinary and Higher National Diploma in
Business Studies.

Fellow of the Institute of Roofing, including ten years
on the Board of Governors, with a term as Chairman.

People, famous and infamous, whom I have encountered over the years.

IN ORDER OF APPEARANCE

CHAPTER 3
Arthur Gilligan ....England international cricketer
Norman Wisdom ....Comedian and film star
Jimmy Edwards...Comedian and film star

CHAPTER 5
Johnny Haynes ....England international footballer
Bill Foulkes ....England international footballer
Noel Cantwell...Republic of Ireland
international footballer
Jimmy Greaves ....England international footballer
Katy Boyle..Television personality

CHAPTER 7
Terry Biddlecombe...National Hunt jockey
HRH Princess Margaret ....Royalty
Lord Snowdon ....Royalty by marriage,
photographer and film maker
John Mayall ....Musician
Eric Clapton...Musician
Peter Frampton ....Musician
Zoot Money ....Musician and television actor
Des Decker ....Musician
Eddie Grant ....Musician
Ringo Starr ....Musician and film star
George Harrison...Musician and film star
Olivia Newton John ....Musician and film star
Justin Hayward ....Musician
John Peel ....Disc jockey and journalist

CHAPTER 8
Dave Davis..Musician

CHAPTER 9
HM Queen Elizabeth II

CHAPTER 10
Geraldine James ....Actress

CHAPTER 11
Sir Owen Ashier...Entrepreneur

CHAPTER 12
Colin Blunstone .... Musician

CHAPTER 14
Nicholas Van Hoogstraten .... Entrepreneur

CHAPTER 16
James Bolam .... Actor

CHAPTER 17
Brian Barnes .... Ryder Cup golfer

CHAPTER 18
Sir Jack Walker .... Chairman of Blackburn Rovers
and entrepreneur

Steve Gatting .... Arsenal, Brighton and Charlton
footballer

Mike Gatting .... England international cricketer

CHAPTER 19
Gordon Roddick .... Entrepreneur and philanthropist
Anita Roddick .... Entrepreneur and philanthropist

CHAPTER 20
Eric Bristow .... World Champion darts player
John Lowe .... World Champion darts player
Jocky Wilson .... World Champion darts player
Bobby George .... World Champion (finalist)
darts player
Sir Cliff Richard .... Musician and film star

PLATES:
Sir Stanley Mathews .... England international footballer
Nancy Roberts .... Television personality, hostess
on *Double your Money* programme

Bands I have played in and the musicians I have performed with:

1964 – 1966 **THE SKEYNES**

Founder Members: John Madell, John (Tango) Tangstram, Jim Chatfield and Colin Bailey.

Other Members: John Bowyer and Viv James

1967 – 1971 **THE INVENTIVE MR. JEFF** (To become **BIG BERTHA**)

Founder Members: John Madell, Alan (Ally) Jones, Roger Cross, Mick Pretty and Bernie Humphries.

Other Members: Pete Reynolds and John (Katy) Katon.

1979 – 1980 **THREE'S A CROWD**

Founder Members: John Horan and Jeff Linter

Other Member: John Madell

1980 – **FRED AND THE FERRETS** (Also known as **KESTREL** and **DAYTRIPPER**)

Founder Members: John Horan, John Madell, Steve Smith and John Hunt.

Other Members: Steve Davies, Elaine Bayford, Fleur, Melody Price, Peter Harris and Alan Hackett.

1995 – 1997 **THE ELDERLY BROTHERS**

Founder Members: Doug Eaton, Steve Davis and John Madell

Other Member: Paul Murdan.

1997 – 1999 **SIX FIVE SPECIAL**

Founder Members: John Madell, Steve Davies and Paul Murdan

I have only included bands I have played with professionally. I performed in the New Life Church Band throughout the Eighties and Nineties. I don't know the total number of gigs I have completed; if I include every performance since 1963 when I first acquired a drum kit I guess it must exceed 1000. I have also played for other bands whilst still an active member of Fred and the Ferrets.

Last Chance

Verse 1

The first half has come and gone,
Sad to see you off your game,
The second half you got all wrong,
You only have yourself to blame.

Chorus

Last chance to do your best,
Last chance to pass the test,
Last chance to make the grade,
Last chance so do not fade.

Verse 2

The second half had much at stake,
Admit it you lacked the nerve,
The third half will make or break,
Choose right now who you serve.

Chorus

Last chance to do your best,
Last chance to pass the test,
Last chance to make the grade,
Last chance so do not fade.

(Middle eight and lead break)

Can't love, can't cry,
Might stay, might fly,
Don't wait, don't die,
Will cope, will try,

Verse 3

The first half is the distant past,
The second half did not last,
The third half you cannot mask,
Well on the way to complete your task.

Chorus

Last chance to do your best,
Last chance to pass the test,
Last chance to make the grade,
Last chance so do not fade.

LIST OF PHOTOGRAPHS

Unless otherwise stated on the following page, the photographs in this book are taken from the author's collection.

I am grateful to the following for their kind permission to use the images mentioned:

David Sawyer: the images of the wedding group, and my five sons.

Paul Millen: the image of Janet Madell.

Graham Allfrey: the image of The Skeynes.

Gordon Fraser: the image of Fred and the Ferrets.

J. M.

Imperial Linear measurements (Length and Distance)

Imperial		Metric equivalents
1 inch		25.4 millimetres
1 foot	(12 inches)	0.3048 metre
1 yard	(3 feet)	0.9144 metre
1 mile	(1,760 yards)	1.6093 kilometres

Imperial Height measurements (Examples)

Imperial		Metric equivalents
5' 0"	(Five feet)	1.524 metres
6' 2"	(Six feet, two inches)	1.8796 metres
6' 5"	(Six feet, five inches)	1.956 metres

Imperial Weight measurements

Imperial		Metric equivalents
1 ounce		28.35 grams
1 pound	(16 ounces)	0.45359237 kilogram
1 stone	(14 pounds)	6.35 kilograms
1 hundredweight	(112 pounds)	50.80 kilograms
1 ton	(2,240 pounds)	1.016 tonnes

Imperial Volume measurements

Imperial		Metric equivalents
1 pint		568.26 millilitres
1 gallon	(8 pints)	4.546 litres